SEVENTH EDITION

GRAMMAR IN CONTEXT 1

SANDRA N. ELBAUM

Australia · Brazil · Mexico · Singapore · United Kingdom · United States

National Geographic Learning,
a Cengage Company

Grammar in Context 1, Seventh Edition
Sandra N. Elbaum

Publisher: Sherrise Roehr

Executive Editor: Laura Le Dréan

Development Editor: Lisl Bove

Director of Global Marketing: Ian Martin

Heads of Regional Marketing:

  Joy MacFarland (United States and Canada)

  Charlotte Ellis (Europe, Middle East, and Africa)

  Kiel Hamm (Asia)

  Irina Pereyra (Latin America)

Product Marketing Manager: Tracy Bailie

Content Project Manager: Beth F. Houston

Media Researcher: Leila Hishmeh

Art Director: Brenda Carmichael

Senior Designer: Lisa Trager

Operations Support: Rebecca G. Barbush, Hayley Chwazik-Gee

Manufacturing Planner: Mary Beth Hennebury

Composition: MPS North America LLC

For permission to use material from this text or product,
submit all requests online at **cengage.com/permissions**
Further permissions questions can be emailed to
permissionrequest@cengage.com

Grammar in Context 1 ISBN: 978-0-357-14023-9
Grammar in Context 1 + OLP ISBN: 978-0-357-14049-9

National Geographic Learning
200 Pier 4 Boulevard
Boston, MA 02210
USA

Locate your local office at **international.cengage.com/region**

Visit National Geographic Learning online at **ELTNGL.com**
Visit our corporate website at www.cengage.com

Printed in China
Print Number: 01   Print Year: 2019

CONTENTS

1 STUDENT LIFE

2 PLACES TO VISIT

3 HOUSING

4 WHAT'S IN A NAME

5

SAVING THE PLANET

6

OUR FUTURE

7

IN FLIGHT

8

SHOPPING

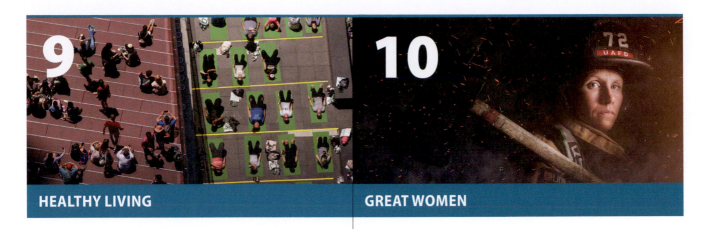

9

HEALTHY LIVING

10

GREAT WOMEN

AMERICAN EXPERIENCES

PEOPLE ON THE MOVE

APPENDICES

WELCOME TO *GRAMMAR IN CONTEXT*, SEVENTH EDITION

Grammar in Context, the original contextualized grammar series, brings grammar to life through engaging topics that provide a framework for meaningful practice. Students learn more, remember more, and use language more effectively when they study grammar in context.

ENHANCED IN THE SEVENTH EDITION

National Geographic photographs introduce unit themes and pull students into the context.

UNIT
10

Adjectives and Adverbs
Noun Modifiers
Too/Very/Enough

A portrait of a firefighter
in Columbus, Ohio, USA

FIREFIGHTER

72

UAFD

GREAT
WOMEN

What you do makes a difference,
and you have to decide what kind of
difference you want to make.

JANE GOODALL

Unit openers include an inspirational quote to help students connect to the theme.

New and updated readings introduce the target grammar in context and provide the springboard for explanations and practice.

New Think About It questions give students the opportunity to personalize and think critically about what they are reading.

CROWDFUNDING

Read the following article. Pay special attention to the words in bold. 🔊 9.3

Have you ever **had** an idea for a business but no way to fund it? **Have** you **asked** relatives and friends for money to help you? If you **have done** these things, you know it isn't easy to get people interested in investing in your dream. After getting money from relatives and friends, it's hard to find more people willing to invest. Lately people **have found** a different way to raise cash: through crowdfunding. Crowdfunding is a method of "collecting small amounts of money from a lot of different people, usually by using the Internet." While the idea **has been** around for possibly hundreds of years, the word "crowdfunding" **has** only **existed** since 2006.

Crowdfunding websites, which started to appear on the Internet in 2010, **have helped** individuals raise billions of dollars worldwide. So how does it work? A person demonstrates his idea in a short video and states his financial goal and the time frame for raising money. Usually the first investors are family and friends. Little by little strangers become interested and donate money.

Not all crowdfunding plans are for profit. Some people **have used** crowdfunding websites that are specifically for philanthropic¹ projects. These sites **have attracted** people who want to make the world a better place. The 97 Supermarket in Changchun, China is one example of this. Jiang Naijun used crowdfunding to get the money to open a supermarket. She named her market 97 because that was her age when she did this. Since she became profitable, she **has given** at least half the money she earns to charity², to help children in need. "I wanted to do more for society," she said.

If you want more information, just google "crowdfunding" and you will find a number of different sites specializing in different types of projects.

¹ philanthropic: intended to help others
² charity: an organization that helps people in need

Crowdfunding has become one of the most popular ways for people to raise money for a cause, project, or event. In 2017, $34 billion was raised globally. This number is expected to grow to more than $300 billion by 2025.

98-year-old Jiang Naijun used crowdfunding to start her supermarket and donates the profits to charity.

234   Unit 9

COMPREHENSION Based on the reading, write T for *true* or F for *false*.

1. _____ Sometimes strangers help fund a crowdfunding project.
2. _____ The idea of crowdfunding is old, but it has become easier to do with the Internet.
3. _____ The "97 Supermarket" project didn't reach its financial goal.

THINK ABOUT IT Discuss the questions with a partner or in a small group.

1. What would you like to crowdfund for? Why?
2. What might be some challenges with crowdfunding? Explain.

9.4 The Present Perfect—Overview of Uses

EXAMPLES	EXPLANATION
People **have used** crowdfunding since 2010. Google **has been** in existence for over 20 years.	We use the present perfect to show that an action or state started in the past and continues to the present.
I **have used** my laptop in coffee shops many times. How many articles about crowdfunding **have** you **read**?	We use the present perfect to show that an action repeated during a period of time that started in the past and includes the present.
Have you ever **asked** relatives for money?	We use the present perfect to show that an action occurred at an indefinite time in the past.

EXERCISE 7 Tell if the sentences show continuation from past to present (C), repetition from past to present (R), or an indefinite time in the past (I).

1. Larry Page has been interested in computers since he was a child. ___C___
2. How many e-mails have you received today? _____
3. I've had my laptop for one year. _____
4. The word "crowdfunding" has been in existence since 2006. _____
5. Internet security has become a big problem. _____
6. Has your computer ever had a virus? _____
7. My cousin has used crowdfunding two times. _____
8. Have you ever used your laptop in a coffee shop? _____

GRAMMAR IN USE
When an event happened in the recent past, and the effect is still felt, we often use the present perfect. This is especially common for speakers of British English. In American English, we use either the present perfect or the simple past.

Someone **has** *just* **donated** $10,000!
I **have forgotten** my password again.
Have you **heard** the news?

The Present Perfect, The Present Perfect Continuous   235

New Grammar in Use notes highlight practical usage points to help students communicate more effectively.

New listening comprehension activities encourage students to listen for meaning through natural spoken English.

EXERCISE 17 Listen to the information about the U.S. Census. Write T for *true*, F for *false*, or NS for *not stated*. 🔊 9.6

1. _____ At first, children were not counted in the census.
2. _____ All census information is available to everyone.
3. _____ Most Americans complete the census questionnaire.

New Fun with Grammar allows the class to practice grammar in a lively game-like way.

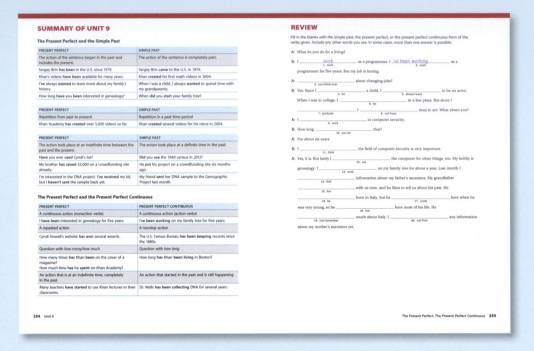

Summary and Review sections help students revisit key points and assess their progress.

From Grammar to Writing gives editing advice and practice to set students up to successfully apply the grammar to writing.

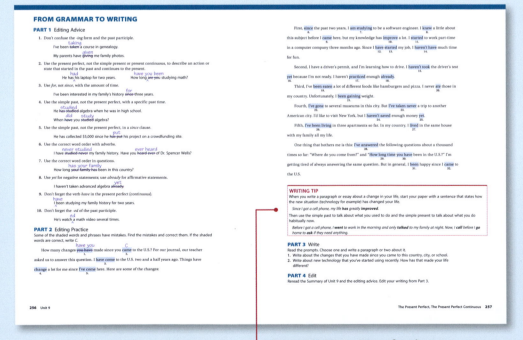

New Writing Tips further connect the grammar to the unit writing task.

ADDITIONAL RESOURCES

FOR STUDENTS The **Online Practice** provides a variety of interactive grammar activities for homework or flexible independent study.

GO TO ELTNGL.COM/MYELT

FOR TEACHERS The **Classroom Presentation Tool** allows the teacher to project the student book pages, open interactive activities with answers, and play the audio program.

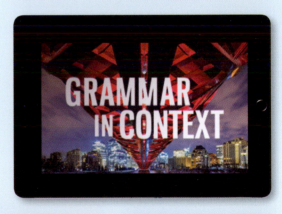

The Teacher's Website hosts the teacher's guide, audio, and ExamView® Test Center, so teachers have all the materials they need in one place.

ELTNGL.COM/GRAMMARINCONTEXTSERIES

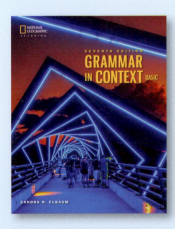
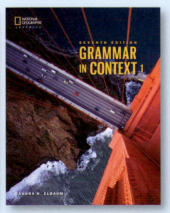
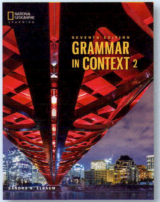

ACKNOWLEDGMENTS

The Author and Publisher would like to acknowledge and thank the teachers who participated in the development of the seventh edition of *Grammar in Context*.

A special thanks to our Advisory Board for their valuable input during the development of this series.

ADVISORY BOARD

Andrea Gonzalez, BYU English Language Center, Provo, UT, USA

Ellen Rosen, Fullerton College, Fullerton, CA, USA

Erin Pak, Schoolcraft College, Livonia, MI, USA

Holly Gray, Prince George's Community College, Largo, MD, USA

John Halliwell, Moraine Valley Community College, Palos Hills, IL, USA

Katherine Sieradzki, FLS Boston, Boston, MA, USA

Maria Schirta, Hudson County Community College, Jersey City, NJ, USA

Oranit Limmaneeprasert, American River College, Sacramento, CA, USA

Susan Niemeyer, Los Angeles City College, Los Angeles, CA, USA

REVIEWERS

Adriana García, Institut Nord-America, Barcelona, Spain

Alena Widows, Institut Nord-America, Barcelona, Spain

Augustine Triantafyllides, So Easy, Athens, Greece

Bilal Aslam, GTCC, High Point, NC, USA

Carmen Díez, CFA Les Corts, Barcelona, Spain

David Finfrock, QU, Doha, Qatar

Deanna Henderson, LCI, Denver, CO, USA

Ellen Barrett, Wayne State University, Detroit, MI, USA

Francis Bandin, UAB, Barcelona, Spain

Jonathan Lathers, Macomb Community College, Warren, MI, USA

Karen Vallejo, University of California, Irvine, CA, USA

Kathy Najafi, Houston Community College, Houston, TX, USA

Katie Windahl, Cuyahoga Community College, Cleveland, OH, USA

Laura Jacob, Mt. San Antonio College, Walnut, CA, USA

Leah Carmona, Bergen Community College, Paramus, NJ, USA

Luba Nesterova, Bilingual Education Institute, Houston, TX, USA

Marcos Valle, Edmonds Community College, Lynnwood, WA, USA

Marla Goldfine, San Diego Community College, San Diego, CA, USA

Milena Eneva, Chattahoochee Technical College, Marietta, GA, USA

Monica Farling, University of Delaware, Newark, DE, USA

Naima Sarfraz, Qatar University, Doha, Qatar

Natalia Schroeder, Long Beach City College, Long Beach, CA, USA

Paul Schmitt, Institut d'Estudis Nord-Americans, Barcelona, Spain

Paula Sanchez, Miami Dade College, Miami, FL, USA

Paulette Koubek-Yao, Pasadena City College, Pasadena, CA, USA

Robert Yáñez, Hillsborough Community College, Tampa, FL, USA

Samuel Lumbsden, Essex County College, Newark, NJ, USA

Sarah Mikulski, Harper College, Palatine, IL, USA

Steven Lund, Arizona Western College, Yuma, AZ, USA

Teresa Cheung, North Shore Community College, Lynn, MA, USA

Tim McDaniel, Green River College, Auburn, WA, USA

Tristinn Williams, Cascadia College, Seattle, WA, USA

Victoria Mullens, LCI, Denver, CO, USA

A WORD FROM THE AUTHOR

My parents immigrated to the United States from Poland and learned English as a second language as adults. My sisters and I were born in the United States. My parents spoke Yiddish to us; we answered in English. In that process, my parents' English improved immeasurably. Such is the case with many immigrant parents whose children are fluent in English. They usually learn English much faster than others; they hear the language in natural ways, in the context of daily life.

Learning a language in context, whether it be from the home, from work, or from a textbook, cannot be overestimated. The challenge for me has been to find a variety of high-interest topics to engage the adult language learner. I was thrilled to work on this new edition of *Grammar in Context* for National Geographic Learning. In so doing, I have been able to combine exciting new readings with captivating photos to exemplify the grammar.

I have given more than 100 workshops at ESL programs and professional conferences around the United States, where I have gotten feedback from users of previous editions of *Grammar in Context*. Some teachers have expressed concern about trying to cover long grammar units within a limited time. While ESL is not taught in a uniform number of hours per week, I have heeded my audiences and streamlined the series so that the grammar and practice covered is more manageable. And in response to the needs of most ESL programs, I have expanded and enriched the writing component.

Whether you are a new user of *Grammar in Context* or have used this series before, I welcome you to this new edition.

Sandra N. Elbaum

For my loves
Gentille, Chimene, Joseph, and Joy

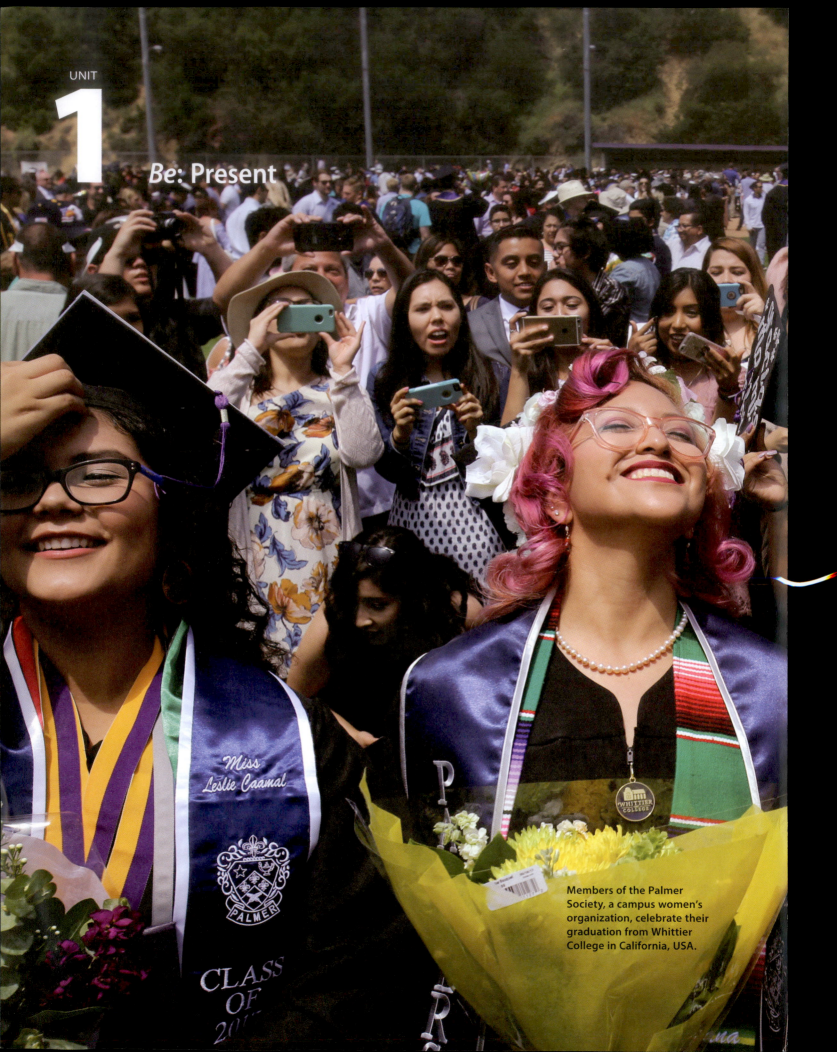

Members of the Palmer Society, a campus women's organization, celebrate their graduation from Whittier College in California, USA.

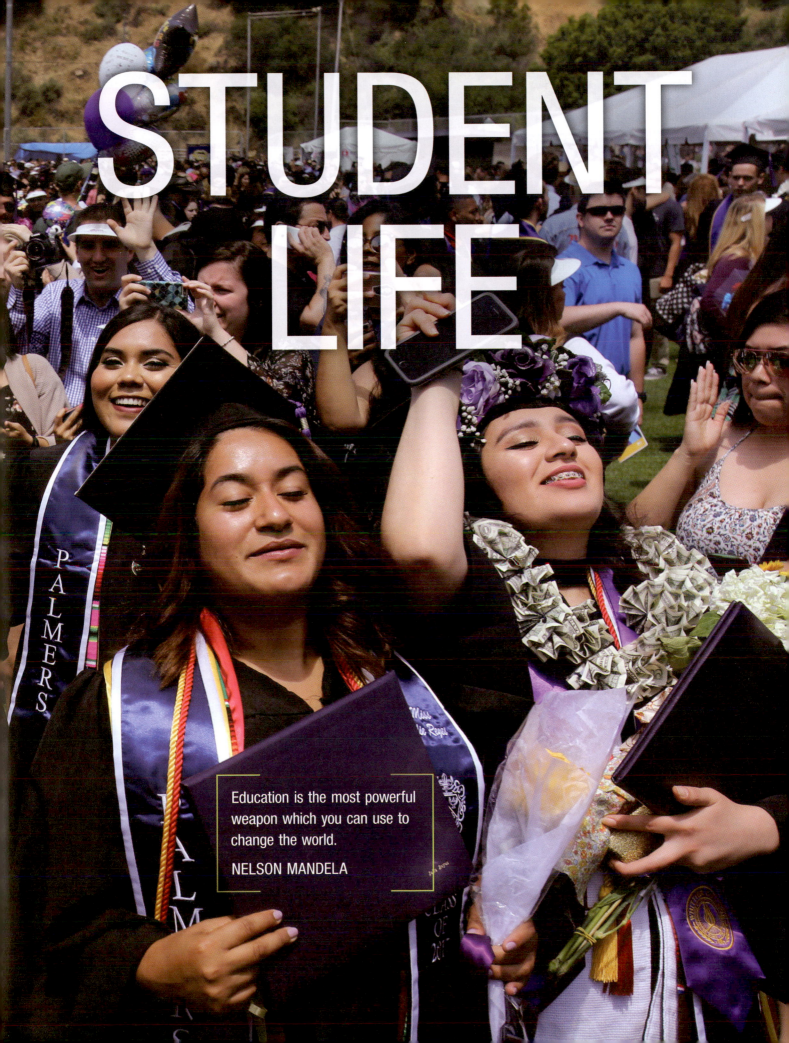

STUDENT
LIFE

Education is the most powerful weapon which you can use to change the world.

NELSON MANDELA

COMMUNITY COLLEGE FAQs

Read the following article. Pay special attention to the words in bold. 🎧 1.1

Q: **Is** community college a popular choice for students in the United States?

A: Yes, it **is**. About 34 percent of all college students in the U.S. **are** community college students.

Q: Why **is** it a popular choice?

A: Community colleges **are** usually less expensive than four-year colleges. Also, a community college degree **is** only two years.

Q: How old **is** the typical community college student?

A: The average age **is** 28.

Q: **Are** most community college students in school full time?

A: No, they **aren't**. About 66 percent of community college students **are** in school part time.

Q: Why **are** so many community college students in school part time?

A: Because most of them work. Twenty-two percent work full time, and 41 percent work part time.

Q: **Is** it difficult for these students to take classes?

A: It **isn't** usually a problem. At community colleges, classes **are not** only during the day. They **are** also at night and on weekends. The schedule **is** very helpful for busy students like me.

Q: **Is** your community college easy to get to?

A: It **is** near public transportation. It**'s** very convenient[1].

Q: **Is** it a good idea to go to community college?

A: Yes, it **is**! The yearly salary for a person with a community college degree **is** about $4,500 more than for a person without a degree.

---

[1] convenient: easy to get to

Aerial view of Shelton State Community College in Tuscaloosa, Alabama, USA

COMPREHENSION Based on the reading, write T for *true* or F for *false*.

1. _____ Many students in the U.S. go to a community college.

2. _____ Most community college students study full time.

3. _____ Community colleges are good for busy students.

THINK ABOUT IT Discuss the questions with a partner or in a small group.

1. Is community college a good choice for you? Explain.

2. Do you think it's a good idea for students to work and go to college at the same time? Explain.

1.1 *Be*—Present Forms

The verb *be* has three forms in the present: *am, is,* and *are.*

SUBJECT	BE	
I	**am**	a professor.
She		from Chicago.
My professor		excellent. ← *very good*
He	**is**	from the Philippines.
The college		convenient.
It		near public transportation.
We		ESL students.
You	**are**	a good teacher.
They		nice.

Notes:

1. The subject is a noun (*professor, college,* etc.) or a pronoun (*I, you, he, she, it, we, they*).
2. We begin sentences with the subject.

   The teacher is intelligent. (NOT: *Is intelligent the teacher.*)

EXERCISE 1 Listen to a student talking about his classes. Write T for *true*, F for *false*, or NS for *not stated*. 🎧 1.2

1. _____ Rolando works during the day.

2. _____ Susana's classes are in the evening.

3. _____ Rolando is 35 years old.

EXERCISE 2 Listen again. Then fill in the blanks with the words you hear. 🎧 1.2

My name ____is____ Rolando Lopez. I _____ from Guatemala.
    1.   **2.**

I _____ a student at a community college. My major _____ engineering. My
    3.   **4.**

engineering classes _____ at night, and my English class _____ on Saturdays.
    5.   **6.**

continued

My wife, Susana, _____ a student here, too. Susana _____ in the nursing
                              7.   8.
program. Her classes _____ in the morning. She _____ home with our
                              9.   10.
children in the evening. They _____ in school during the day.
                                        11.
The students in my ESL class _____ from nine different countries. Some students
                                          12.
_____ in their forties or fifties, but some _____ in their twenties. I
        13.   14.
_____ 35 years old.
        15.

1.2 *Be*—Uses

EXAMPLES	EXPLANATION
Evening classes **are convenient**. The tuition **is low**. Chicago **is a city**. Illinois **is a state**.	We use *be* with a description of the subject. We use *be* when we define or classify the subject or say what the subject is.
My community college **is in Chicago**. The college **is near public transportation**.	We use *be* with the location of the subject.
I **am from Guatemala**. My wife **is from Mexico**.	We use *be* with the place of origin of the subject.
Rolando **is 35 years old**.	We use *be* with the age of the subject.
It **is cold** in Chicago in the winter.	We use *is* with weather. The subject for weather is *it*.
It **is 6 o'clock** now.	We use *is* with time. The subject for time is *it*.

GRAMMAR IN USE

The verb *be* is the most common verb in English. It connects the subject to a noun, adjective, or prepositional phrase. You cannot leave it out. Some languages do not have a similar verb.

He *is* from Saudi Arabia. (NOT: He from Saudi Arabia.)   They *are* students. (NOT: They students.)

EXERCISE 3 Fill in the blanks with a form of *be*.

1. My name _____ is _____ Rolando Lopez.

2. I _____ from Guatemala.

3. My wife _____ from Guatemala, too.

4. My wife and I _____ students.

5. Guatemala _____ a country in Central America.

6. My classmates _____ from nine different countries.

7. We _____ immigrants.

8. You _____ interested in nursing.

9. My major _____ engineering.

10. It _____ warm in Guatemala all year.

EXERCISE 4 Match each subject with the correct phrase. Then write a sentence using each subject and phrase with the correct form of *be*.

1. Trains and buses ___d___   **a.** is in Chicago.

2. My community college _____   **b.** the cost of college courses.

3. Some adult education classes _____   **c.** from many different countries.

4. ESL students _____   **d.** forms of transportation.

5. Tuition _____   **e.** an ESL student.

6. I _____   **f.** hot in Guatemala in the summer.

7. Spanish _____   **g.** the language of Mexico.

8. It _____   **h.** free.

1. _Trains and buses are forms of transportation._____

2. _____

3. _____

4. _____

5. _____

6. _____

7. _____

8. _____

EXERCISE 5 Fill in the blanks to make true statements.

1. My classroom is on _the second floor_____.
   _{location}

2. Chicago and Los Angeles are _____.
   _{description}

3. The school is in _____.
   _{location}

4. The teacher is about _____ years old.
   _{age}

5. The teacher is from _____.
   _{place}

6. It is _____ now.
   _{time}

7. It is _____ today.
   _{weather}

8. My school is _____.
   _{description}

1.3 Subject Pronouns and Nouns

EXAMPLES	EXPLANATION
You are a good student. **I** am in the United States. **It** is Monday.	The subject pronouns are *I, you, he, she, it, we,* and *they.*
Chicago is very big. **It** is in Illinois. **My wife** is a student. **She** is from Mexico. **My parents** are in Guatemala. **They** are happy.	Subject pronouns (*it, she, they*) can take the place of subject nouns (*Chicago, wife, parents*).
My classmates are from different countries. **They** are immigrants. **English and math** are my favorite subjects. **They** are useful subjects.	We use *they* for plural people and things.
You are a good teacher. **You** are good students.	*You* can be a singular or plural subject pronoun.
My wife and I are in the United States. **We** are in Chicago.	When the subject is another person and *I*, we put the other person before *I*.

GRAMMAR IN USE

In conversation, you sometimes hear sentences like "Me and my friend are from Mexico." This is common but not correct. *Me* is not a subject pronoun. The correct sentence is "My friend and I are from Mexico."

EXERCISE 6 Fill in the blanks with the correct subject pronoun.

1. Nicaragua and Guatemala are countries. _____*They*_____ are in Central America.

2. My wife and I are students. _____ are students at a community college.

3. Guatemala is a small country. _____ is south of Mexico.

4. _____ is warm in Guatemala all year.

5. Some students are international students. _____ are from China, Japan, and Spain.

6. _____ am an ESL student.

7. English is a useful language. _____ is necessary in the United States.

8. Adult classes at my college are free. _____ are for ESL students.

9. My book is new. _____ is *Grammar in Context*.

10. I am a student. _____ are the teacher.

11. My teacher is a nice woman. _____ is from Boston.

12. My classmates and I are interested in American life. _____ are new here.

EXERCISE 7 Put the words in the correct order to make a statement. Use a capital letter at the beginning and a period at the end.

1. a two-year college/my college/is

   My college is a two-year college.

2. am/I/a student

   _____

3. my parents/in Guatemala/are

   _____

4. expensive/is/a four-year college

   _____

5. is/convenient for me/my college

   _____

6. my teacher/is/40 years old

   _____

7. is/from New York/my teacher

   _____

8. eight weeks long/my class/is

   _____

9. Rolando/married/is

   _____

10. cold/it/is/in the winter

    _____

1.4 Contractions with *Be*

EXAMPLES		EXPLANATION
I am You are She is He is It is We are They are	**I'm** in Minneapolis. **You're** a student. **She's** a young teacher. **He's** 74 years old. **It's** cold in winter. **We're** busy. **They're** big.	We can make a contraction with a subject pronoun + *am, is,* or *are*. We put an apostrophe (') in place of the missing letter.
Rolando is Guatemala is	**Rolando's** from Guatemala. **Guatemala's** in Central America.	We can make a contraction with most nouns + *is*.
Here is	**Here's** a class schedule.	We can make a contraction with *here is*.
My clas<u>s</u> **is** big. Beli<u>ze</u> **is** in Central America. Engli<u>sh</u> **is** the language of the United States. Colle<u>ge</u> **is** different here.		We don't make a contraction with *is* if the subject noun ends in *s, se, z, ze, ge, ce, sh, ch,* or *x*.
Textbooks **are** expensive. The classrooms **are** big.		We don't make a contraction with a plural noun and *are*.

GRAMMAR IN USE

We usually use contractions when we speak. The full form sounds very formal.

> **It's** *a beautiful day.*

We sometimes use contractions in informal writing like email.

> **I'm** *happy about my grade.*

EXERCISE 8 Complete the conversation between a new student (A) and a teacher (B). Use contractions with a form of *be*.

A: I 'm _____ late.
　　　　　　　1.

B: That _____ OK.
　　　　　　2.

A: I _____ sorry.
　　　　　3.

B: No problem. It _____ the first day of class.
　　　　　　　　　　　　4.

A: The parking lot _____ very crowded.
　　　　　　　　　　　　5.

B: Yes, it _____ a problem.
　　　　　　　　6.

A: My friend _____ late, too. He _____ in the parking lot.
　　　　　　　　　7.　　　　　　　　　　　　8.

B: Don't worry. The first day _____ always hard.
　　　　　　　　　　　　　　9.

A: I _____ so sorry.
   10.

B: It _____ OK. Really.
   11.

A: You _____ very kind. Oh. Here _____ my friend now.
   12.   13.

B: Good. We _____ ready to begin.
   14.

EXERCISE 9 Complete the paragraph with the correct forms of *be*. Use contractions when possible.

OK, class. It 's_____ time to begin. You _____ all here now. My name
   1.   2.

_____ Peter Lang. Call me "Peter." English _____ my native language. I
   3.   4.

_____ happy to be your teacher. Here _____ a paper with information about
   5.   6.

the school, the class, and the textbook. The information _____ on my class website,
   7.

too. My office _____ on the second floor, Room 2030. The textbook for the course
   8.

_____ *Grammar in Context*. The bookstore _____ on Broadway Avenue.
   9.   10.

The address _____ 4545 North Broadway.
   11.

EXERCISE 10 Complete the paragraph with the correct forms of *be*. Use contractions when possible.

I 'm_____ a student of English at a commumity college. I _____ happy in
   1.   2.

the United States. My teacher _____ American. His name _____ Charles
   3.   4.

Madison. Charles _____ a good teacher. He _____ patient with students.
   5.   6.

My class _____ big. All the students _____ immigrants, but
   7.   8.

we _____ from different countries. Five students _____ from Asia. One
   9.   10.

woman _____ from Poland. She _____ from Warsaw, the capital of Poland.
   11.   12.

Many students _____ from Mexico. We _____ ready to learn English, but
   13.   14.

English _____ a hard language for me.
   15.

1.5 Be + Adjective Descriptions

EXAMPLES				EXPLANATION
Subject	**Be**	**Very**	**Adjective**	
My teacher	is		kind.	After a form of *be*, we can use an adjective to describe the subject. *Very* can come before an adjective.
The desks	are	very	small.	
The college	is		interesting.	
I	am		tired.	
I'm **thirsty**. We're **afraid**.				We use *be* with physical or mental conditions: *hungry, thirsty, cold, hot, tired, happy, afraid,* etc.

Note:

Some adjectives end in *-ed* or *-ing*.

    bored/boring, confused/confusing, interested/interesting

ABOUT YOU Write sentences about your school. Use a singular or plural subject and the correct form of *be*. Use contractions when possible. Then compare your answers with a partner.

1. _____ My teachers are _____ intelligent.

2. _____ expensive.

3. _____ cheap.

4. _____ new.

5. _____ big.

6. _____ friendly.

7. _____ hard.

8. _____ interesting.

EXERCISE 11 Complete the sentences with the correct form of *be* and an adjective.

1. The classroom __is clean_____ .

2. The college _____ .

3. The school library _____ .

4. The school cafeteria _____ .

5. The textbook for the course _____ .

6. The parking lot _____.

7. The teachers at the school _____.

8. American students _____.

9. Schools in the United States _____.

10. Students in the United States _____.

1.6 *Be* + (Adjective +) Noun Descriptions

SINGULAR SUBJECT	BE	A/AN	ADJECTIVE	SINGULAR NOUN
Harvard	is	a	large	university.
I	am	an	international	student.
You	are	a	fast	reader.
PLURAL SUBJECT	**BE**		**ADJECTIVE**	**PLURAL NOUN**
You and I	are		new	students.
They	are		good	friends.

Notes:

1. We use the articles *a* and *an* for singular nouns. We don't use *a* or *an* for plural nouns.
2. We use *a* before a consonant sound. We use *an* before a vowel sound. The vowels are *a, e, i, o,* and *u.*
3. We use *a* when a beginning *u* is not a vowel sound.
   English is **a useful** language.

EXERCISE 12 Fill in the blanks with the correct form of *be.* Add *a* or *an* when necessary.

1. Nursing and technology _____ *are* _____ popular college programs.

2. Broward College _____ community college in Florida.

3. Harvard _____ old university.

4. Chicago _____ interesting city.

5. My friend and I _____ students here.

6. You _____ teacher.

7. I _____ immigrant.

8. Some students _____ international students.

9. My dictionary _____ useful book.

Complete the sentences to make true statements about your college or school. Use the correct form of *be* and *a* or *an* when necessary.

1. _____Math 101 is an_____ easy course.

2. _____ hard courses.

3. _____ useful website.

4. _____ heavy book.

5. _____ noisy places.

6. _____ quiet place.

7. _____ American teachers.

8. _____ good students.

9. _____ crowded place.

1.7 Negative Statements with *Be*

EXAMPLES	EXPLANATION
I **am not** married. Rolando **is not** from Mexico.	We put *not* after a form of *be* to make a negative statement.

Two Kinds of Contractions

	CONTRACTION WITH SUBJECT PRONOUN AND *BE*	CONTRACTION WITH *BE* AND *NOT*
I **am not**	I**'m not**	—
you **are not**	you**'re not**	you **aren't**
he **is not**	he**'s not**	he **isn't**
she **is not**	she**'s not**	she **isn't**
it **is not**	it**'s not**	it **isn't**
we **are not**	we**'re not**	we **aren't**
they **are not**	they**'re not**	they **aren't**

Notes:

1. We cannot make a contraction with *am + not*. (NOT: *I amn't*)

2. We can make negative contractions with most nouns.

   Rolando is not Mexican. = *Rolando's **not** Mexican.* OR *Rolando **isn't** Mexican.*

3. Remember: We cannot make a contraction with certain words + *is*. (See Chart 1.4.)

   English is not my native language. = *English **isn't** my native language.* (NOT: *English's not my native language.*)

EXERCISE 13 Fill in the blanks with a subject pronoun and a negative form of *be*. Use both ways of making contractions when possible.

1. The classroom is clean and big.

   _____It isn't_____ dirty. _____It's not_____ small.

2. My husband and I are in the classroom.

   _____ in the library. _____ in the cafeteria.

3. Today's a weekday.

   _____ Saturday. _____ Sunday.

4. I'm a student.

   _____ a teacher.

5. The students are busy.

   _____ lazy. _____ tired.

6. You're on time.

   _____ early. _____ late.

7. My classmates and I are in an English class.

   _____ in the cafeteria. _____ in the library.

ABOUT YOU Write T for *true* or F for *false* next to each statement. If it's false, make the statement negative and write a true statement. Use pronouns and contractions. Share your answers with a partner.

1. Today is the first day of class. _____F_____

   _Today's not the first day of class. It's the third day of class._____

2. The students in my class are from different countries. _____

   _____

3. I'm an immigrant. _____

   _____

4. I'm married. _____

   _____

5. The school is convenient for me. _____

   _____

6. My parents are proud of me. _____

_____

7. The parking lot is free here. _____

_____

8. The school is near public transportation. _____

_____

9. The semester is eight weeks long. _____

_____

10. Arabic is my native language. _____

_____

The Foggy Bottom–GWU metro station is on the George Washington University campus in Washington, DC.

High school seniors at their graduation ceremony

Public School FAQs

Read the following questions and answers about education in the United States. Pay special attention to the words in bold. 🎧 1.3

Are you interested in American education? **Are** you confused about some things? Here are some frequently asked questions (FAQs):

Q: **Is** education for children **in the United States** free?

A: Yes, it **is**. It's free **in public schools** through high school.

Q: **Are** all children in public schools?

A: No, they **aren't**. Eighty-eight percent of children are in public schools. Nine percent are **in private schools**. Private schools aren't free.

Q: What about the other 3 percent?

A: 3 percent are homeschooled. The parents are the children's teachers.

Q: **How many** months a year **are** students **in school**?

A: They're in school for 10 months a year.

Q: **What's** a freshman?

A: A freshman is a student in the first year of high school or college. A sophomore is a student in the second year. A junior is a student in the third year. A senior is a student in the fourth year.

Q: **How many** years **are** students in school?

A: Most students are in school for 12 years. It depends on the state.

Q: **Are** rules different from state to state?

A: Yes, they **are**.

The chart shows the different possibilities for a 12-year education in the United States.

8 years elementary school
4 years high school

6 years elementary school
2 years middle school
4 years high school

5 years elementary school
3 years middle school
4 years high school

COMPREHENSION Based on the reading, write T for *true* or F for *false*.

1. _____ Middle school is always three years in the United States.

2. _____ All students in the United States are in public schools.

3. _____ A freshman is a first-year student in high school or college.

THINK ABOUT IT Discuss the questions with a partner or in a small group.

1. How many years are students in school in your country?

2. Why do you think some children are homeschooled?

1.8 *Yes/No* Questions and Short Answers with *Be*

STATEMENT	YES/NO QUESTION	SHORT ANSWER
I **am** a student.	**Am** I a good student?	Yes, you **are**.
You **are** in college.	**Are** you at a community college?	No, I'm **not**.
He **is** a teacher.	**Is** he a good teacher?	Yes, he **is**.
She **is** in high school.	**Is** she a junior?	No, she **isn't**.
It **is** June.	**Is** it vacation time?	Yes, it **is**.
We **are** in high school.	**Are** we freshmen?	Yes, we **are**.
They **are** students.	**Are** they in public school?	No, they **aren't**.
Education **is** free in public schools.	**Is** education free in college?	No, it **isn't**.

Notes:

1. We use a contraction for a short *no* answer. We don't use a contraction for a short *yes* answer.

> Is the school open on December 25? No, it **isn't**.

> Is a C a passing grade? Yes, it **is**. (NOT: Yes, it's.)

2. We use a pronoun in a short answer.

> Is Rolando a freshman? Yes, **he** is. (NOT: Yes, Rolando is.)

EXERCISE 14 Complete the conversation between two students. Use contractions when possible.

A: Hi. My name 's_____ Hector. I _____ new here.
                        1.   **2.**

B: Hi. My name _____ Eduardo.
                        3.

A: I'm from Mexico. _____ from Mexico, too?
                              4.

B: No, _____ . I'm from Brazil.
              5.

A: I'm a sophomore. _____ a sophomore, too?
                              6.

B: Yes, _____ .
              7.

A: _____ in the same ESL class?
      8.

B: Yes, we _____ .
                9.

A: _____ the teacher American?
      10.

B: No, _____ . She's Canadian.
            11.

A: _____ time for class now?
      12.

B: Yes, it _____ . _____ almost ten o'clock. Let's go.
               13.   14.

EXERCISE 15 Find a partner. Ask and answer *yes/no* questions about your school and this class. Use the words given and the correct form of *be*. Use contractions in your answers when possible.

1. the school/big

   A: *Is the school big?*

   B: *Yes, it is.*

2. it/near public transportation

3. the cafeteria/on the first floor

4. it/open now

5. the library/closed now

6. the course/free

7. the textbooks/free

8. the teacher/American

9. the classroom/clean

10. it/big

11. you/a freshman

1.9 *Wh-* Questions with *Be*

STATEMENT	*WH-* QUESTION
I **am** late.	**How** late **am** I?
You **are** from South America.	**Where are** you from?
He **is** my teacher.	**Who is** he?
It **is** late.	**What** time **is** it?
We **are** lost.	**Where are** we?
They **are** here on Fridays.	**When are** they here?
The teacher **isn't** here today.	**Why isn't** the teacher here today?

Notes:

1. We can make a contraction with a *wh-* word + *is*: *who's, what's, when's, where's, how's, why's.*

2. After *what*, we can use a noun.

   what kind, what nationality, what country, what time

3. We use *how* to ask about health or an opinion.

   How are you? I'm fine.

   How is your English class? It's hard.

4. After *how*, we can use an adjective or an adverb.

   how long, how late, how old, how big, how much, how many

EXERCISE 16 Complete the conversation between two students. Use contractions when possible.

A: You're in my math class, right?

B: Yes, I am. <u>   *What's*   </u> your name?
             1.

A: Aya Barghouti.

B: Nice to meet you. I'm Joao Santos.

A: _____ your English teacher?
              2.

B: Peter Lang.

A: He's my teacher, too! Are we in the same class?

B: _____ your class?
            3.

A: It's on Mondays and Wednesdays at 10:00 a.m.

B: My class is on Tuesdays and Thursdays at 9:00 a.m.

A: _____ nationality is Mr. Lang?
            4.

B: He's Canadian, I think. I'm from Brazil. _____ you from?
                                                              5.

A: I'm from Syria.

B: _____ Syria?
            6.

A: It's in the Middle East.

B: _____ your native language?
            7.

A: It's Arabic. Mr. Lang speaks Arabic, too.

B: Mr. Lang isn't here today.

A: _____ here today? Is he sick?
            8.

B: No, he isn't. His daughter is in a play.

GRAMMAR IN USE

Many *wh-* questions with *is ('s)* are common in conversation:

What's up?	*How's the weather?*
What's the matter?	*How's the food?*
What's that?	*Where's the bus?*
Who's there?	*When's the test?*

EXERCISE 17 Choose the correct word(s) to complete the phone conversation between a student in the United States (A) and his brother back home (B).

A: Hello?

B: Hi, Sayed. It's Ali. How are you?

A: I'm fine.

B: Where (*are you*/*you are*) now?
        1.

A: I'm in my dorm. (*Are you*/*You are*) at home?
                    2.

B: Yes, (*I am*/*I'm*). It's 4:15 p.m. here. (*What time is it*/*What time it is*) there?
       3.   **4.**

A: It's 1:15 a.m. here. It's late but I'm not tired.

B: Why (*aren't you*/*you aren't*) tired?
        5.

A: I'm nervous about my test tomorrow.

B: (*How's*/*What's*) college life in the United States? (*It is*/*Is it*) very different from here?
    6.   **7.**

A: Yes, (*is it*/*it is*). My new classmates are so interesting. (*They're*/*Are they*) from many different countries
        8.   **9.**

    and are all ages. One man in my class is older than everyone else.

B: (*How old is he*/*How is he old*)?
           10.

A: He's 75.

B: Really? (*Where he's*/*Where's he*) from?
            11.

A: South Korea. (*Where are Mom and Dad*/*Where Mom and Dad are*) now?
              12.

B: At work. (*They're*/*They*) worried about you.
          13.

A: Why (*they are*/*are they*) worried about me?
          14.

B: Because you're alone in the United States.

A: (*It's*/*Is*) not a problem for me. I'm on the dean's list.
    15.

B: (*What's*/*Who's*) the dean's list?
        16.

A: It's a list of students with high grades.

B: (*I'm*/*I*) proud of you.
    17.

ABOUT YOU Fill in the blanks to make true statements. Then use the words given to write questions. Use contractions when possible.

1. I'm from _____Bosnia_____.

   where _Where are you from?_____

2. My name is _____.

   what _____

3. My family is _____.

   how big _____

4. The president/prime minister of my country is _____.

   who _____

5. The flag from my country is _____.

   what color _____

6. My country is in _____.

   where _____

7. I'm _____ feet, _____ inches tall.

   how tall _____

8. My birthday is in _____.

   when _____

9. My favorite subject in school is _____.

   what _____

10. It's _____ in my hometown.

    what time _____

EXERCISE 18 Find a partner (from a different country, if possible). Ask and answer your questions.

   A: *I'm from Bosnia. Where are you from?*

   B: *I'm from Taiwan.*

EXERCISE 19 Complete the phone conversation between two friends.

A: Hello?

B: Hi, Cindy. This is Maria.

A: Hi, Maria. How _____are you_____?
    1.

B: I'm fine.

A: _____ your first day of class?
        2.

B: Yes, it _____. I'm at school now, but I'm not in class.
            3.

A: Why _____ in class?
          4.

B: Because it's break time now.

A: How _____ the break?
          5.

B: It's 10 minutes long.

A: How _____?
                        6.

B: My English class is great. My classmates are very interesting.

A: Where _____ from?
                        7.

B: They're from all over the world.

A: _____ your teacher American?
          8.

B: Yes, she _____. She's from California. _____?
              9.   **10.**

A: It's 3:35.

B: Oh, I'm late.

A: Let's get together soon. _____ free this weekend?
                                  11.

B: Yes, I am. I'm free on Saturday afternoon.

A: I have a class on Saturday.

B: When _____ free?
              12.

A: On Sunday afternoon.

B: Sunday's fine, after 1:00. Talk to you later.

1.10 Prepositions of Place

We use prepositions to show where things are (location) and where they are from (origin).

PREPOSITION	EXAMPLES	
on	The books are **on** the table. The cafeteria is **on** the first floor.	
at	I am **at** school. My brother is **at** home. My parents are **at** work.	
in	The students are **in** the classroom. The wastebasket is **in** the corner.	
in front of	The board is **in front of** the students.	
in back of/behind	The board is **in back of** the teacher. The wall is **behind** the board.	
between	The empty chair is **between** the students.	
over/above	The exit sign is **over** the door. The clock is **above** the lockers.	
below/under	The books are **below** the desks. The desks are **under** the chairs.	
by/near/close to	The chair is **by** the window. The chair is **near** the window. The chair is **close to** the window.	
next to	The light switch is **next to** the door.	

PREPOSITION	EXAMPLES
across from	Room 202 is **across from** Room 203.
far from	Los Angeles is **far from** New York.
in (a city)	My community college is **in Los Angeles**.
on (a street)	It's **on Stevens Creek Boulevard**.
at (an address)	It's **at 21250 Stevens Creek Boulevard**.
from (a place)	Rolando is **from Guatemala**.

Note:

A preposition usually comes at the end of a question.

> *Where is Rolando's wife **from**?*

> *What street is the college bookstore **on**?*

GRAMMAR IN USE

Prepositions often appear in fixed expressions. For example, *at* is used in:

at home	*at the movies*
at work	*at a party*

ABOUT YOU Complete the sentences to make true statements about the location of things or people. Use the correct form of *be* and a preposition.

1. My phone _____*is in my bag*_____ .

2. My classroom _____ .

3. I _____ .

4. The library _____ .

5. The cafeteria _____ .

6. The teacher _____ .

7. We _____ .

8. Our books _____ .

9. The parking lot _____ .

10. The school _____ .

11. The classroom computer _____ .

12. The nearest exit _____ .

Students work on a sample SAT at a test-prep school in Massachusetts, USA.

TEST for COLLEGE ADMISSION

Read the following conversation between a teenager and his younger brother. Pay special attention to the words in bold. 1.4

A: What's **this**? Is it an application for college?

B: No, it isn't. It's an application for the SAT.

A: The SAT? What's **that**?

B: It's a test for college admission[1].

A: What are **those** dates?

B: They're the dates of the test. The test is only a few times a year.

A: What's **that**?

B: It's a test preparation book. The questions are similar to the questions on the SAT.

A: What kind of questions are **those**?

B: They're multiple-choice questions. And **these** are essay questions.

A: Is **this** a test for all subjects?

B: The main test is for reading, math, and writing.

A: What about other subjects, like history and science?

B: Tests for **those** subjects are separate.

A: What are all **these** prices?

B: **This** price is for the main test. **These** prices are for the subject tests.

_____

[1] admission: permission to enter college

COMPREHENSION Based on the reading, write T for *true* or F for *false*.

1. _____ The SAT is a college admissions test.

2. _____ The SAT has only multiple-choice questions.

3. _____ The main SAT has questions about science and history.

1. What is on the university admissions test in your country?

2. Do you think it is a good idea to use a test preparation book before a test like the SAT? Why or why not?

1.11 *This, That, These, Those*

EXAMPLES		EXPLANATION
Singular	**This** is my application. **That** is my professor.	We use *this* (near) and *that* (not near) to identify singular objects and people.
Plural	**These** are the prices. **Those** are the dates.	We use *these* (near) and *those* (not near) to identify plural objects and people.
This question is hard. **Those dates** are convenient.		A noun can follow *this*, *that*, *these*, and *those*.

Notes:

1. Only *that is* can form a contraction (*that's*).

   That's my professor.

2. When the question contains *this* or *that*, the answer uses *it*.

   Is **that** your math book? No. **It's** my English book.

3. When the question contains *these* or *those*, the answer uses *they*.

   What are **those** papers? **They're** applications.

EXERCISE 20 Choose the correct word(s) to complete the conversation between a father and his son.

A: What's (*this*/*these*)?
          1.

B: (*Its*/*It's*) my application for a scholarship.
   2.

A: What are (*that*/*those*)?
          3.

B: (*They*/*They're*) applications for different colleges. (*This*/*These*) college is nearby. (*That*/*Those*)
   4.   5.   6.

colleges are in different states. (*It's*/*They're*) more expensive. Colleges (*are*/*is*) more expensive for
                                  7.   8.

out-of-state students.

A: What's (*that*/*these*) price? (*It is*/*Is it*) the price of a college course?
         9.   10.

B: No. (*That's*/*They're*) the price of the test.
      11.

A: Oh. (*It's*/*Is*) expensive! College, books, tests—(*they're*/*those*) all so expensive.
      12.   13.

B: That's why (*is*/*it's*) important for me to get a scholarship.
          14.

A: Yes, it is. (*This is*/*This's*) very important.
         15.

SUMMARY OF UNIT 1

Forms of *Be: Am, Is, Are*

AFFIRMATIVE STATEMENT	She **is** a senior.	You **are** late.
NEGATIVE STATEMENT	She **isn't** a junior.	You **aren't** on time.
YES/NO QUESTION	**Is** she a senior in college?	**Are** you new here?
SHORT ANSWER	No, she **isn't**.	Yes, I **am**.
WH- QUESTION	**Where is** that college?	**Why are** you late?
NEGATIVE WH- QUESTION	**Why isn't** she in class today?	**Why aren't** you on time?

Uses of *Be*

USE	EXAMPLES
DESCRIPTION	Chicago **is a big city**.
LOCATION	Chicago **is in Illinois**.
PLACE OF ORIGIN	The teacher **is from Chicago**.
AGE	I **am 25 (years old)**.
TIME	It **is 6:00 p.m.**
WEATHER	It **is warm** today.

Contractions with *Be*

	EXAMPLES
With pronouns	I'm, you're, he's, she's, it's, we're, they're
With nouns	the teacher's, Rolando's
With *that*	that's
With question words	what's, when's, where's, why's, how's, who's
With *not*	isn't, aren't

Prepositions of Place

on	at	in	in front of
in back of/behind	between	over/above	below/under
by/near/close to	next to	across from	far from
in (a city)	on (a street)	at (an address)	from (a place)

This/That/These/Those

	SINGULAR	PLURAL
Near	**This** is a college application.	**These** are multiple-choice questions.
Not near	**That**'s a test application.	**Those** are essay questions.

REVIEW

Choose the correct word(s) to complete the conversation between two students. If both answers are correct, circle both choices.

A: Hi, Sofia. How's your English class?

B: Hi, Danuta. (*It's*/*She's*) wonderful. (*I*/*I'm*) very happy with it.
        1.   **2.**

A: What level (*you are*/*are you*) in?
              3.

B: Level 2. My English teacher (*is*/*'s*) Kathy Lee.
                    4.

A: (*Is she*/*She's*) American?
    5.

B: Yes, (*she's*/*she is*). She's (*from*/*of*) New York. (*She's*/*She is*) a very good teacher.
      6.   **7.**   **8.**

    (*Who's your teacher*/*Who your teacher is*)?
           9.

A: Bob Sanchez. He's (*a teacher very good*/*a very good teacher*). But (*I'm not*/*I amn't*) happy with my class.
                  10.   **11.**

B: Why (*you aren't*/*aren't you*) happy with your class?
      12.

A: The classroom's (*on*/*in*) the third floor. It's (*next*/*next to*) the cafeteria, so it's noisy.
            13.   **14.**

B: (*How big is your class*/*How is your class big*)?
        15.

A: Thirty-five students.

B: (*Those*/*That's*) a big class. My (*class's not*/*class isn't*) big—only 15 students.
    16.   **17.**

    The students (*in*/*on*) my class (*'re*/*are*) from seven different countries.
        18.   **19.**

A: Where (*are the students from*/*are from the students*)?
         20.

B: They're from Mexico, Russia, India, Peru, Iraq, Poland, and Vietnam.

A: (*That's*/*This's*) an interesting group. In my class, we (*'re*/*are*) all from Mexico.
    21.   **22.**

B: (*Is American Mr. Sanchez*/*Is Mr. Sanchez American*)?
         23.

A: No, (*he's not*/*he isn't*). He's from Mexico. (*English's not*/*English isn't*) his first language.
        24.   **25.**

    But (*that's not*/*that isn't*) a problem. His English (*'s*/*is*) very good.
        26.   **27.**

B: (*Ms. Lee's*/*Ms. Lee is*) about 55 years old. How (*is Mr. Sanchez old*/*old is Mr. Sanchez*)?
    28.   **29.**

A: (*He's a young man*/*He's young man*). He's about 25.
    30.

FROM GRAMMAR TO WRITING

PART 1 Editing Advice

1. Don't repeat the subject noun with a pronoun.

    My teacher ~~he~~ is from Los Angeles.

2. Use the correct word order.

    My class is small
    ~~Is small my class~~.

    is your teacher
    Where ~~your teacher is~~ from?

3. Every sentence has a subject. For time and weather, the subject is *it*.

    It's
    ~~Is~~ six o'clock now.

    It's
    ~~Is~~ very cold today.

4. Don't confuse *this* and *these*.

    This
    ~~These~~ is my book bag.

    These
    ~~This~~ are my books.

5. Don't use a contraction for *am not*.

    I'm not
    ~~I amn't~~ an American.

6. Put the apostrophe in place of the missing letter.

    It's
    ~~Its~~ late.

    isn't
    The teacher ~~is'nt~~ here.

7. Use *a* or *an* before a singular noun. Don't use *a* or *an* before a plural noun.

    an
    Biology is ^ interesting subject.

    Mr. Sanchez and Ms. Lee are ~~a~~ good teachers.

8. Don't use a contraction for a short *yes* answer.

    I am
    Are you from Mexico? Yes, ~~I'm~~.

PART 2 Editing Practice

Some of the shaded words and phrases have mistakes. Find the mistakes and correct them. If the shaded words are correct, write C.

A: Hi. My name is Leo. *C* I from Latvia. *I'm* What's your name?
    1.   2.   3.

B: My name's Diane.
    4.

A: Nice to meet you, Diane. Where you are from?
    5.

B: I from Rwanda.
    6.

A: Where Rwanda is?
    7.

B: Its in Central Africa. Rwanda is a country very small. Is a city or a country Latvia?
    8.   9.   10.

A: Latvia is country. Is in Europe. Tell me more about Rwanda. What's the language of Rwanda?
    11.   12.

B: My native language is Kinyarwanda. Whats your native language?
    13.   14.

A: Latvian. Russian's also a language in Latvia. You are married?
15.   16.

B: Yes, I'm. My husband is'nt from Rwanda. He's from Burundi. Are you married?
17.   18.   19.   20.

A: No, I amn't. I'm only 18. I'm in the United States with my parents and sister.
21.   22.

B: I'm here with my husband and kids. This are pictures of my kids, Jimmy and Lance.
23.

A: The teacher he's here. Is time for class.
24.   25.

WRITING TIP
Be sure to indent (move in) the first line of each new paragraph. A new paragraph begins a new idea, and the indent helps the reader understand your ideas.

PART 3 Write
Fill in the blanks with affirmative or negative forms of *be*. Then rewrite the paragraphs with an affirmative statement after each negative statement.

My name _____is_____ _____ . I _____ from an English-speaking country. I
1.   your name   2.

_____ a student at a community college. My classmates _____ all very young. We
3.   4.

_____ all from the same country. We _____ all immigrants.
5.   6.

I _____ a freshman. This _____ my first course here. The school _____
7.   8.   9.

convenient for me. My teacher _____ American. She/He _____ very young. The
10.   11.

classroom _____ very nice. It _____ clean. I _____ in my English class now.
12.   13.   14.

I _____ happy with my school.
15.

My name is Muneer. I am not from an English-speaking country. I am from an Arabic-speaking country.

PART 4 Edit
Reread the Summary of Unit 1 and the editing advice. Edit your writing from Part 3.

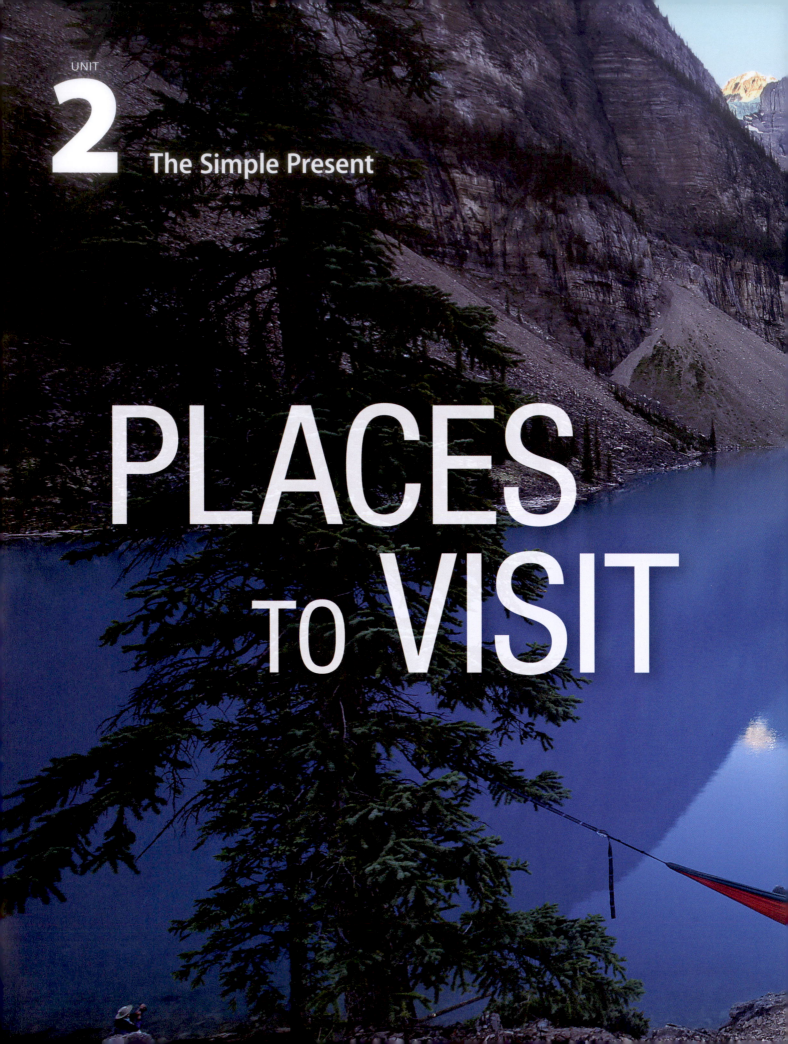

PLACES TO VISIT

A tourist lies in a hammock as the sun rises in Banff National Park in Alberta, Canada.

The real voyage of discovery consists not in seeking new landscapes, but in having new eyes.

MARCEL PROUST

Washington, DC

Read the following article. Pay special attention to the words in bold. 🎧 2.1

Tourists from all over the world **visit** Washington, DC, the capital of the United States. Is DC a state? No, it isn't. What, exactly, is DC? *DC* **means** "District of Columbia." The District of Columbia is a special government district. More than 700,000 people **live** in Washington, DC.

Washington **doesn't have** factories. Government and tourism are the main businesses of Washington. Washington **doesn't have** tall buildings like other big cities.

Many Washington workers **don't live** in Washington. They **live** in nearby states: Virginia and Maryland. Washington **has** a good subway system. It **connects** Washington to nearby cities in Virginia and Maryland.

Tourists **come** to see the White House, where the president **lives**. They also **want** to see the Capitol. The Capitol, the building where Congress **meets**, is on a hill. Senators and representatives from each state **work** on Capitol Hill. They **make** the country's laws.

Besides government buildings, Washington also **has** many interesting museums and monuments. The Smithsonian Institution **has** 17 museums in Washington. Tourists **don't pay** to see government buildings and museums. But people **need** tickets to reserve a time to see many places because they are crowded.

A trip to Washington, DC, is an enjoyable and educational experience.

The United States Capitol Building

COMPREHENSION Based on the reading, write T for *true* or F for *false*.

1. _____ It's expensive to visit government buildings in Washington, DC.

2. _____ The president works in the Capitol Building on Capitol Hill.

3. _____ The District of Columbia isn't a state.

THINK ABOUT IT Discuss the questions with a partner or in a small group.

1. Does Washington, DC, sound like a good place for you to visit? Why or why not?

2. Do you know another city like Washington, DC? What is it, and why is it similar?

2.1 The Simple Present—Affirmative Statements

A simple present verb has two forms: the base form and the -*s* form.

EXAMPLES			EXPLANATION
Subject	**Base Form**		
I You We They My friends	**live**	in Washington.	We use the base form when the subject is *I, you, we, they,* or a plural noun.
Subject	**-s Form**		
He She It The president My family	**lives**	in Washington.	We use the -*s* form when the subject is *he, she, it,* or a singular noun. *Family* is a singular noun.
I **have** friends in Washington, DC. Washington **has** many museums.			*Have* is an irregular verb. The -*s* form is *has*.

EXERCISE 1 Listen. Then write T for *true*, F for *false*, or NS for *not stated*. 🎧 2.2

1. _____ The speaker wants to see the White House.

2. _____ The speaker lives in Washington, DC.

3. _____ The National Museum of the American Indian is one of the most popular museums in the world.

EXERCISE 2 Listen again. Fill in the blanks with the words you hear. 🎧 2.2

For my vacation next month, I _____*plan*_____ to go to Washington, DC, with my family.

　　　　　　　　　　　　　　　　　1.

Washington _____ many interesting museums and government buildings. We

　　　　　　　　2.

_____ to visit the National Museum of the American Indian. My son _____ a

3.　　　　　　　　　　　　　　　　　　　　　　　　　　　　　　　　　　　　　4.

continued

school project. He _____ to know more about American Indian culture and history. The
                          5.

museum _____ big. It _____ four levels. We _____ about
               6.   **7.**   **8.**

three or four hours to see everything.

We also _____ to visit the Air and Space Museum. I _____ some
                      9.   **10.**

information about this museum. It's one of the most popular museums in the world! About 7 million

people _____ each year. The museum _____ the history of space exploration.
              11.   **12.**

We also _____ to visit the zoo. The zoo _____ giant pandas. My daughter
                      13.   **14.**

_____ pandas.
       15.

2.2 The Simple Present—Use

EXAMPLES	EXPLANATION
The president **lives** in the White House. The president **meets** with leaders of other countries.	We use the simple present with general truths or customs.
We **take** a vacation every summer. We sometimes **go** to Washington, DC.	We use the simple present with regular activities or repeated actions.
I **come** from New York. He **comes** from California.	We use the simple present with a place of origin.

Notes:

1. For a place of origin, we can use *come from* or *be from*.

   He **comes from** California. = He **is from** California.

2. We can follow some verbs with an infinitive (*to* + the base form).

   Tourists **like to see** the White House.

EXERCISE 3 Choose the correct form of the verb to complete each statement.

1. Visitors (*like*/*likes*) the museums.

2. The president (*live*/*lives*) in the White House.

3. Many people in Washington, DC, (*work*/*works*) for the government.

4. Washington (*have*/*has*) many beautiful museums.

5. Millions of tourists (*visit*/*visits*) Washington every year.

6. The subway (*connect*/*connects*) Washington to nearby cities.

7. You (*need*/*needs*) a ticket for some museums.

8. *DC* (*mean*/*means*) "District of Columbia."

9. I (*want*/*wants*) to visit Washington, DC.

The simple present is very common. We use it to talk about what we want, have, need, like, know, and think, for example.

I **have** a new bicycle. We **like** vanilla ice cream.

We **need** more time for this project. I **don't know** the answer.

ABOUT YOU Complete the sentences to make true statements about yourself. Use the correct form of the verb given. Then share your statements with a partner.

1. In my city, I especially _____ .
   like

2. My family _____ .
   live

3. The capital of my country _____ .
   have

4. Most people in my country _____ .
   speak

5. Tourists in my country _____ .
   visit

6. My city _____ .
   have

7. The leader of my country _____ .
   work

8. Many people in my country _____ .
   want

9. My country _____ .
   need

10. For transportation, most people _____ .
    use

11. For breakfast, most people _____ .
    eat

2.3 Spelling of the -s Form

RULE	BASE FORM	-S FORM
We add -s to most verbs to make the -s form.	hope	hope**s**
	eat	eat**s**
When the base form ends in ss, sh, ch, z, or x, we add -es.	miss	miss**es**
	wash	wash**es**
	catch	catch**es**
	buzz	buzz**es**
	mix	mix**es**
When the base form ends in a consonant + y, we change the y to i and add -es.	carry	carr**ies**
	worry	worr**ies**
When the base form ends in a vowel + y, we add -s. We do not change the y.	pay	pay**s**
	enjoy	enjoy**s**
We add -es to go and do.	go	go**es**
	do	do**es**
Remember: Have is irregular. The -s form is has.	have	**has**

EXERCISE 4 Write the *-s* form of each verb.

1. eat _____ *eats* _____   12. enjoy _____

2. study _____ *studies* _____   13. think _____

3. watch _____   14. say _____

4. try _____   15. change _____

5. play _____   16. brush _____

6. have _____   17. like _____

7. go _____   18. reach _____

8. worry _____   19. fix _____

9. want _____   20. raise _____

10. do _____   21. charge _____

11. push _____   22. see _____

2.4 Pronunciation of the *-s* Form 🎧 2.3

PRONUNCIATION	RULE	EXAMPLES	
/s/	We pronounce the *-s* as /s/ after voiceless sounds: /p, t, k, f/.	hope—hopes eat—eats	pick—picks laugh—laughs
/z/	We pronounce the *-s* as /z/ after voiced sounds: /b, d, g, v, m, n, ŋ, l, r/ and all vowel sounds.*	grab—grabs read—reads hug—hugs live—lives hum—hums run—runs	sing—sings fall—falls hear—hears see—sees go—goes play—plays
/əz/	We pronounce the *-s* as /əz/ after these sounds: /s, x, z, ʃ, tʃ, dʒ/.	miss—misses dance—dances fix—fixes use—uses	buzz—buzzes wash—washes watch—watches change—changes

Pronunciation Note:

The *-s* form of the following verbs has a change in the vowel sound.

do /du/—does /dʌz/

say /seɪ/—says /sɛz/

* See Appendix E for vowel and consonant sounds in English.

EXERCISE 5 Find a partner. Take turns saying the base form and the -s form of each verb in Exercise 4.

EXERCISE 6 Fill in the blanks with the correct form of each underlined verb.

1. I <u>like</u> to visit big cities. My wife _____*likes*_____ to sit by a pool and read.

2. She <u>wants</u> to visit Miami. I _____ to visit Washington, DC.

3. I <u>enjoy</u> museums. She _____ swimming.

4. She <u>prefers</u> a relaxing vacation. I _____ an active vacation.

5. I <u>want</u> to use public transportation. She _____ to rent a car.

6. She <u>gets</u> up late. I _____ up early.

7. I <u>take</u> one small suitcase. She _____ two big suitcases.

EXERCISE 7 Write three sentences about the current U.S. president or the leader of a country you know. Use the simple present. Then find a partner and share your answers.

1. _____

2. _____

3. _____

2.5 The Simple Present—Negative Statements

EXAMPLES	EXPLANATION
The president lives in the White House. The vice president **does not live** in the White House. Washington, DC, has many government buildings. It **doesn't have** tall buildings.	We use *does not* + the base form when the subject is *he, she, it,* or a singular noun. *Doesn't* is the contraction for *does not*.
Visitors pay to enter most museums. They **do not pay** to enter Smithsonian museums. We live in Maryland. We **don't live** in Washington.	We use *do not* + the base form when the subject is *I, you, we, they,* or a plural noun. *Don't* is the contraction for *do not*.

Note:

Compare the negative form with *be* and other simple present verbs.

Washington, DC, **isn't** *a big city.*

It **doesn't have** *tall buildings.*

EXERCISE 8 Fill in the blanks with the negative form of each underlined verb.

1. You <u>need</u> tickets for some museums. You _____*don't need*_____ money for the

   Smithsonian museums.

2. Washington, DC, <u>has</u> monuments. It _____ factories.

3. The subway <u>runs</u> all day. It _____ after midnight on weeknights.

4. You <u>need</u> a car in many cities. You _____ a car in Washington.

5. Washington <u>has</u> a subway system. Miami _____ a subway system.

6. My friend <u>lives</u> in Virginia. He _____ in Washington.

7. I <u>like</u> American history. I _____ geography.

8. The president <u>lives</u> in Washington. He _____ in New York.

9. The president <u>serves</u> a four-year term. He _____ a six-year term.

10. We <u>have</u> a president. We _____ a prime minister.

11. The U.S. Congress <u>makes</u> the laws. The president _____ the laws.

ABOUT YOU Write affirmative or negative statements about your hometown. Use the words given with the correct form of the verb. Then find a partner and share your answers.

1. have a zoo

   *My hometown has a zoo.*_____

2. get a lot of rain

   *My hometown doesn't get a lot of rain.*_____

3. be modern

   _____

4. have very tall buildings

   _____

5. have more than a million people

   _____

6. be the capital of my country

   _____

7. have government buildings

_____

8. attract a lot of tourists

_____

9. have a subway

_____

10. have an airport

_____

EXERCISE 9 Complete the paragraphs with the correct form of the verbs given. When *not* is given, make a contraction with *does* or *do*.

Sara Harris _____<u>is</u>_____ a 30-year-old woman. She
    1. be

_____ in Arlington, Virginia. She _____ in
    2. live   **3.** work

Washington, DC, but she _____ there because it's too expensive. Rent is cheaper
    4. not/live

in Arlington. Sara _____ a car, but she _____ it to go
    5. have   **6.** not/use

to work. She _____ the subway to work.
    7. take

Sara _____ for the government. She _____
    8. not/work   **9.** be

a tour guide. She _____ groups on tours of the Capitol. Tourists
    10. lead

_____ to pay to enter the Capitol, but they _____
    11. not/need   **12.** need

a reservation. The Capitol _____ open for tours from 8:30 a.m. to 4:30 p.m.
    13. be

Monday through Saturday.

Sara _____ two roommates. They _____
    14. have   **15.** work

in government offices. They _____ to work on the subway, too. Sara
    16. go

and her roommates _____ very busy, so they
    17. be

_____ much free time.
    18. not/have

The SMOKIES

Read the following article. Pay special attention to the words in bold. 🎧 2.4

The most popular national park in the United States is the Great Smoky Mountains National Park in Tennessee. Sometimes we call the Smoky Mountains "The Smokies." Here are some frequently asked questions (FAQs) about the park.

Q: **How many** visitors **does** this park **receive** a year?

A: It receives more than 11 million visitors a year.

Q: **What do** visitors **do** in the park?

A: Some people like to drive through the Smokies to see the natural beauty. Some people prefer to hike[1]. This park has 800 miles of hiking trails.

Q: **Does** the park **have** many plants and animals?

A: **Yes**, it **does**. It is home to 100 different native species[2] of trees. There are 1,600 species of plants, 60 species of mammals, and 200 species of birds.

Q: **Do** bears **live** in the park?

A: **Yes**. The park has about 1,500 black bears.

Q: **Does** the park **have** educational programs?

A: **Yes**, it **does**. It **has** programs to teach young people about conservation.

Q: **What does** *conservation* **mean**?

A: It means "protection." The park protects plants and animals.

Q: **Why do** the mountains **have** the name *Smoky Mountains*?

A: There is a blue mist[3] that looks like smoke.

Q: **Where do** visitors to the park **stay**?

A: The park has a lodge[4] and campgrounds.

Q: **How much does** it **cost** to enter the park?

A: Entrance to the park is free. If you want to camp, you have to pay.

---

[1] to hike: to walk in nature for exercise
[2] species: a type or category of something
[3] mist: a cloud of tiny water droplets
[4] lodge: a small country house, often that you use on vacation

A sunset view of the Smokies from the Morton Overlook in Tennessee, USA

COMPREHENSION Based on the reading, write T for *true* or F for *false*.

1. _____ Great Smoky Mountains National Park produces smoke from fires.

2. _____ Great Smoky Mountains National Park has educational programs.

3. _____ It is free to camp at Great Smoky Mountains National Park.

THINK ABOUT IT Discuss the questions with a partner or in a small group.

1. Do you like to go hiking? Where?

2. What makes national parks special?

2.6 The Simple Present—*Yes/No* Questions and Short Answers

STATEMENT	*YES/NO* QUESTION	SHORT ANSWER
The park **has** hiking trails.	**Does** the park **have** campgrounds?	Yes, it **does**.
The park **charges** money for camping.	**Does** the park **charge** an entrance fee?	No, it **doesn't**.
Birds **live** in the park.	**Do** bears **live** in the park?	Yes, they **do**.
Parks **get** a lot of visitors in the summer.	**Do** the parks **get** a lot of visitors in the winter?	No, they **don't**.

Notes:

1. For *yes/no* questions with *he, she, it,* and singular subjects, we use:

   Does + *subject* + *base form* . . . ?

   For a short answer, we use:

   Yes, + *subject pronoun* + does.   No, + *subject pronoun* + doesn't.

2. For *yes/no* questions with *I, we, you, they,* and plural subjects, we use:

   Do + *subject* + *base form* . . . ?

   For a short answer, we use:

   Yes, + *subject pronoun* + do.   No, + *subject pronoun* + don't.

3. Compare *yes/no* questions and short answers with *be* and with other simple present verbs.

   Is the park free? Yes, it **is**./No, it **isn't**.

   Does the park **have** a campground? Yes, it **does**./No, it **doesn't**.

GRAMMAR IN USE

We often answer a *yes/no* question with a simple *Yes* or *No*.

Do you like to hike? **Yes./Yeah.**

Are you tired? **No./Nope.**

Yeah is an informal way to say *yes*. *Nope* is an informal way to say *no*.

EXERCISE 10 Reread Exercise 9. Then answer the questions with a complete short answer. Use a subject pronoun in your answers.

1. Does Sara work in Washington, DC? _____Yes, she does._____

2. Does Sara live in Washington, DC? _____

3. Does Sara work for the government? _____

4. Does Sara have a car? _____

continued

5. Does Sara need a car to go to work? _____

6. Do Sara's roommates work for the government? _____

7. Do Sara and her roommates have a lot of free time? _____

8. Do tourists need to pay to enter the Capitol? _____

EXERCISE 11 Complete the conversation with the words given. Use *does* or *do* when necessary.

A: <u>Does the United States have</u> a lot of national parks?
1. the United States/have

B: Yes, it _____ . _____ 60 parks. Grand Canyon
2. **3.** it/have

National Park is very popular.

A: _____ near Great Smoky Mountains National Park?
4. Grand Canyon National Park/be

B: No, it _____ . The Grand Canyon is in Arizona.
5. is/not

A: _____ the Grand Canyon each year?
6. a lot of people/visit

B: Yes. About 6 million tourists visit each year.

A: _____ a lot of time to visit the Grand Canyon?
7. I/need

B: No, you _____ . Many visitors just go to the edge of the canyon.
8.

A: _____ a tour guide to see the park?
9. we/need

B: No, you _____ . You can use your smartphone for a self-guided tour.
10.

A: _____ an entrance fee?
11. this park/charge

B: Yes, it _____ . It charges $35 per car.
12.

A: _____ into the park?
13. buses/go

B: Yes, they _____ . Passengers pay $20.
14.

A: _____ into the canyon?
15. people/go

B: Most people don't go into the canyon. Some people take a helicopter tour.

A: _____ over the canyon?
16. the helicopter/go

B: Yes, it _____ .
17.

A: _____ expensive to take a helicopter tour?
18. it/be

B: Yes, it _____ . It's about $300 for a 45-minute ride.
19.

EXERCISE 12 Read the information about two popular national parks. Then read each sentence about one of the parks. Use the words in the statement to write a *yes/no* question about the other park. Answer with a short answer.

Yosemite National Park, California

- gets about 5 million visitors a year
- has black bears
- giant sequoia trees grow here
- has waterfalls
- entrance fee is $35 per car
- has bicycle trails
- part of the National Park Service

Grand Canyon National Park, Arizona

- gets about 6 million visitors a year
- has black bears
- no giant sequoia trees grow here
- has waterfalls
- entrance fee is $35 per car
- has no bicycle trails
- part of the National Park Service

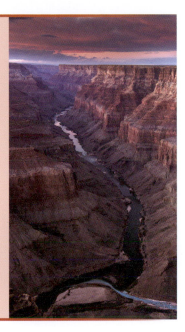

1. Yosemite National Park is in California.

    Is Grand Canyon National Park in California?

    No, it isn't.

2. Grand Canyon National Park gets about 6 million visitors a year.

    _____

    _____

3. Yosemite National Park has black bears.

    _____

    _____

4. Giant sequoia trees grow in Yosemite National Park.

    _____

    _____

5. Grand Canyon National Park has waterfalls.

    _____

    _____

continued

The Simple Present 45

6. The entrance fee for Yosemite National Park is $35 per car.

_____

_____

7. Yosemite National Park has bicycle trails.

_____

_____

8. Yosemite National Park is part of the National Park Service.

_____

_____

EXERCISE 13 Fill in the blanks to complete each conversation.

1. **A:** Most big cities have tall buildings. ___Does Washington, DC, have___ tall buildings?

   B: No, it _____ doesn't _____ . Washington, DC, doesn't have tall buildings.

2. **A:** The trains seem to run all day. _____ 24 hours a day?

   B: No, they _____ . On weekdays, they run from early morning to midnight.

3. **A:** In my city, all passengers pay the same fare on the subway. _____ the

   same fare on the subway in Washington?

   B: No, they _____ . They pay differently by time of day and number of stops

   they travel.

4. **A:** You need a ticket to enter museums in my hometown. _____ a ticket to

   enter museums in Washington?

   B: Yes, you _____ . You need tickets for some museums in Washington.

5. **A:** The Washington Monument is very tall. _____ an elevator?

   B: Yes, it _____ . It has an elevator.

6. **A:** The president works in Washington. _____ on Capitol Hill?

   B: No, he _____ . He works in the White House.

7. **A:** _____ the laws?

   B: No, he _____ . Congress makes the laws.

8. **A:** The president lives in the White House. _____ in the White House?

B: No, he _____ . The vice president lives at the U.S. Naval Observatory.

9. **A:** Washington, DC, is on the East Coast. _____ on the East Coast?

B: No, it _____ . Washington state is on the West Coast.

10. **A:** Many museums in Washington, DC, are free. _____ free?

B: Yes, it _____ . The zoo is free.

2.7 The Simple Present—*Wh-* Questions

Compare statements and *wh-* questions.

STATEMENT	*WH-* QUESTION
The park **receives** many visitors.	**How many** visitors **does** the park **receive** each year?
The park **has** bears.	**What kind** of bears **does** the park **have**?
You **prefer** a vacation in nature.	**Where do** you **prefer** to go?
Visitors **do** many things in the park.	**What do** visitors **do** in the park?
The park **doesn't charge** an entrance fee.	**Why doesn't** the park **charge** an entrance fee?
I **don't like** to camp.	**Why don't** you **like** to camp?

Notes:

1. For *wh-* questions with *he, she, it,* or a singular subject, we use:

Wh- *word* + does + *subject* + *base form . . . ?*

2. For *wh-* questions with *I, we, you, they,* or a plural subject, we use:

Wh- *word* + do + *subject* + *base form . . . ?*

3. For negative *wh-* questions, we use:

Wh- *word* + don't *or* doesn't + *subject* + *base form . . . ?*

4. Compare *wh-* questions with *be* and with other simple present verbs.

What kind *of vacation* **are** *you interested in?*

Why aren't *you interested in tour groups?*

What kind *of places* **do** *you* **like** *to visit?*

Why don't *you* **like** *museums?*

GRAMMAR IN USE

In informal English, we usually put the preposition at the end of a *wh-* question.

Who do you travel **with**? (informal)

In formal English, use *whom,* not *who,* after a preposition.

With whom *do you travel?* (formal)

EXERCISE 14 Listen to the conversation. Fill in the blanks with the words that you hear.

A: _____ *Where do you plan* _____ to go on your next vacation?

1.

B: We want to go to Washington, DC.

A: _____ to see and do there?

2.

B: We want to visit the government buildings, of course, and the museums. We plan to go to the National

Museum of the American Indian.

A: What kind of exhibits _____ there?

3.

B: Some exhibits show the history of the American Indian. Others show their life and culture.

They also _____ a theater.

4.

A: _____ in the theater?

5.

B: Different things like the storytelling, dance, and music of American Indians.

A: It sounds like a big museum. _____?

6.

B: It has four levels.

A: Wow! That's big. _____ to see everything?

7.

B: At least two hours.

A: _____?

8.

B: It's free.

A: Really? Nothing's free! All the museums in my city charge money.

_____ any money in Washington museums?

9.

B: We _____ with our taxes.

10.

National Museum of
the American Indian,
Washington, DC

EXERCISE 15 Complete the conversation between two friends. Use the underlined verbs to help you form each question.

A: I plan to visit a national park next summer.

B: Which park _____ *do you plan* _____ to visit?
1.

A: I plan to visit Yosemite National Park.

B: What month _____ to go there?
2.

A: I want to go in July.

B: It's crowded in July. It gets a lot of visitors.

A: How many visitors _____ ?
3.

B: Let's look on the park website. Maybe we can find the answer there.

A: It doesn't matter. That's the time my wife has vacation.

B: How many weeks of vacation _____ ?
4.

A: Two weeks.

B: Do you plan to camp?

A: My wife doesn't like to camp, but I do.

B: Why _____ to camp?
5.

A: She likes to sleep in a bed, not on the ground.

B: Why _____ to camp?
6.

A: I like to sleep in a tent under the stars.

EXERCISE 16 Write questions with the words given. Use the underlined verbs to help you.

1. The museum has several floors. (how many floors)

   _How many floors does it have?_____

2. We don't pay to go to the museum. (why/not pay to go to the museum)

   _____

3. The museum has programs. (what kind of programs)

   _____

4. The museum opens at 9:00 a.m. (what time/close)

   _____

continued

5. The Grand Canyon <u>gets</u> a lot of visitors. (how many visitors)

_____

6. Great Smoky Mountains National Park <u>is</u> in Tennessee. (where/Grand Canyon National Park)

_____

7. Yosemite National Park <u>charges</u> an entrance fee. (how much money)

_____

8. The United States <u>has</u> a lot of national parks. (how many national parks)

_____

EXERCISE 17 Complete the conversation between two friends. Use the underlined verbs to help you.

A: Let's do something fun today.

B: What _____ _do you want_ _____ to do?
                                    1.

A: I <u>want</u> to go to a museum.

B: I <u>don't like</u> museums.

A: Really? Why _____ museums?
                              2.

B: They're boring.

A: No, they're not. You learn a lot when you go to a museum.

B: Which museum _____ to visit?
                                3.

A: I <u>want</u> to visit the history museum. It's free on Fridays.

B: I <u>don't like</u> history.

A: Why _____ history?
                      4.

B: History is boring. I prefer to go to the movies.

A: Come with me to the museum. Please?

B: What kind of exhibits _____?
                                        5.

A: It <u>has</u> exhibits about American life. Come on, let's go!

B: What time _____ today?
                            6.

A: The museum <u>closes</u> at 5:00 p.m.

B: OK. Let's go to the museum at 3:00 p.m., and then we can go to a movie, OK?

A: Fine.

Find a partner. Ask and answer *yes/no* questions. Use the words given. Then ask an affirmative or negative follow-up *wh-* question.

1. like to travel

   A: *Do you like to travel?*

   B: *No, I don't.*

   A: *Why don't you like to travel?*

   B: *I'm afraid to fly, and I don't like driving.*

2. like museums

3. like to learn about American history

4. visit parks in the summer

5. plan to take a vacation

2.8 Questions about Meaning, Spelling, Cost, and Time

WH- WORD	*DO/DOES*	SUBJECT	VERB	
What	does	*DC*	**mean**?	
How	do	you	**spell**	*government*?
How	do	you	**say**	*government* in your language?
How much	does	it	**cost**	to enter the park?
How long	does	it	**take**	to see the museum?

EXERCISE 18 Fill in the blanks to complete each conversation.

1. **A:** How much _____ *does it cost* _____ to enter the Air and Space Museum?

   B: It doesn't cost anything to enter the Air and Space Museum. It's free.

2. **A:** How long _____ to see the museum?

   B: It takes at least two hours.

3. **A:** How _____ *Yosemite*?

   B: You spell *Yosemite Y-O-S-E-M-I-T-E.*

4. **A:** What _____?

   B: *DC* means "District of Columbia."

5. **A:** How much _____ to enter Great Smoky Mountains National Park?

   B: It doesn't cost anything. It's free to enter.

6. **A:** How _____ *mountain* in Spanish?

   B: In Spanish, you say *montaña.*

EXERCISE 19 Complete the conversation between two students.

A: Are these your children in this photo?

B: Yes, they are.

A: How old _____ *are they* _____?
1.

B: Ana's 23 and Marek's 29.

A: Do they live with you?

B: No. Ana lives in New York, and Marek lives in Maryland near Washington, DC.

A: _____ for the government?
2.

B: Yes, he does. He works for the IRS.

A: What _____ ?
3.

B: *IRS* means "Internal Revenue Service." It's the government tax collection agency.

A: How long _____ Marek to get to work
4.

from Maryland?

B: It only takes about 45 minutes. He uses the subway.

A: My niece lives in Maryland, too.

B: Where _____ in Maryland?
5.

A: She lives in Fallston.

B: I don't know that city. How _____ *Fallston*?
6.

A: *F-A-L-L-S-T-O-N.* My niece loves living there.

B: _____ for the government?
7.

A: No. She's a teacher.

FUN WITH GRAMMAR

Make connections. As a class, create a survey with six questions to find out what you have in common with your classmates. Use *wh-* questions, such as "How many siblings do you have?" Write the questions and your answers on a piece of paper. Then go around the room and survey your classmates. If someone has the same or a similar response to yours, write his or her name next to your response. The person with the most things in common with his or her classmates is the winner.

TIMES SQUARE

Read the following essay. Pay special attention to the words in bold. 🎧 2.6

I live in New York City. New York has so many things to see and do. I especially love Times Square. Times Square is a top tourist attraction in the United States. Times Square is **always** a busy place. More than 300,000 pedestrians[1] pass through Times Square **every day**. It has hotels, restaurants, theaters, and shopping. **Every night** visitors come to see an amazing display of electronic billboards[2].

New Year's Eve is especially wonderful at Times Square. **Every year** New Yorkers and tourists come together at Times Square to count down to the new year. About a million people wait for the Waterford Crystal ball to drop, marking the beginning of the new year. The ball **always** drops **at** exactly **midnight**.

I **usually** go to Times Square with my friends to see the ball drop. I **never** drive there because parking is so expensive. We **always** take the subway. **Sometimes** it's very cold **on New Year's Eve**. If the temperature is below 10 degrees, we **usually** stay home and watch the ball drop on TV.

Times Square is also near the theater district in New York. I **hardly ever** go to the theater because it's so expensive. Some theater tickets cost more than $200! It's **often** hard to get a ticket for the popular shows. The tickets are **almost always** sold out[3].

I love New York City. Tourists from all over the world love it, too.

---

1 pedestrian: a person on foot
2 billboard: a large outdoor sign
3 sold out: all gone

COMPREHENSION Based on the reading, write T for *true* or F for *false*.

1. _____ Times Square is only popular at night.

2. _____ The writer always goes to Times Square on New Year's Eve.

3. _____ Theater tickets in New York are very expensive.

THINK ABOUT IT Discuss the questions with a partner or in a small group.

1. Why do you think Times Square is so popular?

2. Do you like popular places like Times Square? Why or why not?

2.9 Frequency Words and Expressions with the Simple Present

FREQUENCY WORD/EXPRESSION	FREQUENCY	EXAMPLES
always	100 percent	Times Square is **always** crowded.
almost always/usually		Popular shows are **almost always** sold out.
often		It is **often** hard to get theater tickets.
sometimes		It is **sometimes** very cold on New Year's Eve.
seldom/rarely/hardly ever/almost never		I **seldom** go to the theater.
never	0 percent	I **never** drive to Times Square.

GRAMMAR IN USE

When someone asks us how often we do something, we often use expressions like these:

All the time.   *Not much.*

Every few months.   *Not often.*

Once in a while.   *Hardly ever.*

ABOUT YOU Fill in the blanks to make true statements about yourself. Use a frequency word or expression. Then find a partner and compare your answers.

1. I _____*hardly ever*_____ go to the zoo.

2. I _____ celebrate New Year's Eve.

3. I _____ go to the theater.

4. I _____ use public transportation.

5. I _____ go to museums.

6. I _____ eat in restaurants.

7. I _____ visit people in other cities.

8. I _____ receive visitors from other cities.

2.10 Position of Frequency Words and Expressions

EXAMPLES	EXPLANATION
Times Square **is always** busy. It **is almost never** quiet in Times Square.	We put the frequency word or expression after the verb *be*.
I **never drive** to Times Square. We **hardly ever stay** home on New Year's Eve.	We put the frequency word or expression before other verbs.
Sometimes it's cold on New Year's Eve. **Often** it's hard to get theater tickets.	We can put *sometimes, usually,* and *often* at the beginning of the sentence.
Every night people visit Times Square. People visit Times Square **every night**.	We put frequency expressions that start with *each* or *every* at the beginning or at the end of the sentence.

Notes:

1. We don't put *always, hardly ever,* or *never* before the subject.

   I **always** celebrate New Year's Eve. (NOT: *Always I celebrate…*)

2. We can put *sometimes* at the end of a sentence.

   It's cold on New Year's Eve **sometimes**.

EXERCISE 20 Rewrite each sentence. Use the frequency word or expression given. In some cases, more than one correct word order is possible.

1. I travel with my family. (often)

   I often travel with my family.

2. My family and I take a vacation in the summer. (every year)

3. We are interested in seeing something new. (always)

4. We visit major cities, like New York and San Francisco. (often)

5. We visit relatives in other cities. (sometimes)

6. We travel by car. (usually)

7. We fly. (hardly ever)

8. We are bored. (never)

2.11 Questions and Short Answers with *Ever*

We use *ever* to ask a question about frequency. We begin the question with an auxiliary verb (*do/does*) or a form of *be*.

DO/DOES	SUBJECT	EVER		SHORT ANSWER
Do	you	**ever**	travel in the winter?	Yes, we **sometimes** do.
Does	your brother	**ever**	travel with you?	No, he **rarely** does.
BE	SUBJECT	EVER		SHORT ANSWER
Is	Washington	**ever**	hot in the summer?	Yes, it **usually** is.
Is	Times Square	**ever**	crowded?	Yes, it **always** is.

Notes:

1. In a short answer, we put the frequency word or expression between the subject and the verb.

2. We don't use a negative verb in a short answer when the frequency word is *never*.

> A: *Is the school ever open on January 1?*
>
> B: *No, it **never is**.* (NOT: *No, it never isn't.*)

GRAMMAR IN USE

In informal conversations, we often just use *yes/no* + frequency word/expression to answer questions about frequency.

> A: *Do you ever drive to work?*
>
> B: **Yes, always.**
>
> A: *Does your sister ever pick you up from school?*
>
> B: **No, never.**

ABOUT YOU Find a partner. Ask and answer each question. Use frequency words or expressions in your answers.

1. Do you ever take the bus?

   A: *Do you ever take the bus?*

   B: *No, I never do.*

2. Do you ever drive to school or work?

3. Do you ever visit museums?

4. Do you ever use the Internet to plan a trip?

5. Do you ever stay with relatives when you travel?

6. Do you ever celebrate New Year's Eve with friends?

7. Do you ever take pictures when you travel?

8. Do you ever use GPS in a car?

2.12 Questions and Answers with *How Often*

We use *how often* to ask a question about frequency. We use an auxiliary verb after *how often*.

EXAMPLES	EXPLANATION
How often does your family take a vacation? We take a vacation **once a year**. **How often do** you take the subway? I take the subway **twice a day**.	We answer questions beginning with *how often* with frequency expressions such as *once/twice/three times a week/month/year*.
How often do you drive downtown? I drive downtown **once in a while**.	For a less specific answer, we can use *once in a while*.

Note:

When answering a question with *how often*, we can put some frequency expressions at the beginning or the end of the sentence.

> ***Twice a year**, I visit my family.*   *I visit my family **twice a year**.*

ABOUT YOU Find a partner. Ask and answer each question. Use frequency words or expressions in your answers.

1. How often do you travel?

   A: *How often do you travel?*

   B: *I travel about three times a year.*

2. How often do you visit your native country?

3. How often do you go to the movies?

4. How often do you use public transportation?

5. How often do you get a haircut?

6. How often do you post on social media?

EXERCISE 21 Choose the correct word(s) to complete the conversation.

A: Do (*you ever*/*ever you*) travel to other countries?

         1.

B: No, I (*ever/rarely*) do. (*One/Once*) a year, I go back to my country, but that's all.

        2.   3.

A: (*What/How*) often do you travel in the United States?

       4.

B: (*Once a while/Once in a while*), I go to see my aunt in Miami. But I (*ever/never*) go there

       5.   6.

   in the summer because it's too hot.

A: (*It's sometimes/It sometimes is*) hot in New York, too.

       7.

B: Yes, but not like in Miami.

continued

A: Does your aunt (*ever/never*) come to New York to see you here?
⠀⠀⠀⠀⠀⠀⠀⠀⠀⠀**8.**

B: No, she (*ever/never*) does. She says it's too cold here.
⠀⠀⠀⠀⠀⠀**9.**

A: But it's not cold in the summer.

B: She (*always says/says always*) it's too crowded here. What about you? Do you travel a lot?
⠀⠀⠀⠀⠀⠀⠀⠀⠀⠀**10.**

A: No. I like to travel, but my husband doesn't. So we do things here in New York.

B: Do you (*ever go/go ever*) to Times Square on New Year's Eve?
⠀⠀⠀⠀⠀⠀⠀⠀**11.**

A: No, we never (*do/don't*). (*It's always/Always it's*) so crowded. We (*get together often/often get together*)
⠀⠀⠀⠀⠀⠀⠀**12.**⠀⠀⠀⠀⠀⠀⠀⠀**13.**⠀⠀⠀⠀⠀⠀⠀⠀⠀⠀⠀⠀⠀⠀⠀⠀⠀**14.**

with friends on New Year's Eve.

2.13 Prepositions of Time

PREPOSITION	EXAMPLES	EXPLANATION
in	Times Square isn't crowded **in the morning**. We visit museums **in the afternoon**. Theaters are crowded **in the evening**.	We use *in* with general times of day: *the morning, the afternoon, the evening.*
	We elect a U.S. president every four years: **in 2020, in 2024, in 2028**, and so on.	We use *in* with years.
	We like to travel **in the summer**. People go to Times Square even **in the winter**.	We use *in* with seasons: *the summer, the fall, the winter, the spring.*
	New York is cold **in December**.	We use *in* with months.
on	Many people go to Times Square **on New Year's Eve**. We watch the ball drop **on December 31**.	We use *on* with specific dates and days, such as holidays.
	I like to relax **on the weekend**.	We use *on* with *the weekend.*
at	Let's go to Times Square **at 10 o'clock**. The ball drops **at midnight**.	We use *at* with specific times of the day: *noon, 2 o'clock, midnight.*
	There are many people in Times Square **at night**.	We use *at* with *night.*
from … to from … until	The national parks are crowded **from May to October**. The subway in Washington, DC, runs **from 5:00 a.m. until midnight** on weekdays.	We use *from … to/until* with a beginning time and an ending time.

* See Appendix G for more prepositions of time.

GRAMMAR IN USE

When we give an approximate time, we can use *about* or *around* before the time and drop *at*.

*The party starts **(at) around 5 p.m**.*

EXERCISE 22 Fill in the blanks with the correct preposition of time. Then find a partner and ask and answer each question.

1. What do you usually do _____ December 31?

2. Do you like to travel _____ the summer?

3. What do you usually do _____ the morning?

4. What do you usually do _____ Saturday morning?

5. What do you usually do _____ the evening?

6. What do you like to do _____ your birthday?

7. What do you like to do for fun _____ the weekend?

ABOUT YOU Find a partner. Ask and answer each question. Use prepositions of time in your answers.

1. When do students in your country have vacation?

2. What do kids usually do on vacation?

3. When do you do your homework?

4. What hours are you in school?

5. When is your birthday?

FUN WITH GRAMMAR

Play a guessing game. Each person writes three sentences about themselves on a piece of paper: two that are true and one that is not true. The sentences must use frequency words and/or prepositions. For example, "I go to bed at 9:00 p.m." Number these sentences 1–3. One person goes first and reads all three sentences aloud. The class may ask a total of three follow-up questions, and then each person must decide which statement isn't true. Everyone writes the person's name and the number of the sentence they believe isn't true on their piece of paper. Then the person says which sentence wasn't true. Everyone who guesses correctly puts a +1 next to the person's name on their paper. The person with the most points is the winner.

A view of the New York City skyline
and the Statue of Liberty at sunset

SUMMARY OF UNIT 2

The Simple Present—Forms

BASE FORM	-S FORM
You **travel** in the summer.	Sara **lives** in Virginia.
You **don't travel** in the winter.	She **doesn't live** in Washington, DC.
Do you **travel** by car?	**Does** she **live** near the subway?
Yes, we **do**.	Yes, she **does**.
When do you **travel**?	**Where does** she **live**?
Why don't you **travel** by car?	**Why doesn't** she **live** in Washington?

The Simple Present—Use

USE	EXAMPLES
General truths and customs	Washington, DC, **has** over 700,000 people. Many people **celebrate** New Year's Eve in Times Square.
Regular activities	We **take** a vacation every summer. We often **visit** national parks.

Frequency Words and Expressions

always	100 percent
almost always/usually	
often	
sometimes	
rarely/seldom/hardly ever/almost never	
never	0 percent

Questions and Answers with Frequency Words

QUESTION	ANSWER
Does he **ever go** to Washington?	Yes, he **sometimes does**.
How often does he **go** to Washington?	**Twice a year.**

Prepositions of Time

in	Vancouver is cold **in January**.
on	We go outside **on the weekend**.
at	I go to work **at 8:00 a.m.**
from … to from … until	The parks are busy **from May to October**. The store is open **from 9:00 a.m. until 7:00 p.m.**

REVIEW

PART A Fill in the blanks. Use the correct form of the word(s) given.

A: My sister _____ lives _____ in New York, and she really _____ it.
 1. live   **2.** love

B: What _____ in New York?
 3. she/do

A: She _____ to school.
 4. go

B: What _____ for fun?
 5. she/do

A: She _____ a lot of friends. They _____
 6. have   **7.** like

 to go to Central Park or to the MOMA.

B: What _____?
 8. MOMA/mean

A: MOMA _____ "Museum of Modern Art."
 9. mean

B: Museums are expensive. How much _____ to visit the museum?
 10. it/cost

A: It _____ $25. But she _____ only $14 because she
 11. cost   **12.** pay

 _____ a student discount.
 13. get

B: _____ a car?
 14. your sister/have

A: No, she doesn't. She _____ the subway.
 15. use

PART B Choose the correct word(s) to complete the conversation from above.

B: Do (you ever/ever you) visit your sister?
          1.

A: Yes, I (do often/often do). I like to go (in/on) December for winter break.
          2.   **3.**

B: Do you (ever/never) go to Times Square (on/in) New Year's Eve?
          4.   **5.**

A: No, we never (do/don't).
          6.

B: Really? Why (don't you/you don't) go to Times Square? It looks like so much fun.
          7.

A: My sister doesn't (like/likes) crowds. (Always we/We always) watch Times Square on TV.
          8.   **9.**

B: How (often/ever) does your sister (come/comes) home to visit your family?
          10.   **11.**

A: She (comes usually/usually comes) (in/on) the summer. (I'm always/I always am) happy to see her.
          12.   **13.**   **14.**

B: New York (have/has) so many museums and theaters. But they're so expensive.
          15.

A: Some things (cost/costs) a lot of money, but other things are free. Central Park is beautiful, and it
          16.

 (doesn't cost/isn't cost) any money. My sister (have/has) a part-time job now, so that helps.
          17.   **18.**

B: What kind of work (she does/does she do)?
          19.

A: (She's work/She works) in a coffee shop (on/at) Saturdays.
          20.   **21.**

FROM GRAMMAR TO WRITING

PART 1 Editing Advice

1. Use the -*s* form when the subject is *he, she, it,* or a singular noun.

   The president live*s* in the White House.

2. Use the base form after *doesn't.*

   Sara doesn't ~~lives~~ *live* in Washington.

3. Don't forget *do/does* in a *wh-* question.

   How *do* people celebrate New Year's Eve?

4. Use the correct word order in a question.

   Why ~~you don't~~ *don't you* like to travel?

5. Use the correct spelling for the -*s* form.

   She ~~hurrys~~ *hurries* to the train in the morning.

6. Use the correct negative form.

   He ~~not~~ *doesn't* like to travel by car.

7. Put frequency words in the correct place.

   I ~~never am~~ *am never* bored on a vacation.

   ~~Always I~~ *I always* travel in the summer.

8. Don't use *be* with another verb to form the simple present.

   ~~I'm~~ I like to visit national parks.

9. Use correct question formation for meaning and cost.

   What ~~means pedestrian~~ *does pedestrian mean*?

   How much ~~cost the tickets~~ *do the tickets cost*?

10. Use the correct preposition.

    What do you do ~~at~~ *on* New Year's Eve?

PART 2 Editing Practice

Some of the shaded words and phrases have mistakes. Find the mistakes and correct them. If the shaded words are correct, write C.

I'm from Dallas, but ~~I'm~~ live in Chicago now. Chicago has many tourist attractions. My sister
1. (I) **2.** (C)

sometimes visit me in the summer. She and her husband have two small children, Sophie and Carter.
3. **4.** **5.**

The kids are always happy to visit me. I'm take the kids many places. They really likes the zoo. They
6. **7.** **8.**

want always to see the monkeys. Carter likes the snakes too, but Sophie doesn't likes them. She crys if we
9. **10.** **11.** **12.**

goes to the snake house. Carter always says, "Why you don't like snakes? They're so interesting."
13. **14.** **15.**

The kids always want to go to the Museum of Science. They find many interesting things to do there,
16. **17.**

but it's very expensive. My sister sometimes asks me, "How much cost the tickets?" but I doesn't tell her. I
18. **19.** **20.**

want to pay for everyone because they're my guests.
21.

My brother-in-law enjoys baseball, so I usually take him to a baseball game. I not like baseball very
22. **23.** **24.**

much, but I go with him anyway. I'm always bored at baseball games.
25.

Chicago is a great city for tourists. We have a good time when my sister's family come to visit.
26.

WRITING TIP

Before you start writing, you should think about different ways to address a topic. This is called *brainstorming*. If you are writing about an interesting place in your city or another city you know, for example, consider three different places before responding to the prompt. Ask and answer questions to gather information about each place, such as:

Where is this place? Why is it interesting? Are there any other places like this in the world?

The answers to these questions will help you choose one place to write about.

PART 3 Write

Read the prompts. Choose one and write one paragraph about it.

1. Write about an interesting place in your city or in another city you know about.
2. Write about how you celebrate New Year's Eve.

PART 4 Edit

Reread the Summary of Unit 2 and the editing advice. Edit your writing from Part 3.

UNIT

3

Singular and Plural Nouns
There Is/There Are
Articles

The colorful houses of Reitdiephaven,
a new neighborhood in Groningen, the
Netherlands

HOUSING

Home is the nicest word there is.

LAURA INGALLS WILDER

The HIGH COST of HOUSING

Read the following article. Pay special attention to the words in bold. 🎧 3.1

Some **people** live **paycheck** to paycheck. They spend all their money from one paycheck and need to wait for their next paycheck to pay their **bills**. Who are these people? People with low **incomes**? No. They are often middle-class **Americans**, people with good **salaries**. Some of these people are "house rich but cash poor." This means that they put all their **savings** into a **house** or **condo**[1] and have nothing left for **emergencies**. About one-third of American **households** live this **way**. Financial **planners**[2] tell **homeowners** to keep three to six **months** of **expenses** for **emergencies**, but many don't follow this advice.

Some Americans don't want to own a house. They prefer to rent an **apartment** because they don't want debt[3]. This is especially true of **millennials**, people born between 1980 and 2000. But renting is often very expensive. Some **cities** have very high **rent**. New York City, Boston, and San Francisco have some of the highest rents in the United States.

Some single young **adults** prefer not to own and not to rent. They live with their **parents**. Fifteen percent of young American adults between the **ages** of 25 and 35 live with their parents. More **men** than **women** choose to live with their parents. Of course, when mom and dad pay all the bills and don't charge them rent, it's a very good way to save money on living expenses.

---

[1] condo: private housing usually in an apartment building
[2] financial planner: someone who helps people manage their money
[3] debt: money owed to another

COMPREHENSION Based on the reading, write T for *true* or F for *false*.

1. _____ Financial planners tell homeowners to keep money for emergencies.

2. _____ Rent in New York City is very expensive.

3. _____ About 50 percent of U.S. households live paycheck to paycheck.

THINK ABOUT IT Discuss the questions with a partner or in a small group.

1. What are some reasons people live with their parents?

2. Do you prefer to rent or own a home? Why?

3.1 Singular and Plural Nouns

EXAMPLES	EXPLANATION
He lives with his **mother**. He lives with his **parents**.	*Singular* means one. *Plural* means more than one. Plural nouns usually end in -*s*.
Some young **men** and **women** live with their parents. Some **children** live with their grandparents.	Some plural nouns are irregular. They don't end in -*s*.

Note:
Some nouns have no singular form: *pajamas, clothes, pants, (eye)glasses, scissors.*

3.2 Regular Plural Nouns—Spelling

WORD ENDING	SINGULAR FORM	PLURAL ENDING	PLURAL FORM
vowel	expense movie	+ -s	expense**s** movie**s**
consonant	bill month	+ -s	bill**s** month**s**
ss, sh, ch, x	class dish church box	+ -es	class**es** dish**es** church**es** box**es**
vowel + *y*	boy day	+ -s	boy**s** day**s**
consonant + *y*	lady emergency	y + -ies	lad**ies** emergenc**ies**
vowel + *o*	patio radio	+ -s	patio**s** radio**s**
consonant + *o*	mosquito tomato	+ -es	mosquito**es** tomato**es**

Exceptions: *photos, pianos, solos, altos, sopranos, autos, avocados, condos*

-*f* or -*fe*	leaf knife	f + -ves fe + -ves	lea**ves** kni**ves**

Exceptions: *beliefs, chiefs, roofs, chefs*

Singular and Plural Nouns, *There Is/There Are*, Articles   **67**

EXERCISE 1 Listen to the report. Then write T for *true*, F for *false*, or NS for *not stated*. 🎧 3.2

1. _____ Condos have fees.

2. _____ Condo owners have a lot of responsibilities, including lawn care.

3. _____ Condos are more expensive than houses.

EXERCISE 2 Listen again. Fill in the blanks with the words you hear. 🎧 3.2

Maybe you rent an apartment now, but in the future you plan to own a house. You probably

have a lot of _____. For example, what is better, a house or a condo? Here are some
           1.

_____ to consider.
   2.

Do you want control over all your _____? Then a condo probably isn't for you.
                       3.

_____ are part of an association. The association has a lot of _____. For
   4.   5.

example, some _____ don't allow _____.
         6.   7.

Are you very busy? Do you have time to shovel the snow in the winter or take care of the lawn in the

summer? _____ have a lot of _____. If you don't have time for these
         8.   9.

_____, then home ownership is probably not right for you. If you own a condo, the
   10.

association pays someone to do these _____, but you pay a maintenance fee each month.
                       11.

Do you have _____? Maybe you want a yard where they can play and a garage for
           12.

their _____ and _____. Then a house is a better choice.
     13.   14.

EXERCISE 3 Write the plural form of each noun.

1. loaf   *loaves*   8. life _____

2. toy _____   9. story _____

3. brush _____   10. sofa _____

4. country _____   11. key _____

5. half _____   12. age _____

6. book _____   13. kiss _____

7. valley _____   14. potato _____

15. rent	_____	20. video	_____
16. watch	_____	21. month	_____
17. photo	_____	22. studio	_____
18. lip	_____	23. adult	_____
19. tax	_____	24. illness	_____

ABOUT YOU Fill in the blanks with the plural form of the nouns given. Then find a partner and tell whether each statement is true or false in your countries.

1. ___Houses___ are very expensive.
     house

2. Most _____ live with their _____.
              kid   grandparent

3. Most single _____ live with their _____.
                    adult   parent

4. Most _____ live in a house.
              family

5. Most _____ stay in the same house all their _____.
              family   life

6. Most people save money for _____.
                                          emergency

3.3 Regular Plural Nouns—Pronunciation 🎧 3.3

	RULE	EXAMPLES	
/s/	We pronounce the plural ending as /s/ after the voiceless sounds: /p, t, k, f, θ/.	lip—lips cat—cats rock—rocks	cuff—cuffs month—months
/z/	We pronounce the plural ending as /z/ after all vowels and after the voiced sounds: /b, d, g, v, m, n, ŋ, l, r/.	bee—bees cab—cabs lid—lids bag—bags stove—stoves	sum—sums can—cans thing—things bill—bills car—cars
/əz/	We pronounce the plural ending as /əz/ after the sounds: /s, x, z, ʃ, tʃ, ʒ, dʒ/.	class—classes place—places tax—taxes cause—causes	dish—dishes beach—beaches garage—garages bridge—bridges

EXERCISE 4 Find a partner. Say the plural form of each word in Exercise 3.

3.4 Irregular Plural Nouns

SINGULAR	PLURAL	EXPLANATION
man woman tooth foot	men women teeth feet	Some plural nouns have a vowel change from the singular form.
sheep fish deer	sheep fish deer	Some plural nouns are the same as the singular form.
child person mouse	children people mice	Some plural nouns have a different word form.

Note:

The plural of *person* can also be *persons*, but *people* is more common.

Pronunciation Note:

We hear the difference in pronunciation between *woman* (/wʊmən/) and *women* (/wɪmən/) in the first syllable.

EXERCISE 5 Write the plural form of each noun.

1. man _____ men _____

2. foot _____

3. woman _____

4. policeman _____

5. child _____

6. fish _____

7. mouse _____

8. sheep _____

9. tooth _____

10. person _____

EXERCISE 6 Fill in the blanks with the plural form of the nouns given.

1. Some _____ houses _____ are very big.
       house

2. The United States has almost 330 million _____.
                                               person

3. Americans move many _____ in their _____ .
                          time   life

4. Some young _____ and _____ live with their _____ .
                man   woman   parent

5. _____ are very expensive in some _____ .
      home   city

6. In many _____ , adult _____ live with their parents.
              country   child

7. Do you use meters or _____ to measure things in your country?
                           foot

8. Some apartments have a problem with _____ .
                                          mouse

A row of brownstone apartments in New York City

Finding an APARTMENT

Read the following article. Pay special attention to the words in bold. 🎧 3.4

There are several ways to find an apartment. One way is to look online. **There are** a lot of websites to help you find an apartment. **There are** often pictures of the building and the apartment for rent. **There is** sometimes a map to show you the location of the building.

Another way to find an apartment is to look in the newspaper. **There is** an "Apartments for Rent" section in the back of some newspapers. **There are** ads[1] for apartments and houses for rent. Many newspapers also put this information online.

You can also find an apartment by looking at buildings in the neighborhood where you want to live. **There are** often "For Rent" signs on the front of the buildings. **There is** usually a phone number on the sign. You can call and ask the landlord[2] or manager for information. You can ask:

- How much is the rent?
- Is heat included?
- What floor is the apartment on?
- **Is there** an elevator?
- How many bedrooms **are there** in the apartment?
- How many closets **are there** in the apartment?
- Is the apartment available[3] now?

If an apartment interests you, you can make an appointment to see it. When you go to see the apartment, ask:

- **Is there** a lease[4]? How long is the lease?
- **Is there** a janitor or manager?
- **Is there** a parking space for each apartment? Is it free, or do I have to pay extra?
- **Are there** smoke detectors[5]?
- **Is there** a laundry room in the building? Where is it?

The landlord sometimes asks you a few questions, such as:

- How many people **are there** in your family?
- Do you have any pets?

Look at the apartment carefully before you sign the lease. If **there are** some problems, ask the landlord to fix them before you move in.

---

[1] ad (advertisement): a notice about products or services
[2] landlord: a person who owns a house, apartment, or condo and rents it to others
[3] available: free and ready to use
[4] lease: a contract to pay to use an apartment for a period of time
[5] smoke detector: a device that senses smoke from a fire

Based on the reading, write T for *true* or F for *false*.

1. _____ It's not good to ask the landlord or manager questions.

2. _____ Parking spaces are always free.

3. _____ Some apartments don't have a lease.

THINK ABOUT IT Discuss the questions with a partner or in a small group.

1. What do you think is a good way to find an apartment?

2. What is one question you ask before you rent an apartment?

3.5 *There Is/There Are*

We use *there is* or *there are* to introduce a subject, especially with a location or a time.

SINGULAR	*THERE*	*IS*	*A/AN/ONE*	SINGULAR SUBJECT	LOCATION/TIME
Affirmative	There	is	an	air conditioner	in the bedroom.
			one	dryer	in the basement.
			a	rent increase	this year.
	THERE	*ISN'T*	*A/AN*	SINGULAR SUBJECT	LOCATION/TIME
Negative	There	isn't	a	back door	in my apartment.
			an	elevator	in the building.
	THERE	*IS*	*NO*	SINGULAR SUBJECT	LOCATION/TIME
	There	is	no	elevator	in the building.
PLURAL	*THERE*	*ARE*	(PLURAL WORD)	PLURAL SUBJECT	LOCATION/TIME
Affirmative	There	are	—	smoke detectors	near the bedrooms.
			several	windows	in the bedroom.
			two	closets	in the hall.
	THERE	*AREN'T*	(ANY)	PLURAL SUBJECT	LOCATION/TIME
Negative	There	aren't	any	available apartments	this month.
	THERE	*ARE*	*NO*	PLURAL SUBJECT	LOCATION/TIME
	There	are	no	parking spaces	on the street.

Notes:

1. We can write a contraction with *there is*: *there's*. We don't write a contraction with *there are*.

2. When two nouns follow *there*, we use a singular verb (*is*) if the first noun is singular.

There is one closet in the bedroom and two closets in the hall.

We use a plural verb (*are*) if the first noun is plural.

There are two closets in the hall and one closet in the bedroom.

GRAMMAR IN USE

In informal conversations, we can use *there're* (/ˈðɛəɹˌə(ɹ)/) instead of *there are*. Don't use this form in writing.

There're a lot of children in this neighborhood.

You will also hear people say, "There's a lot of children in the neighborhood." This is not correct in writing.

ABOUT YOU Write true statements about your house or apartment. Use *there is* or *there are* and the words given. Then find a partner and compare your answers. (If you live in a dorm, do the About You on the next page.)

1. carpet/in the living room

    There's a carpet in the living room.

2. trees/in front of the building

    There are no trees in front of the building.

3. curtains/on the windows

    _____

4. door/in the kitchen

    _____

5. windows/in my bedroom

    _____

6. closet/in the living room

    _____

7. number/on the front door

    _____

8. overhead light/in the kitchen

    _____

9. microwave/in the kitchen

    _____

10. back door

    _____

11. fireplace

    _____

12. smoke detectors

    _____

curtains

overhead light

fireplace

smoke detector

ABOUT YOU Write statements about your dorm or dorm room. Use *there is* or *there are* and the words given. Then find a partner and compare your answers. (If you live in an apartment or a house, do the About You on the previous page.)

1. window/in the room

   <u>There's a window in the room.</u>

2. curtains/on the window

   <u>There are no curtains on the window.</u>

3. closet/in the room

   _____

4. two beds/in the room

   _____

5. bathroom/on my floor

   _____

6. men/in the dorm

   _____

7. cafeteria/in the dorm

   _____

8. snack machines/in the dorm

   _____

9. noisy students/in the dorm

   _____

10. numbers/on the doors

    _____

11. elevator(s)/in the dorm

    _____

12. laundry room/in the dorm

    _____

3.6 Questions and Short Answers with *There*

	STATEMENT	*YES/NO* QUESTION AND SHORT ANSWER
Singular	**There is** a laundry room in the building. **There is** a smoke detector in the apartment.	A: **Is there** a laundry room in your dorm? B: No, **there isn't**. OR No, **there's not**. A: **Is there** a smoke detector near the bedroom? B: Yes, **there is**.
Plural	**There are** some children in my building. **There are** parking spaces behind the building.	A: **Are there** any children on your floor? B: Yes, **there are**. A: **Are there** parking spaces for all of the apartments? B: No, **there aren't**.
	STATEMENT	*HOW MANY* QUESTION AND SHORT ANSWER
Plural	**There are** 10 apartments in my building.	A: **How many** apartments **are there** in your building? B: (**There are**) 25.

Notes:

1. We often use *any* before a plural noun in a question with *there*.

     Are there **any windows** in the kitchen?

2. In a short answer with *no*, we usually make contractions. We don't make a contraction in a short answer with *yes*.

     No, there **aren't**.

     No, there **isn't**. OR No, there's **not**.

3. In *how many* questions with a location, we sometimes omit *there*.

     How many apartments are (there) in your building?

EXERCISE 7 Find a partner. Ask and answer questions about your partner's apartment (Column A) or your partner's dorm (Column B). Use *there* and the words given.

1. smoke detectors/in the hall

     A: *Are there any smoke detectors in the hall?*

     B: *Yes, there are.*

A	B
2. how many closets/in the bedroom	2. married students/in your dorm
3. children/in the building	3. a computer lab/in your dorm
4. a dishwasher/in the kitchen	4. an elevator/in your dorm
5. a yard/in front of the building	5. graduate students/in your dorm
6. trees/in front of the building	6. a quiet place to study/in your dorm
7. a basement/in the building	7. an air conditioner/in your room
8. a laundry room/in the building	8. a parking lot/near your dorm
9. noisy neighbors/in the building	9. how many rooms/in your dorm
10. an elevator/in the building	10. how many floors/in your dorm
11. how many windows/in the apartment	11. how many students/in your dorm
12. how many apartments/in the building	12. a bike room/in your dorm

EXERCISE 8 Complete the phone conversation between a student (A) and a landlord (B). Use *there is, there are, is there, are there,* and other related words. Use contractions when possible.

A: I'm calling about an apartment for rent on Grover Street.

B: We have two apartments available. _____There's_____ a two-bedroom apartment on the first floor and
              1.
a one-bedroom apartment on the fourth floor. Which one are you interested in?

A: I prefer the smaller apartment. _____ an elevator in the building?
                                         2.

B: Yes, there is. How many people _____ in your family?
                                     3.

A: I live alone. I'm a student. Is this a quiet building?

B: Oh, yes. This is a very quiet building. _____ no kids in the building.
                                             4.

A: That's good. I have a car. _____ parking spaces?
                                   5.

B: Yes. _____ 20 spaces in the back of the building.
          6.

A: How _____ apartments _____ in the building?
           7.   8.

B: _____ 30 apartments.
     9.

A: Twenty parking spaces for 30 apartments? Then _____ enough spaces for everyone.
                                           10.

B: Don't worry. Not everyone has a car. And _____ a lot of spaces on the street.
                                   11.

A: _____ a laundry room in the building?
     12.

B: Yes. _____ washers and dryers in the basement.
        13.

A: I hear a dog. Is that your dog?

B: Yes, but don't worry. I don't live in the building. _____ no dogs in the building.
                                   14.

3.7 *There, They,* and Other Pronouns

EXAMPLES	EXPLANATION
There's a janitor in the building. **He's** in the basement. **There's** a little girl in the next apartment. **She's** 10 years old. **There's** an empty apartment downstairs. **It's** available now. **There are** two washing machines. **They're** in the basement.	To introduce a new noun, we use *there + is/are*. When this noun is the subject of the next sentence, we use the subject pronoun *he, she, it,* or *they*.

Spelling Note:

Don't confuse *there* and *they're*. They have the same pronunciation.

    There are dogs in the next apartment. ***They're*** very friendly.

EXERCISE 9 Fill in the blanks with one of the items from the box. You can use an item more than once.

there's	there are	it's	she's	is she	are they
is there	are there	is it	he's	is he	they're

1. ___There's___ a small apartment for rent in my building. ___It's___ on the fourth floor.

2. _____ an old woman in the next apartment. _____ very quiet.

3. _____ parking spaces in the back of the building. _____ not very big.

4. _____ a young man in the basement. _____ busy with his laundry.

5. _____ a five-year-old girl in the next apartment. _____ in school?

6. _____ a boy in the family? How old _____ ?

7. How many apartments _____ in the building? _____ big?

8. _____ an elevator in the building? _____ next to the front door?

9. _____ a janitor in the building. His name is Marco. _____ busy now.

EXERCISE 10 Complete the conversation between a student (A) and a building manager (B). Use combinations of *there, is, are, it,* and *they.* Use contractions when possible.

A: ___Is there___ a laundry room in the building?
      1.

B: Yes, _____ . _____ in the basement.
         2.   3.

A: I need change for the washing machines.

B: _____ a dollar-bill changer in the laundry room.
      4.

A: How many machines _____ ?
         5.

B: _____ four washers and two dryers.
      6.

A: Only two dryers?

B: Yes. _____ very big.
      7.

A: _____ a bike room in the building?
      8.

B: Yes, _____ . _____ in the basement.
         9.   10.

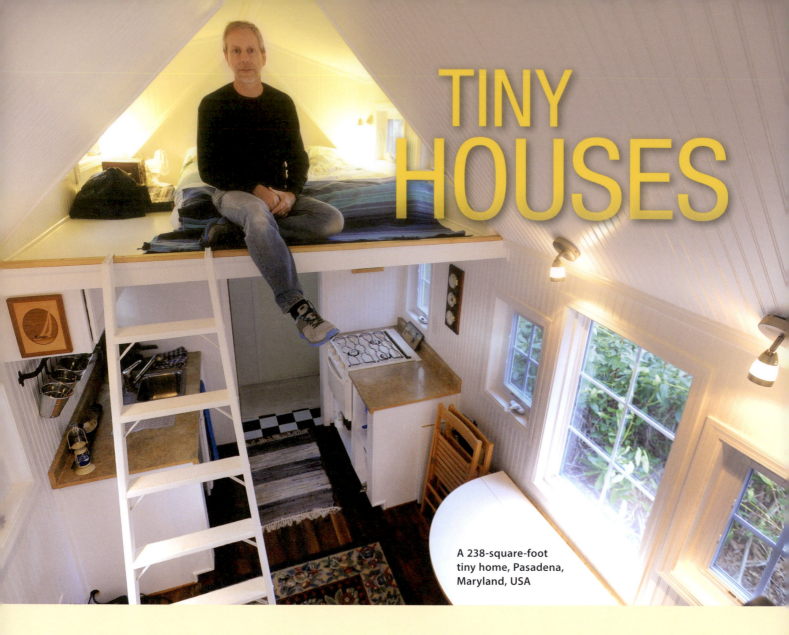

TINY HOUSES

A 238-square-foot tiny home, Pasadena, Maryland, USA

Read the following article. Pay special attention to the words in bold. 🎧 3.5

Do you have **a** dream to own **a** house? Does **the** house of your dreams have many rooms? **The** typical new American home is about 2,600 square feet. **A** big house is expensive. Americans spend one-third to one-half of their salaries on housing costs. Most homeowners have **a** mortgage[1]. They make **a** down payment[2] and then pay **the** mortgage—plus interest—over **a** long period of time. Besides **the** cost of **the** house plus interest, there is insurance, property tax, repairs, and improvements. Over 30 years, **a** $300,000 house can cost over 1 million dollars!

Not everyone wants to own **a** big house. Some people want to own **a** small house. In fact, some people want to own **a** very tiny house. Who wants to live in **a** tiny house? More and more people do. Most tiny-house owners have middle incomes.

Tiny houses come in all shapes and sizes, but they are usually between 100 and 400 square feet. Why do people want **a** very small house? **The** owners of tiny houses want **a** simple life. Some tiny houses cost only about $20,000. Many tiny-house owners do not have **a** mortgage. Without **a** mortgage, they can save more of their paycheck.

There are several websites with pictures of tiny houses. Look at **the** pictures. Is this lifestyle for you?

---

[1] mortgage: a long-term loan from a bank for buying property
[2] down payment: the first payment at the time of buying something (usually 10–20 percent of the cost)

COMPREHENSION Based on the reading, write T for *true* or F for *false*.

1. _____ Most Americans spend more than half of their salaries on housing.

2. _____ Tiny houses are always 100 square feet or less.

3. _____ The average new American home is about 2,600 square feet.

THINK ABOUT IT Discuss the questions with a partner or in a small group.

1. What is your dream house? Where is it? What does it look like?

2. Do you think tiny houses are a good idea? Why or why not?

3.8 Definite and Indefinite Articles, *Some/Any*

EXAMPLES	EXPLANATION
We have **a house**. **The house** has three bedrooms. There's **an apartment** for rent in my building. Do you want to see **the apartment**?	We introduce a singular noun with the indefinite article *a* or *an*. When we refer to this noun again, we use the definite article *the*.
There are **(some) websites** for tiny-house owners. Do you want to see **the websites**? Does your house need **(any) repairs**? How much do **the repairs** cost?	We introduce a plural noun with *some, any,* or no article. When we refer to this noun again, we use the definite article *the*.
The neighbors on my block are friendly. **The mortgage** for our house is expensive.	We use *the* before a noun to talk about a specific person or thing.

Notes:

1. We use *the* before a singular or plural noun if the speaker and listener share an experience and are thinking about the same person or thing.

>   *(husband to wife) We need to pay **the bills** next week.*

2. We use *the* before a singular or plural noun in these expressions: *the next, the first, the second, the last, the only, the same.**

>   *The mortgage is not **the only expense**.*

* See Appendix F for more uses of articles.

GRAMMAR IN USE

We use *the* with certain familiar places and people, even if it's the first time we mention them.

the bank	the beach	the bus	the store
the zoo	the post office	the train	the hospital
the park	the doctor	the movies	the airport

EXERCISE 11 Listen to the conversation. Then write T for *true*, F for *false*, or NS for *not stated*. 🎧 3.6

1. _____ The apartment is very hot.

2. _____ The building manager is very busy.

3. _____ The neighbor's dog is very noisy.

EXERCISE 12 Listen again. Fill in the blanks using *a, an,* or *the.* 🎧 3.6

A: I have _____*a*_____ problem in my apartment.
　　　　　　1.

B: What's _____ problem?
　　　　　2.

A: _____ landlord doesn't provide enough heat. I have to wear _____ sweater all the time in
　　　3.　　　　　　　　　　　　　　　　　　　　　　　　　　　　4.

　_____ apartment.
　5.

B: Why don't you talk to _____ building manager? Maybe _____ heat doesn't work.
　　　　　　　　　　　　　　6.　　　　　　　　　　　　　　7.

A: Maybe. There's one more problem. I have _____ neighbor who has _____ small dog.
　　　　　　　　　　　　　　　　　　　　　　　8.　　　　　　　　　　　9.

　_____ dog makes a lot of noise. We share _____ wall, and I can hear _____ dog
　10.　　　　　　　　　　　　　　　　　11.　　　　　　　　　　　　　12.

　through _____ wall.
　　　　　13.

B: I don't have problems like that. We have _____ very nice building manager. If there's _____
　　　　　　　　　　　　　　　　　　　　　14.　　　　　　　　　　　　　　　　　　　15.

　problem, I send _____ email, and she takes care of it right away.
　　　　　　　16.

EXERCISE 13 Complete the phone conversation between a student (A) and the manager of an apartment building (B). Fill in the blanks with *a, an, the, some,* or *any.*

A: Hello? I want to speak with _____ landlord.
　　　　　　　　　　　　　　　1.

B: I'm _____ manager of _____ building. Can I help you?
　　　　2.　　　　　　　　　　3.

A: I need to find _____ apartment.
　　　　　　　　　4.

B: Where do you live now?

A: I live in _____ big apartment on Wright Street. I have _____ roommate, but
　　　　　　5.　　　　　　　　　　　　　　　　　　　　　　　6.

　he's graduating. I need _____ one-bedroom apartment. Are there _____
　　　　　　　　　　　　7.　　　　　　　　　　　　　　　　　　　　　　8.

　small apartments in your building?

B: There's one.

A: What floor is it on?

B: It's on _____ third floor.
　　　　　　9.

A: Does _____ kitchen have _____ stove and _____
  10.   11.   12.
refrigerator?

B: Yes. _____ refrigerator is old, but it works well. _____ stove is new.
  13.   14.

A: Can I see _____ apartment?
  15.

B: I have _____ questions for you first. Do you have _____ dog?
  16.   17.

A: No, I don't.

B: Do you have _____ pets?
  18.

A: I have _____ snake.
  19.

B: A snake?

A: Don't worry. I keep _____ snake in _____ glass box.
  20.   21.

B: Is _____ box always closed?
  22.

A: Yes, it is. I only open it to feed _____ snake. It eats mice.
  23.

B: Mice?

A: Yes. Can I see _____ apartment?
  24.

B: I'm afraid not. We don't allow pets in _____ building, not even snakes and mice.
  25.

3.9 Making Generalizations

A generalization says that something is true about all members of a group.

EXAMPLES	EXPLANATION
A homeowner pays tax. = **Homeowners** pay tax. **An apartment** is expensive. = **Apartments** are expensive.	To make a generalization about the subject, we can use the indefinite article *a* or *an* before the singular form of the subject. We can also use the plural form of the subject with no article.
I like big **rooms**. I'm not interested in tiny **houses**.	To make a generalization about the object, we use the plural form with no article.

EXERCISE 14 Rewrite each generalization with a plural subject. Make other necessary changes.

1. A homeowner has a lot of expenses.

   Homeowners have a lot of expenses.

2. A house in San Francisco is expensive.

   _____

3. A condo association has a lot of rules.

   _____

4. A building manager takes care of buildings.

   _____

5. A renter pays rent every month.

   _____

6. A yard is good for small children.

   _____

EXERCISE 15 Fill in the blanks with a plural subject. Then find a partner and compare your answers.

1. _____ _Students_ _____ need a cheap apartment.

2. _____ don't want to rent to people with pets.

3. _____ sometimes make a lot of noise in an apartment.

4. _____ need an apartment with an elevator.

5. _____ need a big apartment.

6. _____ are expensive in the United States.

ABOUT YOU Find a partner. Ask and answer questions about the things he or she likes in the place where he or she lives. Use the plural form of each object noun.

1. rug

   A: *Do you like rugs?*

   B: *No, I don't.*

2. white wall

3. curtain on the window

4. picture on the wall

5. plant

6. friendly neighbor

7. bright light

EXERCISE 16 Complete the conversation between two students. Use *a, an, the, some,* or Ø for no article. More than one answer may be possible.

A: I have _____ new apartment. It's great. I'm really happy.
1.

B: I have _____ new apartment too, but it has _____ problems.
2. 3.

A: Really? What problems?

B: I don't like _____ janitor. He's impolite. Also, I want to get _____ dog, but
4. 5.

it's not allowed. _____ landlord says that _____ dogs make a lot of noise.
6. 7.

A: Can you get _____ cat?
8.

B: Yes, but I don't like _____ cats.
9.

A: Is your building quiet?

B: No. There are _____ children in _____ building. When I study, I can hear
10. 11.

_____ children in the next apartment. They watch TV all the time.
12.

A: What about your roommate? Is this a problem for her, too?

B: I don't have _____ roommate now.
13.

A: You need to find _____ apartment in _____ different building.
14. 15.

FUN WITH GRAMMAR

Play a game of picture dictation. Sit back-to-back with a partner and do not look at each other's papers. Each person draws a simple picture of the inside of one room in a house. When the drawings are complete, Partner A describes his or her room to Partner B using sentences with *there is/there are*. Partner B draws this room. Then switch roles. Compare the drawings done from the descriptions to see whose was closest to the original.

SUMMARY OF UNIT 3

Singular and Plural Nouns

REGULAR PLURALS	IRREGULAR PLURALS
boy—boys	man—men
box—boxes	woman—women
story—stories	child—children
tomato—tomatoes	foot—feet
wife—wives	fish—fish

There Is/There Are

SINGULAR	EXAMPLES
AFFIRMATIVE STATEMENT	**There's** a laundry room in my building.
NEGATIVE STATEMENT	**There isn't** an elevator in my building.
YES/NO QUESTION	**Is there** a yard behind your building?
SHORT ANSWER	Yes, **there is**.

PLURAL	EXAMPLES
AFFIRMATIVE STATEMENT	**There are** foreign students in my dorm.
NEGATIVE STATEMENT	**There aren't** any graduate students in my dorm.
YES/NO QUESTION	**Are there** any married students in your dorm?
SHORT ANSWER	No, **there aren't**.
HOW MANY QUESTION	**How many** students **are (there)** in your dorm?

Articles and *Some/Any*

USE	SINGULAR	PLURAL
To introduce a new noun	There's **a tree** in front of my house. My house has **a big yard**.	I have **(some) flowers** in my yard. There aren't **(any) trees** in my yard.
To talk about specific people or things	**The janitor** in my building is very helpful.	**The apartments** in my building are small.
To talk about the only one of something	I don't like **the president** of my condo association.	—
To make a generalization	**A dog** is a popular pet.	**Dogs** are popular pets. I like **dogs**.

REVIEW

Choose the correct word(s) to complete the conversation. Circle Ø for no article. Where you see a blank, write the plural form of the word given.

A: My husband and I have (**a**/*the*/*Ø*) new condo. It has three ___bedrooms___ and two bathrooms.
                                 1.   **2. bedroom**

B: That's big! How many _____ are in your family?
                               3. person

A: Just my husband and me. (*There are*/*They are*/*There's*) 30 _____ in
                                          4.   **5. apartment**

    (*a*/*the*/*Ø*) building. There's (*a*/*an*/*the*) exercise room. (*There's*/*It's*/*There*) not very big, but my husband
      6.   **7.**   **8.**

    likes to use it. There are (*some*/*any*/*a*) weight machines. (*There*/*It's*/*There's*) also (*a*/*the*/*any*) swimming
                             9.   **10.**   **11.**

    pool.

B: How often do you use (*a*/*the*/*Ø*) pool?
                             12.

A: We use it one or two _____ a week. Our _____ really love it.
                             13. day   **14. kid**

    (*There are*/*They're*/*There*) other _____ with small _____ in the building.
                         15.   **16. family**   **17. child**

    I like to sit at (*the*/*a*/*Ø*) pool with a few _____. We talk and watch (*a*/*the*/*Ø*) kids.
                         18.   **19. woman**   **20.**

B: Do you ever invite (*a*/*any*/*the*) _____ to your pool?
                             21.   **22. guest**

A: No. (*A*/*The*/*Ø*) pool is only for _____ of (*a*/*the*/*Ø*) condo association. Other _____
        23.   **24. member**   **25.**   **26. person**

    can't use the pool.

B: Really? Who makes (*the*/*a*/*Ø*) rules?
                             27.

A: (*An*/*The*/*Ø*) condo association makes the rules.
      28.

B: (*There are*/*Are there*/*Are they*) other rules?
                      29.

A: Yes, (*they are*/*there are*/*it is*). (*Pets are*/*The pet is*/*The pets are*) not allowed. (*There's*/*It's*/*They're*) a condo
                      30.   **31.**   **32.**

    for sale in my building. Do you want to see it?

B: I don't like (*a condo*/*condos*/*the condos*). I prefer (*a*/*the*/*Ø*) houses. I don't like to follow
                           33.   **34.**

    (*a rule*/*some rules*/*the rules*) of a condo association. I want to make my own decisions.
        35.

FROM GRAMMAR TO WRITING

PART 1 Editing Advice

1. *People* is a plural noun. Use a plural verb form.

    The people in my building ~~is~~ *are* very nice.

2. Don't confuse *there* with *they're*.

    My apartment has two closets. ~~There~~ *They're* not very big.

3. Don't confuse *it's* and *there's*.

    ~~It's~~ *There's* a closet in my bedroom.

4. Don't confuse *have* and *there*.

    ~~Have~~ *There's* a closet in my bedroom.

5. Don't use *the* if the speaker and the listener don't have the same person or thing in mind.

    I have ~~the~~ *a* new roommate.

6. Don't use *the* with a generalization.

    ~~The h~~*H*ouses are expensive.

7. Don't use *a* before a plural noun.

    There are ~~a~~ big windows in my living room.

8. Don't use an apostrophe for a plural ending.

    The building has three ~~floor's~~ *floors*.

PART 2 Editing Practice

Some of the shaded words and phrases have mistakes. Find the mistakes and correct them. If the shaded words are correct, write C.

    C

I have a new apartment. It's in ~~the~~ *a* nice neighborhood. There are 30 apartments in my building.
    1.   **2.**   **3.**

My apartment is big. They're are four bedrooms and two bathrooms. Has a large closet in each
                           4.   **5.**

bedroom.

I love my kitchen. It's a new dishwasher in a kitchen. I hate to wash a dishes. I don't have a microwave.
                    6.   **7.**   **8.**   **9.**

Some people thinks that's strange, but I don't like the microwaves.
            10.   **11.**

There are five washers and five dryers in the basement. I never have to wait to wash my clothes.
  12.   **13.**

I like my neighbor's. There very nice people. There's a very interesting women across the hall from me.
         14.   **15.**   **16.**   **17.**

We are friends now.

WRITING TIP

When you write a description of a place, it's a good idea to organize your ideas spatially (by space). For example, you can start describing your apartment from the entrance. Then describe each room in the order you see them. Or you can describe your neighborhood in the order you walk through it.

PART 3 Write

Read the prompts. Choose one and write one paragraph about it.

1. Write a description of your neighborhood. Use *there is/there are* in some of your sentences.
2. Write a description of your apartment, house, or dorm room. Use *there is/there are* in some of your sentences.

PART 4 Edit

Reread the Summary of Unit 3 and the editing advice. Edit your writing from Part 3.

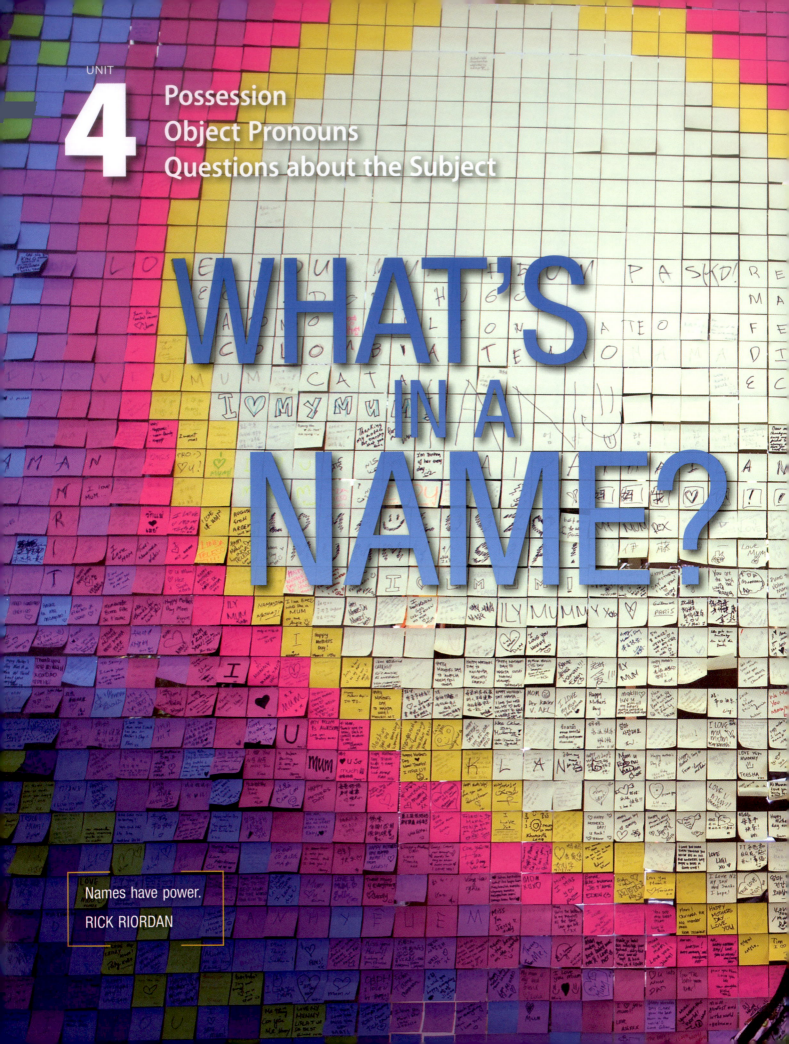

WHAT'S IN A NAME?

Names have power.

RICK RIORDAN

Notes with dedications of love to all the "Moms" of the world in Auckland, New Zealand

The NAME GAME

Read the following article. Pay special attention to the words in bold. 🎧 4.1

Many things go in and out of style. Look at some old photos of **your** parents and grandparents. Maybe **your father's** shorts are very short, and **your mother's** hair is big and curly. In another photo, maybe **your grandparents'** 1960s kitchen has a green refrigerator and dishwasher. Maybe **their** car is large, long, and light green.

Just like hair, clothes, colors, and cars, names also go in and out of style. Every generation, certain names become popular. For example, in the United States some popular **girls'** names from the early 1900s include *Gertrude, Mildred,* and *Viola*. Some popular **boys'** names from that time include *Elmer, Chester,* and *Clarence*. Some popular names from the 1950s and 1960s are *Linda, Judy, Gary,* and *Dennis*. None of these names is very common today. Today, popular names include *Emma, Sophia, Jacob,* and *Liam*.

Sometimes people choose older names *because* they're not very popular. These people want **their** children's** names to be unique. However, they may be in for a surprise: Names from the past sometimes come back in style. At the moment, some old-fashioned names—such as *Hannah, Olivia, Max,* and *Owen*—are becoming popular again.

Some people may have names from another generation[1] for another reason. They may be named after people, usually people in **their** families. This is true of George W. Bush, the 43rd president of the United States. **Whose** name does he have? He is named after **his** father, George H. W. Bush, the 41st president. George W. and **his** wife have two daughters. One **daughter's** name is Jenna. What about the other daughter? **Her** name is Barbara. She is named after **her** grandmother, **George's** mother.

Different names are popular at different times and in different places. Is **yours** popular in **your** country?

---

[1] generation: all of the people of about the same age

Most Popular Names in the United States		
Year	**Boys' Names**	**Girls' Names**
2018	Jackson	Sophia
2010	Jacob	Isabella
2000	Jacob	Emily
1990	Michael	Jessica
1980	Michael	Jennifer
1970	Michael	Jennifer
1960	David	Mary
1950	James	Linda
1940	James	Mary
1930	Robert	Mary
1920	John	Mary

Jars of Nutella hazelnut chocolate spread feature names on the labels at a pop-up store in Hong Kong, China.

COMPREHENSION Based on the reading, write T for *true* or F for *false*.

1. _____ Names, like other things, go in and out of fashion.

2. _____ A lot of old-fashioned names from the past are popular again today.

3. _____ *Linda* is a popular name for girls today.

THINK ABOUT IT Discuss the questions with a partner or in a small group.

1. How do people choose names for children in your country?

2. Does your name have a special meaning?

4.1 Possessive Nouns—Forms

Possessive nouns show ownership or relationship.

	NOUN	RULE	EXAMPLES
Singular nouns	son daughter	Add apostrophe + *s*.	My **son's** name is William. My **daughter's** name is Emma.
Regular plural nouns	girls boys	Add an apostrophe only.	Popular **girls'** names are *Sophia* and *Ava*. Popular **boys'** names are *Noah* and *Jacob*.
Irregular plural nouns	children women	Add apostrophe + *s*.	What are your **children's** names? *Rose* and *Dorothy* are **women's** names.
Names that end in -*s*	James	Add apostrophe + *s*.	Do you know **James's** wife?
Inanimate objects	state	Use *the* _____ of _____. OR _____'s	*Arizona* is **the name of a state**. The **state's** name is *Arizona*.

Notes:

1. We can use two possessive nouns together: ***Emma's husband's** name is William*.
2. When the same noun comes after two different possessive nouns, we can omit the noun to avoid repetition.

   Mary's last name is short. Jennifer's is not. (Jennifer's = Jennifer's last name)

GRAMMAR IN USE

To show possession for inanimate objects (things that are not alive), *of* + noun is more common than noun + *'s* (*the parks **of New York** vs. **New York's** parks*). The *'s* form is more informal and common in speaking.

> ***Boston's streets** are narrow.* (informal)
> *The **streets of Boston** are narrow.* (formal)

EXERCISE 1 Listen to someone talk about names in his family. Fill in the blanks with the words you hear. 🎧 4.2

My name is William Henry White. My nickname is Bill. My _____ name is Elizabeth White.
                                                                                1.
Her nickname is Lizzy. Her name is almost the same as her _____ name. _____
                                                                              2.   3.
name is Elsbeth. Some married women use only their _____ last name, but Lizzy uses both her
                                                                            4.
own name and my name. Our _____ name is Charles. His friends call him "Charley."
                                              5.

continued

_____ teachers prefer to call him by his real name.
                6.

I like to hear about _____ names. The meanings of _____ are so
                                        7.   8.

interesting. For example, the _____ of my name is "protector." And the meaning of my
                                          9.

_____ name is "man." Do you know your _____ meaning?
        10.   11.

EXERCISE 2 Fill in the blanks with the possessive form of the words given.

1. My _____<u>parents' names</u>_____ are Rosa and Paco.
                parents/names

2. My _____ are Lara and Marta.
        sisters/names

3. My _____ is Luis.
        brother/name

4. _____ is four years old.
        Luis/son

5. My _____ are José and María.
        grandparents/names

6. In my country, *José* and *Luis* are common _____.
                                                    men/names

7. In my country, *Rosa* and *Marta* are common _____.
                                                    women/names

8. My _____ has an unusual name: Esma.
        brother/wife

EXERCISE 3 Rewrite these sentences and questions with a possessive noun.

1. The teacher knows the names of the students.

   <u>The teacher knows the students' names.</u>

2. The name of the school is Carson College.

   _____

3. The title of this textbook is *Grammar in Context*.

   _____

4. What are the names of your parents?

   _____

5. Do you use the last name of your father?

   _____

6. What is the name of your best friend?

   _____

7. The names of my sisters are Julie and Jessica.

_____

8. The name of my hometown is Springfield.

_____

4.2 Possessive Adjectives

Possessive adjectives show ownership or relationship.

EXAMPLES	EXPLANATION	
	Subject Pronouns	Possessive Adjectives
I like **my** name. You are a new student. What's **your** name? He likes **his** name. She doesn't like **her** name. Is this your dog? Is it friendly? What's **its** name? We use **our** nicknames. These are my friends. **Their** last name is Johnson.	I you he she it we they	my your his her its our their
My sister loves **her** husband. (NOT: My sister loves his husband.) My uncle lives with **his** daughter. (NOT: My uncle lives with her daughter.)	A possessive adjective refers to the noun before it, not the noun that follows it.	
My sister's name is Linda. **Her son's** name is Noah.	We can use a possessive adjective and a possessive noun together.	

Notes:

1. Do not confuse the possessive adjective _its_ with _it's_ (_it is_).
2. We use the same possessive form for singular and plural nouns.

   her brothers (NOT: _hers brothers_)

GRAMMAR IN USE

Don't confuse _their, there, and they're_. These three words sound the same but have different meanings.

   There _are 24 students in the class._
   They're _all from China._
   Their _textbook is Grammar in Context._

EXERCISE 4 Fill in the blanks with the correct possessive adjective.

1. I don't like _____ my _____ name.

2. He loves _____ mother.

continued

3. She loves _____ father.

4. This tree is losing _____ leaves.

5. Some American women don't change _____ last names when they get married.

6. Do you use _____ father's last name?

7. I use _____ middle name.

8. We put _____ names at the top of the page.

4.3 Questions with *Whose*

We use *whose* + noun to ask about possession or ownership.

QUESTIONS				ANSWERS
Whose + Noun	*Do/Does*	*Subject*	*Verb*	
Whose last name	do	you	use?	I use **my husband's** name.
Whose last name	does	your son	use?	He uses **his father's** name.
Whose + Noun	*Be*	*Subject*		
Whose book	is	this?		It's **Noah's** book.
Whose papers	are	these?		They're **his** papers.

EXERCISE 5 Write a question with *whose* to complete each conversation.

1. **A:** Do you want to see my family photos?

   B: Those are cute children. Are they your kids?

   A: No, they're not.

   B: _Whose kids are they?_____

   A: They're my sister's kids.

2. **A:** There's a book on the floor.

   B: Let me see who it belongs to.

   A: _____

   B: It's Rita Patel's book.

3. **A:** My husband and I have different last names.

   B: _____

   A: Our son uses my husband's last name.

4. A: Do you have your new class schedule?

   B: Yes, I do.

   A: _____

   B: I have Mr. Green's class for math.

5. A: What's your cat's name?

   B: That's not my cat.

   A: _____

   B: I don't know. It's always near my front door.

6. A: Look! I'm first on the list.

   B: That's because your last name is Aaron. Your name is always first.

   A: _____

   B: Mine is. My name is always last. My last name is Zyzik.

4.4 Possessive Pronouns

We use possessive pronouns to avoid repetition of a possessive adjective + noun.

EXAMPLES	EXPLANATION	
Your name is easy to pronounce. **Mine** is hard. (*mine = my name*) His signature is hard to read. **Hers** is easy to read. (*hers = her signature*)	**Possessive Adjectives** my your his her its our their	**Possessive Pronouns** mine yours his hers — ours theirs

ABOUT YOU Write sentences that tell the names of people in your life. Use possessive adjectives or pronouns.

father _His name is Kei._   English teacher _____

mother _____   cousin _____

best friend _____   aunt _____

neighbor _____   uncle _____

EXERCISE 6 Write the correct possessive pronoun for the underlined words.

1. Your name is long. ~~My name~~ is short.
   Mine

2. My sister likes her name. I don't like <u>my name</u>.

3. I like my first name. Do you like <u>your first name</u>?

4. My sister uses her middle name. My brother doesn't use <u>his middle name</u>.

5. My wife and I have different last names. My last name is Roberts. <u>Her last name</u> is Paulson.

6. Your last name is easy to pronounce. <u>Their last name</u> is hard.

7. My brother's children are grown up. <u>Our children</u> are still small.

EXERCISE 7 Choose the correct words to complete the conversation.

A: Do you live with (ⓨour/yours) parents?
　　　　　　　　　　　　　　1.

B: No, I don't. Do you live with (*your/yours*)?
　　　　　　　　　　　　　　　　　2.

A: No. (*Mine/Mines*) are back home in South Korea. They live with (*my/mine*) brother.
　　　　　3.　　　　　　　　　　　　　　　　　　　　　　　**4.**

B: (*Your/Yours*) brother is single, then?
　　　5.

A: No, he's married. He lives with (*his/her*) wife and (*our/ours*) parents.
　　　　　　　　　　　　　　　　6.　　　　　　**7.**

　　In (*our/ours*) country, married children often live with (*his/their*) parents.
　　　8.　　　　　　　　　　　　　　　　　　　**9.**

B: Here, grown children don't usually want to live with (*their/theirs*) parents.
　　　　　　　　　　　　　　　　　　　　　　　　　　　　10.

　　My mom and dad live in another state.

A: Isn't that hard for you?

B: Not really. I have (*my/mine*) life, and they have (*their/theirs*).
　　　　　　　　　11.　　　　　　　　　　　　**12.**

FUN WITH GRAMMAR

Play a guessing game. Closes your eyes. Your teacher will collect one small object from everyone in a bag, for example, a pencil, phone, or coffee cup. You may open your eyes when your teacher gets to you, but try to decide which object to give beforehand so you can put it in the bag quickly and quietly. Your teacher will place all of these objects in a central location and then ask everyone to open their eyes. Use the objects to write sentences with possessive nouns, for example: "The pencil is Raquel's." Write one sentence for each object. When everyone is finished, your teacher will point to an object, ask a volunteer to read his or her sentence about it, and check for accuracy. Use possessive pronouns when you answer your teacher.

　　Volunteer: The pencil is Raquel's.
　　Teacher:　Is the pencil yours, Raquel?
　　Raquel:　Yes it's mine./No, it's not mine.

The teacher will go around the room asking for volunteers to read their sentences until all the owners are identified correctly. Put a mark next to each correct sentence on your paper. The person with the most correct sentences wins.

A father lifts his baby son.

NAMING CUSTOMS

Read the following conversation. Pay special attention to the words in bold. 🎧 4.3

A: Tell **me** about your name. What's your full name?

B: William James Thomas Junior.

A: Do people call **you** "William James"?

B: No. No one calls **me** by my middle name. I never use **it**. I use my middle initial[1] when I sign my name: William J. Thomas, Jr.

A: Why do you use *junior* after your name?

B: My father and I have the same name. His name is William J. Thomas Senior. My mother calls **him** "William," but she calls **me** "Billy." *Bill* and *Billy* are common nicknames for *William*.

A: What's your wife's name?

B: Ann Marie Simms-Thomas. I call **her** "Annie."

A: Why does she have two last names?

B: Simms is her last name, and Thomas is mine. She uses both of **them**.

A: Do you have any children?

B: Yes. We have a son and a daughter. Our son's name is Jacob, but we call **him** "Jake." Our daughter's name is Madison, but everybody calls **her** "Maddie."

A: What do your children call **you**?

B: They call **us** "Mommy" and "Daddy," of course.

_____

[1] initial: the first letter of your first, middle, or last name

COMPREHENSION Based on the conversation, write T for *true* or F for *false*.

1. _____ William has a middle name.

2. _____ William's mother calls William's father "Billy."

3. _____ William's wife doesn't use William's last name.

Discuss the questions with a partner or in a small group.

1. In your country, whose last name do women usually use when they get married?

2. Do you have a nickname? How did you get it?

4.5 The Subject and the Object

EXAMPLES	EXPLANATION
s v o Madison has a nickname. I love Maddie.	The subject (s) comes before the verb (v). The object (o) comes after the verb. The object is a person or a thing.
s v p o He always talks **about** his **children**.	An object can follow a preposition (p).
I have **a middle name**. I never use **it**. He has two **last names**. He uses both of **them**.	An object can be a noun/noun phrase or a pronoun.

EXAMPLES	SUBJECT PRONOUNS	OBJECT PRONOUNS
I like my name. My wife calls **me** "Bill."	I	me
You have a unique name. I want to ask **you** about your name.	you	you
He has a nickname. We call **him** "Jake."	he	him
She uses a nickname. I call **her** "Annie."	she	her
It's a nice name. I like **it**.	it	it
We have two kids. They call **us** "Mommy" and "Daddy."	we	us
They are wonderful kids. We love **them**.	they	them

Notes:

1. After a verb or a preposition, we use an object pronoun.

> *My mother calls my sister and **me** her "little babies."* (NOT: *my sister and I*)

2. In the subject position, we use a subject pronoun.

> *My sister and **I** call our mother "Mama."* (NOT: *My sister and me*)

GRAMMAR IN USE

In subjects and objects that include you and another person, always put yourself last.

> ***She and I** are old friends.*
> *My parents gave **my brother and me** unusual names.*

EXERCISE 8 Fill in the blanks with an object pronoun that matches the underlined word(s).

1. <u>I</u> want to know more about your name. Tell _____*me*_____ something about it.

2. I use <u>my middle name</u> when I sign my name, but I don't use _____ any other time.

3. My children's names are <u>Madison and Jacob</u>. We call _____ "Maddie" and "Jake."

4. <u>You</u> are a new student. I don't know _____.

5. <u>My English teacher</u> is Ms. Kathleen Novak. We call _____ "Kathy."

6. My teacher's name is <u>Mr. Frank</u>. Do you know anything about _____?

7. <u>We</u> have two nephews. They call _____ "Auntie" and "Unc."

EXERCISE 9 Complete the conversation between an international student (A) and an American student (B). Use the correct object pronoun.

A: Americans are informal about names. Our teacher calls _____us_____ by our first names.
   1.

B: What does your teacher call _____ in your country?
   2.

A: In my country, when teachers talk to a woman, they call _____ "Miss" or "Madam." When
   3.

   they talk to a man, they call _____ "Sir."
   4.

B: I like it when the teacher calls _____ by our first names.
   5.

A: I don't. There's another strange thing: in my country, we never use a first name for our teachers. We

   always call _____ "Professor" or "Teacher." In the United States, our teacher doesn't like it
   6.

   when we call _____ "Teacher." She says it's impolite. But in my country, "Teacher" is a
   7.

   term of respect.

B: Only small children in the United States call their teacher "Teacher." If you know your teacher's name,

   use _____.
   8.

A: I can't call _____ "Sophia." It's hard for _____ to change my customs
   9.   10.

   after a lifetime of following _____.
   11.

EXERCISE 10 Fill in the blanks with *I, I'm, my, mine,* or *me.*

1. _____I'm_____ a foreign student.

2. _____ 20 years old.

3. _____ study at the University of Wisconsin.

4. _____ English isn't perfect.

5. Your parents live in Japan. _____ live in the United States.

6. Sometimes my parents visit _____ at the university.

Find a partner. Complete the sentences with *you, your, you're, yours,* or specific names. Then ask and answer the questions. Take turns.

1. What does _____ mother call _____ ?

2. What do _____ call _____ father?

3. My nickname is _____ . What is _____ ?

4. My favorite name for a boy is _____ . What is _____ ?

5. What is _____ favorite name for a girl?

6. Really? I think _____ joking. That's a terrible name!

EXERCISE 11 Fill in the blanks with *he, he's, his,* or *him.*

1. I have a good friend. _____His_____ name is Paul.

2. _____ an accountant.

3. _____ has his own company.

4. The company is _____ .

5. He works with _____ son, Bill.

6. Bill helps _____ with the business.

EXERCISE 12 Fill in the blanks with *she, she's, her,* or *hers.*

1. I have a sister. _____Her_____ name is Diane.

2. _____ an interesting person.

3. I call _____ on the phone once a week.

4. _____ has two children.

5. My children go to Dewey School. _____ go to King School.

6. _____ husband is a teacher.

EXERCISE 13 Fill in the blanks with *it, it's,* or *its.*

1. What do you think of your name? Are you happy with _____it_____?

2. _____ a beautiful name.

3. Look at the list of popular names. Is your name on _____?

4. The name *William* is very popular. _____ on the list almost every year.

5. Look at this website. _____ has a list of popular names in the United States.

6. I have a new book. _____ title is *What to Name Your Baby.*

EXERCISE 14 Fill in the blanks with *we, we're, our, ours,* or *us.*

1. _____We're_____ foreign students.

2. _____ come from different countries.

3. _____ in class now.

4. _____ teacher is American.

5. The teacher asks _____ a lot of questions.

6. Your classroom is on the second floor. _____ is on the third floor.

EXERCISE 15 Fill in the blanks with *they, they're, their, theirs,* or *them.*

1. Diane and Richard are my friends. _____They_____ live near me.

2. _____ Americans.

3. _____ have two children.

4. _____ children go to public school.

5. My house is small. _____ is big.

6. I have dinner with _____ once a week.

FUN WITH GRAMMAR

Draw your family tree. Look up examples on the Internet if you need to. Then exchange family trees with a partner. Write six sentences about the relationships in your partner's family.

David's Aunt Anne is his mother's sister.
He has 16 cousins.
His dad has two brothers.

Take turns reading your sentences to each other and checking that the relationships are correct. Total the number of sentences with family relationships you both got correct. The partners with the most correct sentences win.

WHO NAMES Hurricanes?

Read the following article. Pay special attention to the words in bold. 🎧 4.4

How do hurricanes get their names? Here are some frequently asked questions (FAQs) about naming hurricanes and tropical storms[1].

Q: Who names hurricanes?

A: The World Meteorological Organization (WMO) names hurricanes and tropical storms.

Q: When does a storm get a name?

A: It gets a name when its winds reach 39 mph.

Q: What kind of names does the WMO use?

A: It uses both men's and women's names. The first storm of the year begins with an *A*. The next storm begins with a *B*, and the next one begins with a *C*. If the first storm has a woman's name, the next storm has a man's name.

Q: Why does the WMO use names?

A: Names are easy to remember.

Q: Do Atlantic and Pacific storms have the same names?

A: No, they don't.

Q: Does the WMO use the same list of names every year?

A: No, it doesn't. It uses six lists of names. Every six years, the WMO uses the same list as before. The 2011 list and the 2017 list are the same. The 2013 list and the 2019 list are the same.

Q: Some storms are very serious and deadly[2], like Hurricane Katrina in 2005 or Hurricane Maria in 2017. **What does the WMO do** with those names?

A: The WMO doesn't use those names again. A committee[3] chooses a new name for that letter of the alphabet.

Q: What name takes the place of *Maria*?

A: *Margot* takes the place of *Maria*.

---

[1] tropical storm: heavy rains with high wind
[2] deadly: so dangerous as to cause death
[3] committee: a group of people organized for a purpose

COMPREHENSION Based on the reading, write T for *true* or F for *false*.

1. _____ The WMO uses the same list of names for hurricanes every year.

2. _____ The list of hurricane names is alphabetical.

3. _____ Hurricanes have names of both men and women.

THINK ABOUT IT Discuss the questions with a partner or in a small group.

1. Why do you think we don't repeat the names of deadly hurricanes?

2. Would you like your name to become the name of a hurricane? Why or why not?

4.6 Subject Questions and Non-Subject Questions

EXAMPLES	EXPLANATION
A: **What name follows** *Maria*? B: *Nate* follows *Maria./Nate* does. A: **Who is** in charge of names for hurricanes? B: A committee is in charge./A committee is.	We use *what/which* (+ noun) or *who* + verb to ask about the subject of a sentence. We can use the subject + *do/does/is/are* in a short answer.
A: **Who do you know** on the committee? B: I don't know anyone on the committee. A: **Why does the WMO use** names? B: It uses names because they are easy to remember.	We use a *wh-* word + *do/does* + subject + the base form of the verb to ask a question about something that is not in the subject. For example, to ask a question about an object of a sentence or the reason for something.

Notes:
1. In informal English, we use *who* to ask about the object. In formal English, we use *whom*.

    Who *do you know on the committee?* (informal)

    Whom *do you know on the committee?* (formal)

2. In informal English, we put a preposition at the end of a question. In formal English, we put the preposition before the *wh-* word, at the beginning of the question.

    Who *do you live* **with**? **What** *do you dream* **about**? (informal)

    With whom *do you live?* **About what** *do you dream?* (formal)

EXERCISE 16 Complete the questions with the correct form of the word(s) given. Complete the answers with *do* or *does*. Remember to add *do/does* to non-subject questions.

1. **A:** Who _____ has _____ an uncommon name in your family?
                       a. have

   B: My brother _____. His name is Ezekiel. But only a few people call him that.
                             b.

   A: Who _____ him that?
             c. call

   B: Our parents _____.
                  d.

   A: What _____ him?
             e. you/call

   B: I call him "Zeke."

2. **A:** Who _____ a nickname?
             a. have

   B: I _____.
             b.

   A: What's your nickname?

   B: Alex. My real name is Alejandro. Everyone except one person calls me "Alex."

   A: Who _____ you "Alejandro"?
             c. call

   B: Only my mother _____.
                  d.

3. **A:** Whose name _____ over 10 letters?
                  a. have

   B: Mine _____.
             b.

   A: How many letters _____?
                  c. it/have

   B: It has 12 letters: *Scheherazade.*

   A: Wow! That's a long name. How _____ it?
                            d. you/spell

   B: *S-C-H-E-H-E-R-A-Z-A-D-E.*

A: Where _____?
   e. your name/come from

B: It's the name of a queen in a story. What about your name?

A: My name is unusual, too. But it's short: Pax.

B: That's an interesting name. What _____?
   f. it/mean

A: It means "peace."

4. **A:** My name is Katrina.

B: _____ your name?
   a. you/like

A: I like it, but it's the name of a bad hurricane in 2005.

B: Don't worry. The name is not on the list anymore.

A: Really? Who _____ the names?
   b. replace

B: A committee of the WMO _____.
   c.

A: That's good. What's the new name?

B: I think it's *Katia*.

A: Someone in my family has that name.

B: Who _____ that name?
   d. have

A: My aunt _____.
   e.

4.7 Who, Whom, Whose, Who's

EXAMPLES	EXPLANATION
A: Who names hurricanes? **B:** The WMO does.	We use *who* to ask a question about the subject.
A: Who(m) do you live with? **B:** I live with my parents.	We use *who* or *whom* to ask a question about the object. *Whom* is very formal.
A: Whose name begins with *X*? **B:** Mine does. It's Xavier.	We use *whose* (+ noun) to ask about ownership or relationship.
A: Who's that man? **B:** That's my dad.	*Who's* is a contraction of *who is*.

EXERCISE 17 Complete the conversation with *who, whom, whose,* or *who's.*

A: _____Whose_____ last name do you use?
      1.

B: I use my father's last name. But I don't live with my father.

A: Why not?

B: My parents are divorced.

A: _____ do you live with, then? Your mother?
          2.

B: No. I live with Nina.

A: _____ that?
          3.

B: That's my older sister. I love her, but she's so lazy. She never washes the dishes.

A: _____ washes the dishes, then?
          4.

B: I do. When I ask "_____ turn is it?" she always says, "I know it's my turn,
                          5.

but I'm so busy today."

A: Then don't ask. Just tell her it's her turn. _____ pays the rent?
                                                    6.

B: We both do.

A: I guess you need her, then.

B: I guess I do—for now.

EXERCISE 18 Choose the correct word(s) to complete the conversation.

A: (Whose/Who) name is the same as a hurricane?
        1.

B: (Mine/My) is.
        2.

A: What's your name?

B: Irene.

A: (Who/Whom) names hurricanes?
        3.

B: The WMO does.

A: Do they ever repeat a name?

B: Yes. They repeat names every six years.

A: Who (*decide*/*decides*) on the names?
　　　　　　　 4.

B: A committee does.

A: What (*happens*/*does happen*) to names like *Irene* and *Katrina*?
　　　　　　　　　 5.

B: The WMO doesn't use them anymore because the names give people a bad feeling.

EXERCISE 19 Choose the correct word(s) to complete the conversation.

A: The teacher wants us to talk about names. My name is Lisa Simms-Evans.

B: Do you like (*your*/*you're*) name?
　　　　　　　　1.

A: No, (*its*/*it's*) too long. I have both of my (*parents'*/*parent's*) last names.
　　　　 2.　　　　　　　　　　　　　　　3.

B: Do you have any brothers or sisters?

A: I have one brother. (*He's*/*His*) name is Leslie. (*He's*/*His*) not happy with (*his*/*her*) name, either.
　　　　　　　　　　　 4.　　　　　　　　 5.　　　　　　　 6.

B: Why not?

A: Leslie can be a (*girls*/*girl's*) name. (*Her*/*His*) wife calls him "Les." My parents and (*I*/*me*) call him
　　　　　　　　　　 7.　　　　 8.　　　　　　　　　　　　　　　 9.

　　"More or Less."

B: That's funny. In your family, who (*have*/*has*) a good name?
　　　　　　　　　　　　　　　 10.

A: My goldfish! (*Its*/*It's*) name is Goldie.
　　　　　　 11.

B: Well, class is over. (*Whose is that coat*/*Whose coat is that*)? Is it (*your's*/*yours*)?
　　　　　　　　　　　　　 12.　　　　　　　　　　　　 13.

A: No. It's not (*my*/*mine*).
　　　　　　　 14.

B: What about that book on the floor? Is it (*yours*/*your*) or (*mines*/*mine*)?
　　　　　　　　　　　　　　　　 15.　　　　　 16.

A: (*Who's*/*Whose*) name is in the book?
　　 17.

B: It says, "Soo Won Park." Let's take it and give it to (*him*/*his*).
　　　　　　　　　　　　　　　　　　　 18.

FUN WITH GRAMMAR

Play a guessing game. Pick a famous person, and complete the sentences below about him or her. Each sentence should have more specific information. Walk around the classroom and read your sentences to your classmates. You get a point for each classmate who guesses your person. The person with the most points wins.

I am a person who(m) people know because _____.

I am a person who's _____.

I am a person whose _____.

SUMMARY OF UNIT 4

Possessive Nouns—Forms

	EXAMPLES
Singular nouns	My **father's** name is Harry.
Regular plural nouns	My **parents'** names are Rose and Harry.
Irregular plural nouns	*Sophia* and *Liam* are common **children's** names.
Names that end in -*s*	Can you spell **Charles's** name?
Inanimate objects	What's the name **of our textbook**? What's our **textbook's name**?

Pronouns and Possessive Adjectives

SUBJECT PRONOUN	OBJECT PRONOUN	POSSESSIVE ADJECTIVE	POSSESSIVE PRONOUN
I	me	my	mine
you	you	your	yours
he	him	his	his
she	her	her	hers
it	it	its	—
we	us	our	ours
they	them	their	theirs
who	who(m)	whose	whose

EXAMPLES			
SUBJECT PRONOUN	OBJECT PRONOUN	POSSESSIVE ADJECTIVE	POSSESSIVE PRONOUN
I come from Cuba.	The teacher helps **me**.	**My** name is Rosa.	Your name is common. **Mine** isn't.
They come from South Korea.	The teacher helps **them**.	**Their** names are Kim and Lee.	Your name is short. **Theirs** is long.
Who comes from Poland?	**Who(m)** does the teacher help?	**Whose** name do you like?	This is my book. **Whose** is that?

Subject Questions and Non-Subject Questions

EXPLANATION	EXAMPLES
We use *what* (+ noun)/*which* (+ noun)/*who* + verb to ask about the subject of a sentence.	**What is** the definition of a hurricane? **Who knows** when hurricane season starts?
We use a *wh-* word + *do/does* + subject + the base form of the verb to ask a question about something that is not the subject.	**Who(m) do you know** with the same name as a hurricane? **Why do we name** hurricanes?

REVIEW

Choose the correct word(s) to complete the conversation between two students.

A: (Who/*Who's*/Whose) your English teacher?
1.

B: (*My*/Mine/Me) teacher is Charles Flynn. Who's (*your*/your's/*yours*)?
2.   3.

A: Marianne Peters. She's (*Charle's*/*Charles*/*Charles's*) wife.
4.

B: Oh, really? (*His*/He's/He) last name is different from (*she*/her/*hers*).
5.   6.

A: Yes. She uses (*her*/hers/his) own last name, not her (*husband's*/husbands'/husbands).
7.   8.

B: Do they have children?

A: Yes.

B: (*Whose*/Who's/Who) name do the children use?
9.

A: (*They're*/Their/*They*) use both last names.
10.

B: How do you know so much about (you're/*your*/yours) teacher and (*his*/her/hers) children?
11.   12.

A: We talk about (us/*our*/ours) names in class. We often ask (her/she/*him*) about American customs. She
13.   14.

explains her customs, and we explain (our/us/*ours*).
15.

B: Mr. Flynn doesn't talk about (her/*his*/he's) family in class.
16.

A: Do you call (her/*him*/he) "Mister"?
17.

B: Of course. (He/*He's*/His) the teacher. In my country, (*it's*/its/its') not polite to call a teacher by his or
18.   19.

her first name.

A: (Its/*It's*/It) not polite in my country either. But Marianne is American. (She/*She's*/Her) prefers
20.   21.

her first name.

B: It doesn't seem right. We need to show respect for our teachers. I prefer to call (they/*them*/him) by
22.

(they/they're/*their*) last names. That's the way we do it in my country.
23.

A: In (me/*my*/mine), we just say "Professor." But (we/*we're*/us) in the United States now, so we need to follow
24.   25.

American customs.

FROM GRAMMAR TO WRITING

PART 1 Editing Advice

1. Don't confuse *you're* (*you are*) and *your* (possessive form).

   ~~Your~~ **You're** interested in hurricanes.

   What's ~~you're~~ **your** name?

2. Don't confuse *he's* (*he is*) and *his* (possessive form).

   ~~He's~~ **His** name is Paul.

   ~~His~~ **He's** a good student.

3. Don't confuse *it's* (*it is*) and *its* (possessive form).

   ~~Its~~ **It's** a tropical storm. ~~It's~~ **Its** wind is over 50 mph.

4. Don't confuse *his* and *her*.

   My brother loves ~~her~~ **his** daughter.

   My sister loves ~~his~~ **her** son.

5. Don't confuse *they're* (*they are*) and *their* (possessive form).

   I have two American friends. ~~They're~~ **Their** names are Haley and Mike.

   ~~Their~~ **They're** very nice people.

6. Don't use a possessive pronoun before a noun. Use a possessive adjective.

   How do hurricanes get ~~theirs~~ **their** names?

7. Don't confuse subject pronouns and object pronouns.

   My father and ~~me~~ **I** have the same name.

   I have a daughter. I love ~~she~~ **her** very much.

8. Put the apostrophe in the right place.

   My ~~parent's~~ **parents'** names are Harry and Marge.

9. Don't use an apostrophe for plural nouns.

   My parents have many ~~friend's~~ **friends**.

PART 2 Editing Practice

Some of the shaded words and phrases have mistakes. Find the mistakes and correct them. If the shaded words are correct, write *C*.

        My
~~Mine~~ name is Marta López-Hernández. People often ask me, "Why do you have two last name's?" I
  1.   **2.**   **3.**

come from Mexico, and Mexicans use both parent's names. My father's last name is López. My mother's
                                 4.   **5.**   **6.**

last name is Hernández.

    When a Mexican woman gets married, she drops hers mother's name and adds his husbands' last
                                                      7.   **8.** **9.**

name. My sister is married. Her name is Celia López de Castillo. His husband is Luis Castillo-Sánchez.
                                10.   **11.**

Celia and Luis have two kids, Jorge and Rosa. Theirs friends call them "George" and "Rosie."
                                                12.   **13.**

Me and my sister call Rosa "Rosita" and Jorge "Jorgito."
        14.

    Some people think ours customs are strange because everyone in the family can have a different last
                                     15.

name. Maybe your confused, but it isn't confusing for us.
                16.   **17.**

    In the United States, some Mexicans use only one last name. Their afraid that Americans don't know
                                                18.

what to do with all these names. I prefer the Mexican way. Its our custom, and I'm proud of it.
                                              19.   **20.**

WRITING TIP

When you're deciding between two ideas to write about, it's helpful to use a T-chart. List your ideas for one topic on the left and the other topic on the right. For example, here is the beginning of a T-chart for the first prompt below.

Traditional Names	Unusual Names
easy to say	can be difficult to say

PART 3 Write

Read the prompts. Choose one and write one paragraph about it.

1. Do you prefer traditional names or unusual names? Explain your answer.
2. Write about naming customs in your culture.

PART 4 Edit

Reread the Summary of Unit 4 and the editing advice. Edit your writing from Part 3.

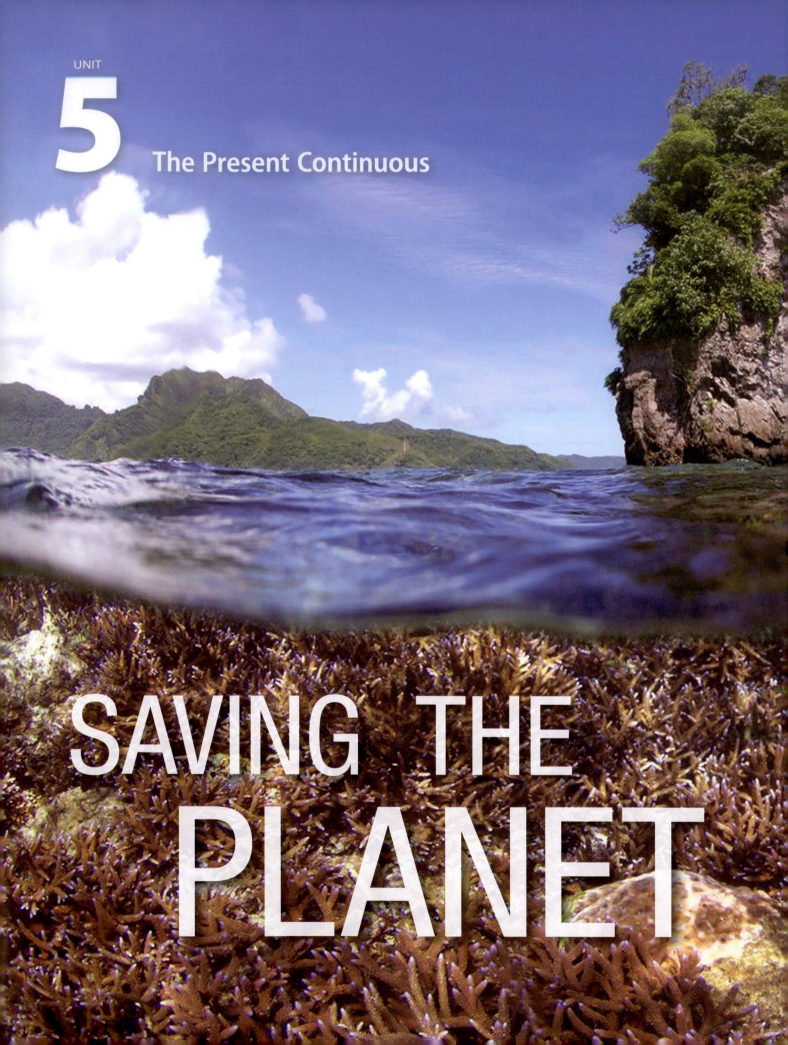

SAVING THE
PLANET

Earth provides enough to satisfy every
man's needs, but not every man's greed.

MAHATMA GANDHI

Humans have an impact on the climate.
A coral reef in American Samoa is
damaged by warm waters, which are a
product of climate change.

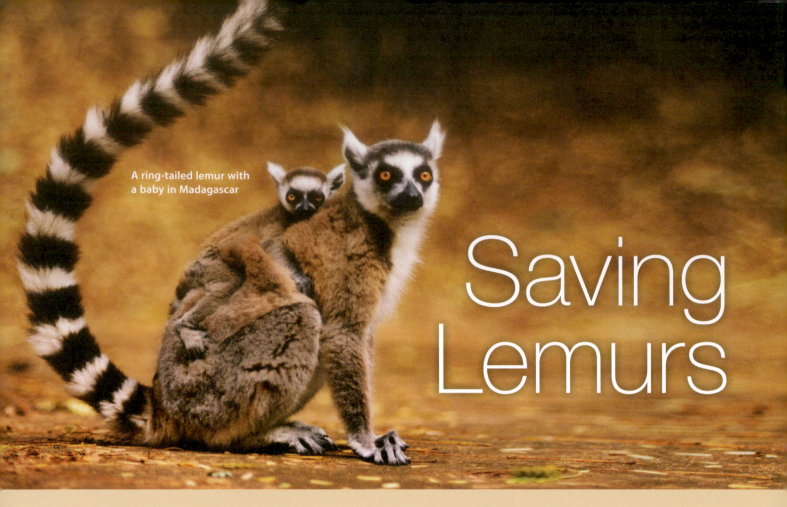

A ring-tailed lemur with a baby in Madagascar

Saving Lemurs

Read the following conversation. Pay special attention to the words in bold. 🎧 5.1

A: What **are** you **watching**?

B: I'm **watching** a video about baby lemurs. Scientists **are raising** about 240 lemurs at Duke University in North Carolina. They**'re breeding**[1] them there.

A: Why **are** they **doing** that? Why **aren't** the lemurs **living** in the wild[2]?

B: Lemurs are the most endangered[3] mammals[4] on the planet. Scientists **are trying** to increase the lemur population. Lemurs **are disappearing** from their native Madagascar. Some species only have a few hundred individuals.

A: Aren't all lemurs from the same species?

B: No. There are about 100 species. In this video, scientists **are working** at Duke University. Other scientists **are working** with the people of Madagascar. They**'re teaching** the local people how to protect the lemur population. Lemurs are close relatives of humans.

A: Really? Oh look! They're so cute. They**'re looking** at the scientists. Those babies **are playing**. That one**'s climbing** a tree. Oh, and that baby**'s jumping** onto its mother. It looks like the scientists **are enjoying** their job.

B: Shh! I want to hear this part.

[Video] *"We're weighing the babies. We want to make sure they're gaining weight. If they're gaining weight, they're healthy. Some babies aren't gaining weight. That means they're not healthy."*

A: I think those scientists **are doing** a wonderful thing.

B: I agree. It costs over $8,400 a year to care for a lemur. I**'m thinking** of sending money to help the Duke Lemur Center.

---

[1] to breed: to help animals produce babies
[2] the wild: a natural area where animals live
[3] endangered: at risk of disappearing
[4] mammal: a warm-blooded animal; the female gives her babies milk

COMPREHENSION Based on the reading, write T for *true* or F for *false*.

1. _____ Lemurs come from Madagascar.

2. _____ Humans and lemurs are closely related.

3. _____ There are 240 species of lemurs.

THINK ABOUT IT Discuss the questions with a partner or in a small group.

1. Why is the Duke Lemur Center important?

2. What other endangered species do you know about?

5.1 The Present Continuous—Forms

AFFIRMATIVE STATEMENTS

SUBJECT	BE	VERB + -*ING*
I	am	
He She It A lemur	is	playing.
You We They The babies	are	

Notes:

1. Remember: We can make a contraction with a subject pronoun and a form of *be*.

I am	→	*I'm*	*You are*	→	*You're*
He is	→	*He's*	*We are*	→	*We're*
She is	→	*She's*	*They are*	→	*They're*
It is	→	*It's*		

2. Most nouns can also form a contraction with *is*, except if they end in *s, se, z, ze, ge, ce, sh, ch*, or *x*.

   A **man's** talking about lemurs.

3. We don't make a contraction with a plural noun and *are*.

   Lemurs are endangered

   NOT: *Lemurs're endangered.*

4. When the subject is doing two things, we don't repeat the verb *be* after *and*.

   *The lemurs **are climbing** and **jumping**.*

5. We can put an adverb like *still* or *also* between *be* and the main verb.

   *Scientists are working with lemurs at Duke University. They **are also working** with people in Madagascar.*

6. The present continuous is sometimes called the present progressive.

continued

NEGATIVE STATEMENTS

SUBJECT	BE	NOT	VERB + -ING
I	am		
He She It	is	not	sleeping.
You We They	are		

Notes:

1. The contraction for *is not* = *isn't*. The contraction for *are not* = *aren't*.

> The baby **isn't** gaining weight.

> Those lemurs **aren't** sleeping.

2. There is no contraction for *am not*.

3. We can make a contraction in a negative statement with a subject pronoun and *am, is,* or *are*.

> **She's** not watching the program.

> **They're** not sleeping.

EXERCISE 1 Listen to the conversation. Fill in the blanks with the words you hear. Use the correct form of *be* and the verbs from the box. You will use one verb more than once. 🎧 5.2

cutting	living	losing	studying	watching
dying	looking	not doing	trying	working

A: I *'m watching* _____ an interesting show. Do you want to watch, too?
  _{1.}

B: I _____ much now. Maybe. What is it about?
  _{2.}

A: It's about parrots. These parrots _____ in the wild in Africa. A scientist,
  _{3.}

Steve Boyes, _____ Cape parrots of South Africa. Boyes and other
  _{4.}

scientists _____ to protect the land where these parrots live. People
  _{5.}

_____ down forests. Parrots _____ places to
  _{6.}   _{7.}

make their nests. They _____ for food, but they can't find enough.
  _{8.}

So many of them _____ . Boyes _____ with
  _{9.}   _{10.}

local people on a project to plant trees. He _____ to give these parrots a place
  _{11.}

to make their nests.

A South African
Cape parrot

5.2 Spelling of the *-ing* Form

RULES	BASE FORM	-*ING* FORM
We add *-ing* to the base form of most verbs.	eat go study	eat**ing** go**ing** study**ing**
For a one-syllable verb that ends in a consonant + vowel + consonant (CVC), we repeat the final consonant and add *-ing*.	p l a n ↓ ↓ ↓ C V C s t o p ↓ ↓ ↓ C V C	plan**ning** stop**ping**
We do not repeat a final *w, x,* or *y*.	show mix stay	show**ing** mix**ing** stay**ing**
For a two-syllable verb that ends in CVC, we repeat the final consonant only if the last syllable is stressed.	r e f e r ↓ ↓ ↓ C V C b e g i n ↓ ↓ ↓ C V C	refer**ring** begin**ning**
For a two-syllable verb that ends in CVC, we don't repeat the final consonant if the last syllable is not stressed.	<u>o</u>pen of<u>fer</u>	open**ing** offer**ing**
If the verb ends in a consonant + *e* or *ue*, we drop the *e* and add *-ing*.	write rescue	writ**ing** rescu**ing**
If the verb ends in *-ie*, we change the *ie* to *y* and add *-ing*.	lie tie	**lying** **tying**

EXERCISE 2 Write the *-ing* form of each verb. In two-syllable verbs that end in CVC, the stressed syllable is underlined.

1. play _____ playing _____   13. raise _____

2. make _____   14. fix _____

3. hit _____   15. rescue _____

4. suffer _____   16. do _____

5. cut _____   17. breed _____

6. admit _____   18. lose _____

7. try _____   19. wait _____

8. happen _____   20. serve _____

9. stay _____   21. visit _____

10. grow _____   22. occur _____

11. hurry _____   23. die _____

12. grab _____   24. disappear _____

EXERCISE 3 Fill in the blanks with the present continuous form of the verbs given. Use contractions when possible.

Some African parrots _____ are suffering _____ from diseases. They _____
1. suffer   2. lose

their feathers and their beaks. They _____ quickly. Today there are fewer than 2,000 left.
3. disappear

Steve Boyes _____ them. He and his team _____
4. rescue   5. work

to help these birds.

The African gray parrot _____ other problems, too. Some people
6. have

_____ and _____ them. It is illegal to catch and sell these
7. catch   8. sell

birds, but people _____ them from their nests. Boyes has a blog about his work
9. steal

with parrots. He _____ to educate people about these birds.
10. try

5.3 The Present Continuous—Use

EXAMPLES	EXPLANATION
We **are watching** a show on TV now. Oh look! That baby lemur **is jumping** onto its mother.	We use the present continuous to describe an action that is in progress at this exact moment.
The babies **are gaining** weight. Steve Boyes **is trying** to teach people about parrots.	We use the present continuous to show a longer action that is in progress. It may not be happening at this exact moment.

GRAMMAR IN USE

Use the present continuous with time expressions like *now, this week/month/year, currently, at the moment.*

Don't use the present continuous with adverbs of frequency like *always* and *never.*

> *He's working at a restaurant **this summer**.*
>
> NOT: *He's never doing his homework.*

EXERCISE 4 Write true affirmative or negative statements with the present continuous and the words given.

1. African parrots/lose their homes

   <u>African parrots are losing their homes.</u>

2. the teacher/show us a video about lemurs

   <u>The teacher isn't showing us a video about lemurs.</u>

3. we/learn about animals in this unit

   _____

4. I/write sentences about animals

   _____

5. Steve Boyes/study lemurs

   _____

6. Boyes/try to rescue parrots

   _____

7. many lemurs/live at the Duke Lemur Center

   _____

8. the unhealthy baby lemurs/gain weight

   _____

5.4 Questions with the Present Continuous

YES/NO QUESTIONS AND SHORT ANSWERS

BE	SUBJECT	VERB + -ING	SHORT ANSWER
Am	I	growing?	No, you're not.
Is	he she it the lemur		Yes, he is. No, she isn't. Yes, it is. No, it's not.
Are	you we they the babies		Yes, I am. No, we're not. Yes, they are. No, they aren't.

Note:

Compare statements and *yes/no* questions.

> **The lemurs are** playing.
>
> **Are the lemurs** playing?

WH- QUESTIONS

WH- WORD	BE (+ N'T)	SUBJECT	VERB + -ING	
What	are	they	studying?	
Why	is	Boyes	writing	a blog?
Why	aren't	some babies	gaining	weight?

Note:

Compare statements and *wh-* questions.

> **The lemurs are** playing.
>
> Where **are the lemurs** playing?

> **The lemurs aren't** sleeping.
>
> Why **aren't the lemurs** sleeping?

SUBJECT WH- QUESTIONS

WH- WORD AS SUBJECT	BE	VERB + -ING	
Who	is	studying	lemurs?
How many lemurs	are	living	at the Lemur Center?

Note:

Compare statements and subject questions.

> **Someone** is studying lemurs.
>
> **Who** is studying lemurs?

EXERCISE 5 Fill in the blanks to complete each conversation. Use *not* when necessary. Use contractions when possible.

1. **A:** Steve Boyes is studying animals. _____*Is he studying*_____ parrots?

a.

   B: Yes, he _____*is*_____. He _____ parrots in Africa.

b.   c.

   A: Why _____ parrots?

d.

   B: He's studying parrots because they're dying and he wants to know why.

2. **A:** _____ a lot about animals?

a.

   B: Yes, I _____. I'm learning about lemurs and parrots.

b.

   A: What _____?

c.

   B: I'm learning that these animals are in danger.

3. **A:** Some parrots are losing places to make their nests.

   B: Why _____ places to make their nests?

a.

   A: Some people are cutting down forests.

   B: I'm asking you a lot of questions. _____ you?

b.

   A: No. You're not bothering me. You're asking interesting questions.

4. **A:** _____ an article about parrots?

a.

   B: No, I _____. I'm reading an article about lemurs.

b.

   A: Why _____ about lemurs?

c.

   B: I'm writing an essay about the Duke Lemur Center.

continued

Steve Boyes on the Okavango
River in Angola

5. **A:** What _____ your brother watching on TV?
   a.

   B: He _____ a program about animals.
   b.

   A: Why _____ his homework?
   c.

   B: He isn't doing his homework because he needs to see the program first.

6. **A:** Who _____ care of the lemurs at Duke University?
   a.

   B: Scientists are taking care of them.

   A: How _____ care of them?
   b.

   B: They're breeding them to increase their population.

7. **A:** _____ all the lemurs doing well at the Duke Lemur Center?
   a.

   B: No, they _____. Some of them aren't gaining weight.
   b.

   A: Why _____ weight?
   c.

   B: Because they're not healthy.

8. **A:** _____ an essay now?
   a.

   B: Yes, I _____. I'm writing an essay for my science class.
   b.

   A: What _____ about?
   c.

   B: I'm writing about endangered species.

ABOUT YOU Find a partner. Ask and answer questions with the words given. Use the present continuous.

1. learn about parrots

   A: *Are you learning about parrots?*

   B: *Yes, I am.*

2. take an online class this semester

3. what other courses/take this semester

4. think about endangered animals

5. plan to read more about nature

6. how/your life changing

FUN WITH GRAMMAR

Play a game of charades. Form two teams. One member from each team goes to the front of the room. Your teacher will secretly tell the two team members an action in the present continuous (e.g., opening the door, walking upstairs). They will act this out for their teams to guess. Teams must use the present continuous in their guesses. The first team to guess the action correctly wins a point. The game continues with two new team members acting each turn. The winner is the team with the most points after everyone has had one turn OR the first team to win 10 points.

> *You're opening a door!*
>
> OR
>
> *She's opening a door!*
>
> OR
>
> *Are you opening a door?*

DISAPPEARING BIRDS

Read the following article. Pay special attention to the words in bold. 🎧 5.3

Birds are amazing animals. They **live** in all parts of the planet, from hot deserts to the ice of Antarctica. They **fly** nonstop for days. They **find** food easily. They **find** safe places to rest. They **carry** seeds. They **control** bugs. One out of five birds **migrates**[1]. These birds **arrive** at their exact destinations[2]. But, unfortunately, all of this **is changing**.

The bird population **is going** down. This **is happening** to birds in all parts of the planet, from hot places to cold places. Birds **are losing** places to live and make their nests. Their food supply **is going** down. Some penguins of Antarctica **are starving**[3]. Some seabirds, like puffins, **are disappearing**. Thirteen thousand species of birds (that's one out of eight) **are disappearing**.

There is another reason for this change. Chemicals in the environment **are affecting** bird populations. In Michigan, near an old chemical factory, robins **are dying**. The songs of some birds **are changing**. Some birds **are having** fewer babies. Some birds **are losing** their ability to find their way. Clearly, birds are in trouble. Why **is** this **happening**?

Insects, fish, and other animals **take in** chemicals from the environment. Birds **eat** insects and fish. Some birds **eat** dead animals. This **is giving** birds health problems. If birds **are having** health problems, what **are** these chemicals **doing** to humans? Scientists like Christy Morrissey **are trying** to find out. Morrissey is a scientist at the University of Saskatchewan in

Canada. She **studies** nature and harmful things in our environment. She **wants** to know how chemicals **affect** these birds and people.

Many birds, such as owls and eagles, **live** for a long time. Morrissey and other scientists **catch** birds, **test** them, **let** them go, and then **catch** them years later. This **helps** the scientists understand changes in the environment. Birds usually **have** a stable[4] population. When the bird population **goes** down, it usually **means** something in the environment **is hurting** them.

According to Morrissey, these birds **are sending** us messages about the health of the planet and even our own health. We **need** to listen to these messages.

---

[1] to migrate: to move from one place to another
[2] destination: a place where someone is going to
[3] to starve: to not have enough food to live
[4] stable: strong and steady

Two puffins in the North Atlantic

COMPREHENSION Based on the reading, write T for *true* or F for *false*.

1. _____ There are birds in every part of the world.

2. _____ All birds migrate.

3. _____ Birds can help us understand dangers to humans.

THINK ABOUT IT Discuss the questions with a partner or in a small group.

1. Why do you think birds are losing places to live?

2. What message are birds sending to humans?

5.5 The Present Continuous vs. the Simple Present—Forms

	SIMPLE PRESENT	PRESENT CONTINUOUS
Affirmative Statement	The gray parrot **lives** in Africa.	Morrissey **is studying** birds.
Negative Statement	It **does not live** in Europe.	She **isn't studying** lemurs.
Yes/No Question	**Does** it **live** in Europe?	**Is** she **studying** seabirds?
Short Answer	No, it **doesn't**.	Yes, she **is**.
Wh- Question	**Where does** it **live**?	**Why is** she **studying** birds?
Negative *Wh-* Question	**Why doesn't** it **live** in Europe?	**Why isn't** she **studying** lemurs?
Subject *Wh-* Question	**What** birds **live** in Europe?	**Who is studying** lemurs?

EXERCISE 6 Listen to the report. Then write T for *true*, F for *false*, or NS for *not stated*. 🎧 5.4

1. _____ Big cats are in danger.

2. _____ There are only 400 tigers left in the world.

3. _____ Luke Dollar also works with other endangered animals.

EXERCISE 7 Listen again. Fill in the blanks with the words you hear. 🎧 5.4

Many animals _____ their places to live. Humans _____
                              1.   2.

land from animals. Which animals _____ because of humans? Big cats, such as lions,
                                          3.

tigers, snow leopards, and cheetahs, are. The population of these animals _____
                                                                                    4.

quickly. Only about 4,000 tigers remain in the wild. What _____ to protect big cats?
                                                                   5.

Luke Dollar, a National Geographic Emerging Explorer, is a scientist who _____
                                                                                  6.

on the Big Cats Initiative. This program _____ people learn about the problems that
                                                 7.

big cats _____. People _____ education about endangered
              8.   9.

animals. Many people _____ that these animals are in danger and that we
                             10.

_____ much time left to save them. "_____ to live in a world
          11.   12.

without lions in the wild?" asks Luke Dollar.

5.6 The Present Continuous vs. the Simple Present—Use

EXAMPLES	EXPLANATION
Gray parrots **live** in Africa. Sometimes I **read** articles about the environment.	We use the simple present with: • general truths or customs • regular activities or repeated actions
We **are reading** about big cats now. The population of big cats **is going** down.	We use the present continuous with: • actions in progress now • longer actions in progress at this general time

---

GRAMMAR IN USE

We use the present continuous to describe some kinds of weather.

It's raining/snowing.
The sun is shining.

EXERCISE 8 Complete the conversation. Use the present continuous or the simple present form of the verbs given. Use contractions when possible. Include any other words you see.

A: What _____*are you doing*_____ here?
　　　　　　　　　　1. you/do

B: I _____ lunch. I always
　　　　　　2. eat

_____ lunch here.
　　　　3. eat

I _____ a video about birds
　　4. also/watch

for my class in environmental science. This week

we _____ the relationship
　　　　　　5. study

between chemicals and bird populations.

A: What _____ ?
　　　　　　　　6. you/learn

B: I _____ about chemicals in
　　　　　　7. learn

lakes and oceans. These chemicals harm fish. A lot of birds

_____ fish. Look
　　　8. eat

at this video. Do you see that pelican? It

_____ to catch a fish.
　　　9. dive

A: Where _____ ?
　　　　　　　10. pelicans/live

B: They _____ close to water.
　　　　　　11. live

An American
White Pelican
catching a fish

CLIMATE CHANGE

Read the following article. Pay special attention to the words in bold.  5.5

The ice on Antarctica **looks** the same from day to day. But scientists **know** this: the ice **is melting**[1].

Ice sheets are very big. Changes in the climate cause them to change very slowly. It usually **takes** a long time for ice sheets to melt. So what **is happening** now?

The ocean **is warming**, and big pieces of ice **are breaking** away and **going** into the ocean. This **is causing** the ocean level to rise. The ice **is melting** six times faster now than in 1979. Why **is** this **happening**?

Human activity is responsible. Transportation, electricity production, and industry are activities that warm the planet. What **does** this **mean** for us?

Coastal cities, like New York, London, and Tokyo, are in danger of being underwater by the end of the 21st century. We **need** to make changes now to prevent[2] this. Some scientists **think** that climate change is unstoppable[3]. We **hope** it's not too late.

---

1 to melt: to change from a solid to a liquid state
2 to prevent: to stop something from happening
3 unstoppable: impossible to stop

The Japanese icebreaker *Shirase* **researching global warming in Lutzow-Holm Bay, Antarctica**

COMPREHENSION Based on the reading, write T for *true* or F for *false*.

1. _____ Ice sheets don't change much from day to day.

2. _____ The ocean level is rising.

3. _____ Human activity affects the climate.

THINK ABOUT IT Discuss the questions with a partner or in a small group.

1. What changes do you notice in your environment that are the result of global warming?

2. What can humans do to stop or slow these changes?

5.7 Action and Nonaction Verbs

EXAMPLES	EXPLANATION
Scientists **are studying** climate change. Ice **is melting**. Pieces of ice **are breaking** away.	Some verbs are action verbs. These verbs express physical or mental activity. We can use the present continuous with action verbs.
We **need** to make changes now. We **hope** it's not too late. The problem of climate change **seems** difficult. We **care about** the planet.	Some verbs are nonaction verbs. These verbs express a sense or a feeling, not an action. We don't usually use the present continuous with a nonaction verb, even if we are talking about now.
We **are looking at** a photo of an ice sheet. (action) She **is looking for** her notes. (action) An ice sheet **looks** the same from day to day. (nonaction)	*Look* can be both an action and a nonaction verb. *Look at* and *look for* are action verbs. *Look*, as something we sense, is a nonaction verb.
I **am thinking about** the environment. (action) **Are** you **thinking of** studying science? (action) I **think that** climate change is real. (nonaction)	*Think* can be both an action and a nonaction verb. *Think about* and *think of* are action verbs. *Think that*, to show an opinion, is a nonaction verb.
Some birds **are having** a hard time finding a place to build a nest. (action) **Do** you **have** time to read the article? (nonaction)	When *have* means to experience something, it is an action verb. When *have* shows possession or relationship, it is a nonaction verb.
We**'re looking at** a video. (action) We **see** a photo of an ice sheet. (nonaction) **Are** you **listening** to the teacher? (action) **Do** you **hear** the birds outside? (nonaction)	*Look at* and *listen* are action verbs. *See* and *hear* are nonaction verbs.

Note:

Groups of common nonaction verbs include:

- Senses (usually followed by *like* or an adjective): *smell, taste, look, sound, feel, seem*
- Feelings and wishes: *like, love, hate, hope, want, need, prefer, care (about), matter*
- Mental states: *believe, know, hear, see, notice, agree, understand, remember, think (that), realize*
- Other verbs: *mean, cost*

GRAMMAR IN USE

We use both the simple present and present continuous in greetings.

*How **are** you?*   *How **are** you **doing**?*

*What**'s** up?* (informal)   *What**'s going** on?* (informal)

EXERCISE 9 Listen to the report. Fill in the blanks with the verbs you hear. Then work with a partner and circle the nonaction verbs. (Not all simple present verbs are nonaction verbs.) 🎧 5.6

Some people _____ *think* _____ that climate change is nothing new on Earth. They often
      1.

_____ that warming and cooling _____ all the time. This is true. But these
      2.   3.

people _____ one important thing: humans _____ climate change now by our
              4.   5.

activities. Scientists say we _____ to make changes now to stop it. Some companies
                                     6.

_____ the danger of climate change and our part in it. They _____ to make
      7.   8.

changes. But some companies _____ to make these changes. It _____ money
                                   9.   10.

to make changes. Some companies _____ more about money than the environment.
                                        11.

   Some activities of modern life _____ our planet. What _____ we
                                          12.   13.

_____ about it? Some scientists _____, "Not enough and not fast enough."
      14.   15.

EXERCISE 10 Complete the conversations with the correct form of the verbs given. Use any other words you see.

1. **A:** What book ____ *are you reading* ____ ?
              a. you/read

   B: It's a book about birds. I _____ it. I _____ at the
                                        b. not/really/read   **c.** just/look

   pictures. _____ to see some of the pictures?
              d. you/want

   A: Sure. Wow. That bird _____ so beautiful. It _____ so
                                     e. look   **f.** have

   many colors.

   B: These birds are South American parrots. My friend _____ a pet parrot.
                                                                   g. have

   A: How long _____ ?
                    h. parrots/live

   B: Some parrots _____ over 50 years.
                          i. live

2. **A:** _____ a science class this semester?
          a. you/take

   B: Yes. I _____ a class in environmental science this semester.
                  b. have

   I _____ about how humans _____ the environment
        c. learn   **d.** harm

   now. A lot of animals _____ because of us. This is our planet, and we
                             e. die

   _____ to do something now to take care of it.
      f. need

   A: I _____ this human behavior. I _____ that we
            g. not/understand   **h.** think

   don't educate young people enough about these things.

B: I _____ . I _____ of getting a degree in

                    i. agree   **j.** think

     environmental science.

A: What _____ to do with your degree?

              k. you/hope

B: I hope to teach high school science.

A: That _____ like a good idea.

              l. sound

3. A: The water level _____ .

                  a. rise

B: Why _____ ?

          b. it/rise

A: Because the ice on Antarctica _____ fast.

                        c. melt

B: How _____ ?

          d. scientists/know

A: They _____ ways to measure the speed.

              e. have

B: Why _____ ?

          f. it/melt

A: The ocean water _____ warmer.

                g. get

B: My brother _____ that climate change is nothing new. He says

               h. think

     that it _____ all the time.

             i. happen

A: Yes, but it _____ faster now because of human activity.

               j. happen

FUN WITH GRAMMAR

Play team Tic-Tac-Toe. Form two teams: Team X and Team O. Your teacher will draw the Tic-Tac-Toe grid below on the board. Teams will take turns choosing a square and making a correct sentence with the verb in the form indicated. You should use the present continuous for action verbs and the simple present for nonaction verbs. For the student choice squares, teams must state which form of the verb they will use before saying their sentence. If a team makes a correct sentence with their chosen verb, they mark the square with an X or an O. If a team does not make a correct sentence, they do not mark the square, and it remains in play. The first team to mark three squares in a row (vertically, horizontally, or diagonally) wins.

look (action)	think (action)	have (action)
think (nonaction)	have (nonaction)	look (nonaction)
have (student choice)	look (student choice)	think (student choice)

SUMMARY OF UNIT 5

Forms of the Present Continuous (With Action Verbs Only)

AFFIRMATIVE STATEMENT	I'm **watching** a video about lemurs.	The baby lemurs **are playing**.
NEGATIVE STATEMENT	You**'re not watching** the video.	That lemur **isn't gaining** weight.
YES/NO QUESTION	**Is** Steve Boyes **rescuing** birds?	**Are** you **studying** birds?
SHORT ANSWER	Yes, he **is**.	No, I**'m not**.
WH- QUESTION	**What** birds **is** he **rescuing**?	**Why is** Steve Boyes **rescuing** birds?
SUBJECT WH- QUESTION	**Who is studying** lemurs?	**How many** scientists **are studying** lemurs?

Uses of the Present Continuous (With Action Verbs Only)

USE	EXAMPLES
For actions that are happening at this moment	She **is watching** a program on TV now. The program **is explaining** climate change.
For longer actions that are in progress at this general time	The planet **is warming**. I **am studying** science this semester.

Uses of the Simple Present

USE	EXAMPLES
For general truths	Lemurs **live** in Madagascar. Some birds **fly** south for the winter.
For regular activities, habits, and customs	I sometimes **watch** nature programs on TV. People often **train** pet parrots to talk.
With nonaction verbs	I **know** more about birds now. We **need** to protect the planet.

Action and Nonaction Verbs

ACTION	NONACTION
The ice **is melting**.	The planet **has** problems.
I **am thinking about** the environment.	I **think that** climate change is a big problem.
We**'re looking at** a book about birds.	Those birds **look** beautiful.
You**'re studying** science.	You **know** a lot about nature.

REVIEW

Complete the conversation between two students in the library. Use the simple present or the present continuous form of the verbs given. Include any other words you see.

A: Hi, Teresa. What _____are you doing_____ here?
1. you/do

B: Hi, Brooke. I _____ for pictures online for my environmental science course.
2. look

A: You have your laptop with you. Why _____ it?
3. you/not/use

B: The computers in the library _____ big monitors. I
4. have

_____ to see the pictures on a large screen.
5. want

A: _____ to go for a cup of coffee?
6. you/want

B: I _____ time now. I _____ for a classmate.
7. not/have 8. wait

We _____ on a project together for our class.
9. work

A: What kind of project _____ on?
10. you/work

B: We _____ to write a paper on climate change. Some people
11. need

_____ it _____ now.
12. not/believe 13. happen

A: What _____ ?
14. you/think

B: I _____ it's a very serious problem.
15. believe

A: I _____ of taking environmental science next semester.
16. think

_____ this class every semester?
17. your teacher/teach

B: I _____ so.
18. think

A: _____ the class?
19. you/like

B: Yes. I _____ it. I especially _____ the
20. love 21. like

teacher. He _____ tests.
22. not/give

A: Why _____ tests?
23. he/not/give

B: He _____ to give us projects. He _____ we
24. prefer 25. think

learn more that way.

A: I _____ . He _____ like an interesting teacher.
26. agree 27. sound

B: He is. Oh, I _____ my friend now. She _____
28. see 29. walk

toward us.

A: I _____ her. She's in my math class.
30. know

FROM GRAMMAR TO WRITING

PART 1 Editing Advice

1. Don't forget *be* with the present continuous.

   We *are* learning about nature.

2. Don't forget *-ing* with the present continuous.

   She is read*ing* an article about lemurs.

3. Use the correct question form in the present continuous and the simple present.

   Why ~~the Earth is~~ *is the Earth* warming?

   What ~~means "starvation"~~ *does "starvation" mean*?

4. Don't use *be* to form the simple present.

   I ~~am~~ know a lot about birds.

5. Don't use the present continuous with a nonaction verb.

   We ~~are needing~~ *need* to take care of our planet.

6. Don't use the present continuous to describe habits.

   Often I ~~am watching~~ *watch* animal programs on TV.

7. Don't use the simple present to describe an action that is happening at this exact moment.

   I ~~watch~~ *am watching* a program on TV about lemurs right now.

PART 2 Editing Practice

Some of the shaded words and phrases have mistakes. Find the mistakes and correct them. If the shaded words are correct, write C.

I am doing *C* a report on the Sumatran tiger this week. The Sumatran tiger is a beautiful animal.
It ~~is having~~ *has* **1.** black stripes on its orange coat. Unfortunately, this animal is disappearing. There are
2.   **3.**
only 400 left.

The Sumatran tiger is live in the forests of Sumatra, which is an island of Indonesia. Most groups of
4.
these tigers have no more than 50 individuals. Why they are disappearing? Tigers are needing large areas
5.   **6.**   **7.**
of forest to live, but people are cutting down forests.
8.

Why do they destroying forests? Farmers want the land for agriculture. But when they cut down the
9.   **10.**   **11.**
forests, they put the tiger in danger. There is another problem, too. Some people killing these animals and
12.

selling parts such as skin and bones. It is against the law to kill these animals, but some people don't care
13.   **14.**

about the law. We are need to protect these animals.
15.

WRITING TIP

When you need to think of several things to say about a topic, it is helpful to create a mind map to brainstorm and categorize your ideas. For example, here is the beginning of a mind map for the second prompt below.

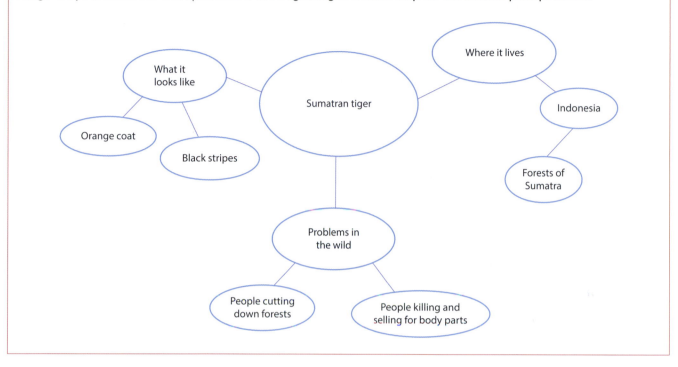

PART 3 Write

Read the prompts. Choose one and write one paragraph about it.

1. Write about an interesting class you are taking. What are you learning? What do you like about this class?
2. Write about a wild animal that you like. What do you know about this animal? Is this animal having problems in the wild?

PART 4 Edit

Reread the Summary of Unit 5 and the editing advice. Edit your writing from Part 3.

OUR FUTURE

> The best thing about the future is that it comes one day at a time.
>
> ABRAHAM LINCOLN

A girl wears her official space suit costume at a space program.

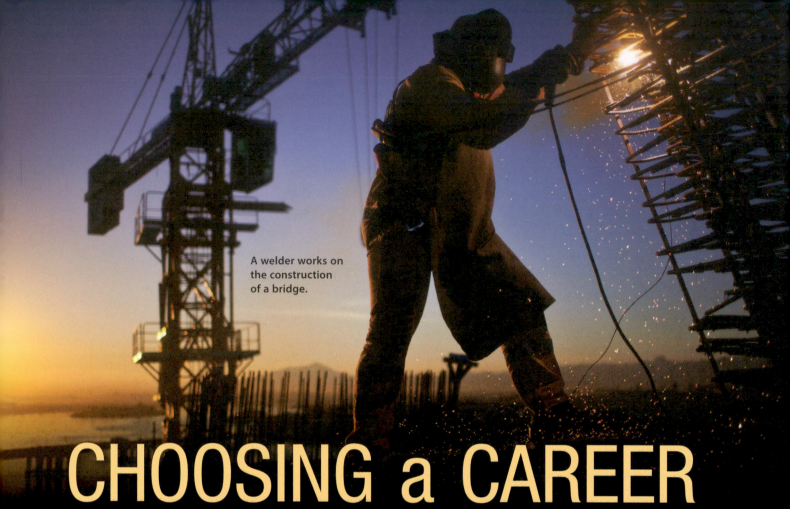

A welder works on the construction of a bridge.

CHOOSING a CAREER

Read the following article. Pay special attention to the words in bold. 🎧 6.1

Deciding on a career can be difficult. There are so many choices. How **will** you **choose** just one? It can help to ask yourself some important questions:

*Will I **find** a job in my field after I graduate?*

It's a good idea to study for a career in a growing field[1]. The Bureau of Labor Statistics (BLS) makes predictions about the fields that **will have** the most job growth. The BLS predicts that health care, construction, and teaching **will be** some of the fastest growing fields of the future. For example, they predict nursing jobs **will increase** by 26 percent in just 10 years.

*What job **will** I **enjoy** doing?*

You**'ll** probably **want** a well-paying job. But it's also important to think about the kind of job you **will enjoy**. Do you love words and writing? Then a career as a journalist or an editor may be right for you. Do you enjoy numbers? Then you may enjoy working as an accountant or engineer.

*What type of workplace **will be** best for me?*

Do you like working in an office? There are many options, such as human resource manager or accountant. Do you hate to be inside? Then a desk job probably **won't work** for you. Jobs that you **will like** better might include park ranger, postal worker, or marine biologist[2].

What kind of lifestyle[3] do I want?

Will you **be** happy working long hours with a lot of pressure? Then you could be a lawyer or a doctor. If not, then you probably **won't like** these jobs. You may prefer a job with more flexibility[4], such as a therapist or an IT consultant.

If you think carefully about these questions, you **will find** your perfect career.

---

[1] field: an area of work
[2] marine biologist: a scientist who studies ocean life
[3] lifestyle: the way a person lives
[4] flexibility: easily changed

COMPREHENSION Based on the reading, write T for *true* or F for *false*.

1. _____ The Bureau of Labor Statistics makes predictions about jobs.

2. _____ Nursing and other health-care professions will grow in the future.

3. _____ An IT consultant has more flexible hours than a lawyer.

THINK ABOUT IT Discuss the questions with a partner or in a small group.

1. Which jobs do you think will go away in the future?

2. Based on the reading and your own experience, what kinds of jobs are good for you?

6.1 The Future with *Will*—Forms

AFFIRMATIVE AND NEGATIVE STATEMENTS

EXAMPLES	EXPLANATION
The number of nursing jobs **will increase**. There **will be** more teaching jobs.	For affirmative statements with *will*, we use *will* + the base form of the verb.
I'll become a nurse. **You'll** be proud of me.	We can make contractions with the subject pronouns + *will*: *I'll, you'll, he'll, she'll, it'll, we'll,* and *they'll*.
A desk job **will not work** for you. Nurses **won't have** trouble finding a job.	For negative statements with *will*, we use *not* after *will*. The contraction for *will not* is *won't*.

Notes:

1. We can put an adverb (*always, never, probably, even, definitely*) between *will* and the main verb.

> Some professions **will definitely grow**.

> She **will probably become** a doctor.

2. The future of *there is* or *there are* is *there will be*.

> **There will be** a job fair next week. **There will be** many STEM companies there.

STATEMENTS, *YES/NO* QUESTIONS, SHORT ANSWERS, AND *WH*- QUESTIONS

STATEMENT	*YES/NO* QUESTION AND SHORT ANSWER	*WH*- QUESTION
She **will become** a nurse.	**A:** **Will** she **become** a hospital nurse? **B:** Yes, she **will**.	**When will** she **become** a nurse?
There **will be** jobs for engineers.	**A:** **Will** there **be** jobs for scientists? **B:** Yes, there **will**.	**What** kind of jobs **will** there **be**?
Health-care jobs **will grow**.	**A:** **Will** farm jobs **grow**? **B:** No, they **won't**.	**Why won't** farm jobs **grow**?
Some jobs **will go** away.	**A:** **Will** IT jobs **go** away? **B:** No, they **won't**.	**Which** jobs **will go** away?

EXERCISE 1 Listen to the article. Then write T for *true*, F for *false*, or NS for *not stated*. 🎧 6.2

1. _____ There will be a lot of jobs online in the future.

2. _____ The number of cashiers will decrease in the future.

3. _____ The Bureau of Labor Statistics is a good source of information about the future of different jobs.

EXERCISE 2 Listen again. Fill in the blanks with the words you hear. 🎧 6.2

Jobs in the future _____<u>will be</u>_____ different from the jobs of today. As people change jobs or retire,
           1.

companies _____ to replace workers. New technology also affects jobs. More people are
        2.

shopping online, so store workers _____ fewer job opportunities. Business practices are
            3.

changing, too. For example, more and more stores are offering self-service checkout. What

_____ this _____ for cashiers? Many people _____ soon
  4.   **5.**   **6.**

_____ without a job. Many factors _____ jobs of the future. The Bureau of Labor
  7.   **8.**

Statistics tries to let us know what the future _____ for workers 10 years from now.
                                9.

EXERCISE 3 Complete the conversation with the verbs from the box. Use *will* and any other words given.
Use contractions when possible. You will use two verbs more than once.

be	find	major	make	remember	show	take

A: I'm planning to study nursing. I'd love to be a doctor, but it <u>'ll take</u> _____ me too long.
                                              1.

    Nursing is a good profession. I know I _____ a job when I graduate. What about you?
                                    2.

B: I'm not sure yet. Both of my parents are teachers, so I _____ in education. I know I
                                           3. probably

    _____ a lot of money as a teacher, but I think it's a wonderful job.
        4. not

A: _____ a lot of jobs in the future? That's important to know.
      5. there

B: I don't know.

A: There's a great website from the Bureau of Labor Statistics. It shows what the future of a

    profession _____ .
                6.

B: Really? How can I find it?

A: Here's my tablet. I _____ you right now. The website says that there
                        7.

    _____ a need for more teachers. As a teacher, you _____ a
        8.   **9.**

    difference in the lives of young people. I _____ my fifth grade teacher. My love
                                  10. always

    of science comes from her.

6.2 The Future with *Will*—Use

EXAMPLES	EXPLANATION
She **will graduate** in four years.	We use *will* for simple facts about the future.
You**'ll be** a great doctor.	We use *will* for predictions.
Do you want to see the BLS website? I**'ll show** it to you on my tablet.	We use *will* for offers. We usually use the contracted form in offers.
A: What do you want to do tonight? **B:** I'm not sure. I**'ll think** of something soon.	We use *will* when the decision or plan about the future comes at the moment of speaking.

GRAMMAR IN USE

When we make a decision at the moment of speaking, we often begin with *I think/I guess* + *I will/I'll*.

  I think I'll take the bus today.

  I guess I'll stay home today.

EXERCISE 4 Find a partner. Take turns making predictions about the future. Use *will* and the words given. Begin each prediction with "I think" or "I don't think."

1. technology/replace teachers

   I don't think technology will replace teachers.

2. there/always/be a need for gardeners

3. workers/stay at the same job for a long time

4. we/always/need the Post Office

5. nurses' salaries/increase a lot

6. the U.S./bring in doctors from other countries

EXERCISE 5 Find a partner. Complete the conversations between students (S) asking for help from a student counselor (C). Write the counselor's offers of help. More than one answer is possible.

1. **S:** I'd like to be an accountant, but I don't know anything about the future of accounting.

   C: I'll show you the BLS website. You can find information there.

2. **S:** I don't have enough money for college.

   C: _____

3. **S:** Where's the financial aid office?

   C: _____

4. **S:** I need a letter of recommendation for the nursing program.

   C: _____

5. **S:** I don't understand the information in this booklet.

   C: _____

RAY KURZWEIL, FUTURIST

Read the following article. Pay special attention to the words in bold. 🎧 6.3

Are computers **going to be** smarter than people someday? Maybe. **Are** they **going to do** even more in the future? Probably. But **are** they **going to tell** stories and **have** a sense of humor[1]? **Will** they **have** feelings? Ray Kurzweil believes this **will happen.**

Who is Ray Kurzweil? He's an author, an inventor, a computer scientist—and a "futurist." He makes predictions about artificial intelligence[2]. He believes that by 2029, computers **are going to do** things better than humans. He predicts that by 2045, computers **will be** 1 billion times more powerful than all human brains together. Just as we now carry little computers (smartphones) in our hands, someday soon, he says, we**'re going to have** little computers in our brains.

Kurzweil is good at making predictions. For example, here are a few of his predictions from his book *The Age of Intelligent Machines*, published in the late 1980s:

- Documents **will include** more than just words. They **will include** voice, music, and other sounds.

- Computers **will be** as common as pencils and books in schools.
- We **will have** wireless networks to share information.

Today's computers search for answers to our questions, but they don't understand what they are searching. Kurzweil is now working on a project that **will improve** the way computers search. He predicts that one day computers **will** actually **understand** our questions before we ask them!

Kurzweil also thinks technology **is going to help** us live longer. In fact, he has a very unusual prediction: he thinks that technology **will help** us live forever[3].

Is this ever **going to happen**? What do you think?

---

[1] sense of humor: an ability to understand and say funny things
[2] artificial intelligence: computer programs that are able to learn and perform human-like thinking tasks
[3] forever: for all future time

COMPREHENSION Based on the reading, write T for *true* or F for *false*.

1. _____ Ray Kurzweil's predictions about the future are often correct.

2. _____ Today's computers understand what they are searching.

3. _____ Kurzweil wants to improve the way computers search.

THINK ABOUT IT Discuss the questions with a partner or in a small group.

1. Which of Kurzweil's predictions for the future do you think will come true? Which ones will not?

2. What are your predictions for the future?

6.3 The Future with *Be Going To*—Forms

AFFIRMATIVE AND NEGATIVE STATEMENTS

EXAMPLES	EXPLANATION
Computers **are going to be** faster. We **are going to live** longer.	For affirmative statements, we use a form of *be* + *going to* + the base form of the verb.
I'm going to read Kurzweil's book. **Technology's going to improve**.	We can make contractions with pronouns and most subject nouns + a form of *be*.
We**'re not going to live** forever. Computers **aren't going to have** feelings.	For negative statements, we use *not* after *is, am,* or *are*.

Note:

We can put an adverb (*always, never, probably, even, actually*) between *be* and *going to*.

   Computers **are probably going to** be smarter than people someday.

Pronunciation Note:

In informal speech, we often pronounce *going to* as *"gonna"* (/gənə/) when a verb comes after *to*.

STATEMENTS, *YES/NO* QUESTIONS, SHORT ANSWERS, AND *WH-* QUESTIONS

STATEMENT	*YES/NO* QUESTION AND SHORT ANSWER	*WH-* QUESTION
Computers **are going to be** faster.	**A: Are** they **going to be** smarter? **B:** Yes, they **are**.	**How are** they **going to be** smarter?
She**'s going to read** an article about Kurzweil.	**A: Is** she **going to read** his book? **B:** No, she**'s not**.	**Why isn't** she **going to read** his book?
There **are going to be** more powerful computers in the future.	**A: Are** there **going to be** better smartphones? **B:** Yes, there **are**.	**What kind of** smartphones **are** there **going to be**?
Some of his predictions **are going to happen**.	**A: Are** all his predictions **going to happen** soon? **B:** No, they **aren't**.	**Which** predictions **are going to happen**?

EXERCISE 6 Listen to the conversation. Then write T for *true*, F for *false*, or NS for *not stated*. 🎧 6.4

1. _____ The speakers are going to watch a television program together.

2. _____ They want to meet Ray Kurzweil.

3. _____ One speaker's brother is coming to visit.

EXERCISE 7 Listen again. Fill in the blanks with the words you hear. 🎧 6.4

A: There *'s going to be* _____ a program about artificial intelligence on TV tonight.
   _{1.}

B: What time _____ on?
   _{2.}

A: At 9:00 p.m. But I _____ it tonight. I _____ it later.
   _{3.} _{4.}

B: Why _____ it tonight?
   _{5.}

A: I have a biology test tomorrow. A friend and I _____ to the library to study.
   _{6.}

Do you want to watch it with me this weekend? I think I _____ it on Friday night.
   _{7.}

_____ free then?
   _{8.}

B: Sorry. My brother _____ in town this weekend, so we have a lot of plans.
   _{9.}

A: When _____ free?
   _{10.}

B: Next weekend.

A: I think I'll watch it this weekend. I _____ an essay about Ray Kurzweil for my
   _{11.}

computer class next week.

B: Who's he?

A: A "futurist." He thinks technology _____ people live forever.
   _{12.}

B: He sounds a little crazy to me.

6.4 The Future with *Be Going To*—Use

EXAMPLES	EXPLANATION
The program **is going to be** on TV at 9:00 p.m.	We use *be going to* with simple facts about the future.
Kurzweil's prediction: Computers **are going to have** feelings.	We use *be going to* for predictions.
I can't watch the program. I**'m going to meet** a friend at the library.	We use *be going to* when there is a previous plan to do something.

Note:
We can also use the present continuous with definite plans for the near future. We usually mention a time.
   I'm meeting a friend at 1:00. = *I'm going to meet* a friend at 1:00.

EXERCISE 8 Find a partner. Take turns making predictions about the future. Use *be going to* and the words given.

1. most cars/not need drivers

   In the future, most cars are not going to need drivers.

2. airplanes/fly without pilots

3. the work environment/ not be the same

4. robots/do the jobs of people

5. technology/create new jobs

6. people/live forever

7. students/learn everything on computers

8. scientists/find a cure for most diseases

ABOUT YOU Make statements about the future, using the verbs below so that they are true for you. Use contractions. Share your statements with a partner.

1. (not) take

   I'm not going to take an online course next semester.

2. (not) buy

3. (not) learn about

4. (not) make

5. (not) call

6. (not) go to

7. (not) stay

EXERCISE 9 Find a partner. Ask and answer questions about the future. Use *will* or *be going to* and the words given.

1. people/travel to another planet *(will)*

   A: *Will people travel to another planet?*

   B: *I think so. People will probably travel to Mars.*

2. people/happier in the future *(be going to)*

3. technology/make our lives better *(will)*

4. technology/make our lives worse *(be going to)*

5. computers/be smarter than people *(will)*

6. Ray Kurzweil/live forever *(be going to)*

6.5 Choosing *Will* or *Be Going To*

	WILL	BE GOING TO
Predictions	Robots **will take** some jobs away from humans.	Robots **are going to take** some jobs away from humans.
Simple facts	A program about Mars **will be** on TV tonight.	A program about Mars **is going to be** on TV tonight.
Offers	I**'ll wash** the dishes.	—
Plans made before the moment of speaking	—	I**'m going to be** a nurse.
Decisions about the future that come at the moment of speaking	**A:** Here's a great article on technology. You can read it. **B:** Thanks! I**'ll return** it tomorrow.	—

Note:

When there is a choice between *will* and *be going to*, *will* sounds more formal.

GRAMMAR IN USE

To ask someone to do something for you, you can use *will*. Use *please* to sound more polite.

Will you get some milk at the store, please? NOT: Are you going to get some milk at the store, please?

EXERCISE 10 Complete the conversation with the verb and any other word(s) given. Use *will* or *be going to*. Sometimes both choices are possible.

A: What _____*are you going to major*_____ in?
      1. major

B: English. When I go back to my country, I _____ an English language school
                                                              2. start

with my brother. English is the most popular language in the world.

A: _____ the most popular language in the world?
      3. it/always/be

B: Probably. It's the language of science, business, and entertainment.

A: I think Chinese _____ the number-one language.
                              4. become

B: I don't think so. I'm reading an interesting article about the future of English.

I _____ you borrow it when I'm finished. I think
      5. let

you _____ it.
        6. enjoy

A: Thanks, but I _____ time to read it. I'm so busy with school
                        7. not/have

and my job.

B: If you have a few minutes, I _____ you a little about it. Over 600 million
                                          8. tell

people speak English as a second language. Some experts believe that by 2020, only 15 percent of English

speakers _____ native speakers.
              9. be

A: This sounds like an interesting article. Maybe I _____ it after all.
                                                              10. borrow

B: I'm almost finished. I _____ it to you tomorrow. By the way, what about
                                11. give

you? What _____ in?
                12. you/major

A: I _____ a nurse.
        13. be

B: You're a very good person. I think you _____ a great nurse.
                                                    14. be

> **FUN WITH GRAMMAR**
>
> Role-play with horoscopes. Two students will come to the front of the class. One is the fortune teller, and one is the customer. The fortune teller should look at the customer's palm and make predictions about that person's future. The customer should ask questions for the fortune teller to answer, too. Set a two-minute timer. Every two minutes, two new volunteers do the role-play until everyone in the class has a had a turn. Then the class will vote on who had the best role-play.

Human Colony on Mars?

Read the following article. Pay special attention to the words in bold. 🎧 6.5

The U.S. space agency, NASA, wants to find out about Mars. **Will** humans **be** able to live on Mars **in the future**? If they **go** to Mars, what **will** they **need**? First, they**'ll need** water and food. They**'ll** also **need** energy. The sun is far away, so Mars is a very cold planet. They **will need** to find energy somewhere else on the planet or bring it with them. NASA **will need** to solve all of these problems **before** humans **go** to Mars.

Another group, Mars One, also wants to go to Mars. The people at Mars One believe that humans can live there. Their goal is to create a permanent[1] human colony[2] there. Mars One interviews people who want to go to Mars. From more than 200,000 applications, Mars One now has a group of 100 people. From those 100 people, Mars One **will choose** 24.

These 24 people **will train** in the Arctic region, where the land and weather are similar to the land and weather of Mars. Mars One **will build** a colony in the Arctic called "Outpost Alpha." **When** the 24 people **do** their training, they **will learn** to grow food, repair computers, and perform simple medical procedures[3]. If they **don't learn** these things, they **will die** when they are on Mars.

When the training **is** over, Mars One **will choose** four people for the first mission. **When will** the training **begin**? No one is sure. Mars One wants to send the first group of people to Mars in 2022, but they are not ready. Mars One doesn't have the technology that they need for Outpost Alpha.

Some people believe that Mars One has too many problems. For example, **if** Mars One **sends** people to Mars, those people **won't come** back. Mars One doesn't have the technology for a round trip. Also, **if** the people in the Mars One colony **have** a problem, it **will take** a long time to reach them. They **will die before** help **arrives**. **Will** Mars One **succeed**? We**'ll have to** wait and see.

---

[1] permanent: continuing forever
[2] colony: a group of people who move to a new place but are still under the government of their home country
[3] procedure: a series of actions

An artist's vision of the future Mars One colony

COMPREHENSION Based on the reading, write T for *true* or F for *false*.

1. _____ Humans on Mars will use energy from the sun.

2. _____ Mars One will build a colony in the Arctic.

3. _____ The four people Mars One sends to Mars will not be able to return.

THINK ABOUT IT Discuss the questions with a partner or in a small group.

1. Why do you think so many people want to go to Mars?

2. Do you want to go to Mars? Why or why not?

6.6 The Future with Time Clauses and *If* Clauses

TIME OR *IF* CLAUSE (SIMPLE PRESENT)	MAIN CLAUSE (FUTURE)	EXPLANATION
If you **go** to Mars,	you **won't come** back.	A clause is a group of words that has a subject and a verb. Some sentences have a time clause or an *if* clause in addition to a main clause. We use the future in the main clause; we use the simple present in the time clause or the *if* clause.
When they **arrive**,	they**'re going to create** a human colony.	
MAIN CLAUSE (FUTURE)	**TIME OR *IF* CLAUSE (SIMPLE PRESENT)**	
I **will go**	**if** they **choose** me.	
They **are going to die**	**before** help **arrives**.	

Note:

If the time clause or the *if* clause comes before the main clause, we use a comma between the two clauses.
If the main clause comes first, we don't use a comma.

> *If they choose me*, *I will go.* (comma)
>
> *I will go if they choose me.* (no comma)

GRAMMAR IN USE

When we are ending a conversation, we often leave out the subject and *will*.

> *Talk to you later. = I'll talk to you later.*
>
> *See you tomorrow. = I'll see you tomorrow.*

EXERCISE 11 Complete the statements about the future. Then find a partner and compare your answers.

1. When the finalists complete the training, _____they will travel to Mars_____.

2. If people go to Mars, _____.

3. If Mars colonists have a problem, _____.

4. If Chinese becomes the international language, _____.

5. If people live a lot longer, _____.

6. If computers become more intelligent than humans, _____.

7. When robots do the work of humans, _____.

8. If the world population continues to grow, _____.

ABOUT YOU Fill in the blanks to make true statements about yourself. Then find a partner and share your statements.

1. When _____ I have more money _____ , I'm going to buy a new cell phone.

2. When _____ , I'll go on vacation.

3. If _____ , I'm not going to graduate.

4. If _____ , I'll probably move.

5. If _____ , I'll probably live longer.

ABOUT YOU Write a prediction or question you have about each of the categories in the chart. Use *will* or *be going to*. Then find a partner and discuss your completed chart.

CATEGORY	FUTURE STATEMENT
1. job/career	I'm going to graduate in two years. When I graduate, will I find a job easily?
2. money	
3. learning English	
4. home	
5. family and children	
6. health	
7. fun and recreation	
8. technology	
9. other	

SUMMARY OF UNIT 6

The Future

THE FUTURE WITH *WILL*	EXAMPLES
AFFIRMATIVE STATEMENT	He **will become** a nurse.
NEGATIVE STATEMENT	He **won't become** a doctor.
YES/NO QUESTION	**Will** he **become** a nurse soon?
SHORT ANSWER	Yes, he **will**.
WH- QUESTION	**When will** he **become** a nurse?
NEGATIVE *WH-* QUESTION	**Why won't** he **become** a doctor?
SUBJECT *WH-* QUESTION	**Who will become** a doctor?

THE FUTURE WITH *BE GOING TO*	EXAMPLES
AFFIRMATIVE STATEMENT	He **is going to study** Chinese.
NEGATIVE STATEMENT	He **isn't going to study** Spanish.
YES/NO QUESTION	**Is** he **going to study** Japanese?
SHORT ANSWER	No, he **isn't**.
WH- QUESTION	**Where is** he **going to study** Chinese?
NEGATIVE *WH-* QUESTION	**Why isn't** he **going to study** Spanish?
SUBJECT *WH-* QUESTION	**Who is going to study** Spanish?

USES OF *WILL* AND *BE GOING TO*	*WILL*	*BE GOING TO*
Predictions	✓	✓
Simple facts	✓	✓
Offers	✓	
Plans before the moment of speaking		✓
Decisions about the future that come at the moment of speaking	✓	

The Future with Time and *If* Clauses

TIME OR *IF* CLAUSE (SIMPLE PRESENT)	MAIN CLAUSE (FUTURE)
After I **finish** the article,	I**'ll give** it to you.
If you **study** nursing,	you**'re going to find** a job easily.

MAIN CLAUSE (FUTURE)	TIME OR *IF* CLAUSE (SIMPLE PRESENT)
I**'m going to teach** English	**when** I **go** back to my country.
I**'ll tell** you about the article	**if** you **have** a few minutes.

REVIEW

Complete the conversation about the future with the word(s) given. Sometimes more than one answer is possible.

A: What <u>are you going to do</u> tomorrow night?
1. you/do

B: Not much. I _____ TV after I _____ my homework.
2. watch   **3.** finish

A: Do you want to go to a lecture with me? One of my professors _____ about her
4. talk

     predictions for the future. The lecture _____ the second in a series of presentations
5. be

     about the future.

B: What time _____?
6. it/start

A: At 8:00 p.m. Afterward we _____ a discussion. In the first lecture, she
7. have

     talked about cities of the future. She thinks cities _____ more
8. have

     parks. Also people _____ bicycles more for transportation. There
9. use

     _____ more bike paths. People _____
10. be   **11.** not/be

     so lazy about exercise. We _____ some of our own food.
12. grow

     We _____ all our food from farmers.
13. not/get

B: How many lectures _____ in this series?
14. there/be

A: Five. I _____ all of them. I _____ you the link to the website
15. attend   **16.** send

     about the lectures. I know she _____ about politics of the future.
17. not/talk

B: Why _____ politics?
18. she/not/discuss

A: That subject makes people angry. So, do you want to go tomorrow?

B: Sure.

A: I _____ to your house around 7:30 p.m.
19. come

B: Thanks. I _____ outside.
20. wait

A: You don't have to wait outside. I _____ you when I _____ to
21. call   **22.** get

     your house.

B: Great.

FROM GRAMMAR TO WRITING

PART 1 Editing Advice

1. For the future with *will*, don't add *be* before the main verb.

    I hope I will ~~be~~ find a good job.

2. Use a verb with *will*.

    I will ^be^ happy when I find a job.

3. Don't combine *will* and *be going to*.

    Technology ^is^ ~~will~~ going to improve. OR Technology will improve.

4. Don't use *be going to* with offers.

    Those books look heavy. ~~I'm going to~~ ^I'll^ help you carry them.

5. Don't use the future in a time or *if* clause.

    When you ~~will~~ graduate from the nursing program, you will find a job.

6. Use a comma after a time clause or *if* clause at the beginning of a sentence.

    If I become a nurse,^ I will help a lot of people.

7. Use a form of *be* with *going to*.

    He ^is^ going to write an essay about our future world.

8. Use *to* after *going* for the future.

    Are computers going ^to^ be smarter than humans?

9. Use the correct word order for questions.

    Why ~~you aren't~~ ^aren't you^ going to read the article?

PART 2 Editing Practice

Some of the shaded words and phrases have mistakes. Find the mistakes and correct them. If the shaded words are correct, write C. Sometimes more than one answer is correct.

           C   *be*

We <u>will see</u> several changes in the future. First, cities <u>will</u> much bigger than they are today. Right

    1.   **2.** ^

now about 3 billion people live in cities. By the year 2050, that number <u>will double</u>. It <u>will</u> necessary to

                                                   3.   **4.**

make changes for so many people to be able to live together. One problem <u>will going to be</u> parking. City

                                                          5.

planners <u>will need</u> to study the problem. Businesses <u>will need</u> to pay for street parking if they <u>want</u> to have

      6.   **7.**   **8.**

customers. I'm glad this will happen. Why <u>they aren't going to do</u> this sooner?

                                           9.

Another change <u>will be</u> with education. Students <u>are going learn</u> more STEM skills (science,

                    10.   **11.**

technology, engineering, and mathematics). Some large companies <u>going to become</u> partners with

                                                        12.

schools. When students <u>will graduate</u> from high school, they <u>will be have</u> the opportunity to work with the

                      13.   **14.**

company and learn from a teacher at the company. This is already happening at some schools in New York.

Other schools in the United States <u>are going to do</u> this in the future.

                                         15.

Many exciting things <u>are going to happen</u> in the future. If I <u>will still work</u> for my company in 2050,

                               16.   **17.**

I <u>will</u> see many changes to my commute and work environment.

  18.

WRITING TIP

Use transition words to organize your ideas in a paragraph. Here are some transitions you can use in a paragraph about your predictions for the future.

> *One prediction . . . /My first prediction . . .*
>
> *Another prediction . . . /My second prediction . . .*
>
> *Finally, . . . /My last prediction . . .*

PART 3 Write

Read the prompts. Choose one and write one paragraph about it.

1. Write about a few of your predictions for the future.
2. Write about a few of your plans or goals for the future.

PART 4 Edit

Reread the Summary of Unit 6 and the editing advice. Edit your writing from Part 3.

IN FLIGHT

The airplane became the first World Wide Web, bringing people, languages, ideas, and values together.
BILL GATES

An airplane flies over a highway in Bangkok, Thailand.

The WRIGHT BROTHERS

Read the following article. Pay special attention to the words in bold. 🎧 7.1

At one time, people only **dreamed** about flying. The Wright brothers, Wilbur and Orville, **were** dreamers who **changed** the world. They **were** the inventors of the first successful airplane.

From a young age, the brothers **were** fascinated[1] with the idea of flying. When Wilbur **was** 11 and Orville **was** 7, their father **gave** them a flying toy.

When they **were** older, Wilbur and Orville **opened** a bicycle shop in Ohio, where they **designed**, **sold**, and **repaired** bicycles. They **used** their bike shop to design an airplane. The brothers **didn't go** to college, but they **studied** a lot about aviation. They **were** interested in the way birds use their wings. They **studied** three necessary things for flying: lift, control, and power. Wilbur **designed** a small flyer with a gasoline engine. The brothers **flew** it for the first time on December 17, 1903. The airplane **stayed** in the air for 12 seconds. It **traveled** a distance of 120 feet. That day they **made** four short flights in their first

"Wright Flyer." Only a few U.S. newspapers **reported** this historic moment. A New York newspaper **wrote**, "They are in fact either fliers or liars."

The Wright brothers **continued** to work on their airplane. For the next two years, they **didn't fly** at all. They **needed** a patent[2] for their invention and customers to buy it. They **contacted** the U.S. government, but the government **wasn't** interested. The government **didn't believe** them. The brothers **went** to Europe in 1908. There they **made** more than 200 flights. People **were** amazed. The brothers **became** famous. News of their success **was** on the front page of newspapers. When they **came** back to America in 1909, they **were** heroes. They **sold** the Wright Flyer to the U.S. Army in 1909.

Airplanes today use the same basic design elements of the Wright Flyer.

---

[1] fascinated: very interested
[2] patent: a government license that prevents others from selling the same item

Wilbur Wright stands and watches Orville Wright's first flight in 1903 at Kitty Hawk, North Carolina, USA.

COMPREHENSION Based on the reading, write T for *true* or F for *false*.

1. _____ The Wright brothers learned about aviation in college.

2. _____ The U.S. government was immediately interested in the Wright brothers' plane.

3. _____ The Wright brothers became famous after they made flights in Europe.

THINK ABOUT IT Discuss the questions with a partner or in a small group.

1. Why do you think people didn't believe the Wright brothers after their first flight?

2. Why are patents important?

7.1 The Simple Past—Forms

EXAMPLES	EXPLANATION
REGULAR VERBS	Regular simple past verbs end in *-ed*.
They **started** a bicycle business. They **repaired** bicycles.	start → start**ed** repair → repair**ed**
IRREGULAR VERBS	Irregular simple past verbs do not end in *-ed*.*
They **made** four short flights in 1903. They **sold** the flyer to the U.S. Army.	make → made sell → sold
Wilbur Wright **was** born in 1867. The Wright brothers **were** inventors.	The verb *be* is irregular. It has two forms in the past: *was* and *were*.

Notes:

1. Except for the verb *be*, the simple past form is the same for all subjects.

> ***They started*** *a business.* ***I started*** *a business.*

2. The verb after *to* does not use the past form.

> *The Wright brothers* ***continued to work*** *on their plane.* (NOT: *continued to worked*)

*See Appendix C for a list of irregular verb forms.

EXERCISE 1 Write the base form of each verb. Write R for *regular verb*. Write I for *irregular verb*. Write B for the verb *be*.

1.	rain	rained	R	9.	_____	worked	_____
2.	write	wrote	I	10.	_____	came	_____
3.	_____	opened	_____	11.	_____	gave	_____
4.	_____	sold	_____	12.	_____	flew	_____
5.	_____	started	_____	13.	_____	were	_____
6.	_____	happened	_____	14.	_____	needed	_____
7.	_____	made	_____	15.	_____	was	_____
8.	_____	died	_____	16.	_____	lived	_____

7.2 The Simple Past—Uses

EXAMPLES	USES
Their father **gave** them a toy.	We use the simple past with single, short past actions.
The Wright family **lived** in Ohio.	We use the simple past with longer past actions.
The Wright brothers **made** four short flights on December 17, 1903.	We use the simple past with repeated past actions.

Note:

We often use *ago* in sentences about the past. *Ago* means "before now."

   *The first flight was over 100 years **ago**.*

EXERCISE 2 Listen to the article. Then write T for *true*, F for *false*, or NS for *not stated*. 🎧 7.2

1. _____ The copy of the original plane was expensive to make.

2. _____ The president came for the celebration.

3. _____ The celebration was a great success.

EXERCISE 3 Listen again. Fill in the blanks with the verbs in the box. You can use some verbs more than once. 🎧 7.2

came	flew	hoped	rained	waited
cost	got	included	repaired	was
failed	hit	needed	stopped	were

   December 17, 2003, _____ was _____ the 100th anniversary of the Wright brothers' first flight.
   1.
There _____ a six-day celebration at Kitty Hawk, North Carolina, the location of the first
   2.
flight. A crowd of 35,000 people _____ to see the flight of a model of the first airplane. The
   3.
audience _____ some famous people, such as Neil Armstrong and Buzz Aldrin. They
   4.
_____ the first men to walk on the moon.
   5.
   It _____ $1.2 million to make a copy of the original plane. People _____ to
   6.   7.
see the Flyer go up in the air. The weather _____ bad that day. It _____ hard.
   8.   9.
The crowd _____ with excitement in the rain. But the Flyer _____ to fly. A
   10.   11.
wing _____ the ground, and the plane _____. Mechanics _____
   12.   13.   14.
the engine and wing. The crowd _____ again for a second try. The plane _____
   15.   16.
wind to lift off, but the winds _____ very calm that day. The Flyer _____ for
   17.   18.
12 seconds in 1903. It never _____ off the ground at all in 2003.
   19.

AMAZING
AVIATORS

Read the following article. Pay special attention to the words in bold. 🎧 **7.3**

At the beginning of the 20th century, flight **was** new. It **was not** for everyone. It **was** only for adventurous people. Two adventurous aviators **were** Charles Lindbergh and Amelia Earhart.

Charles Lindbergh **was** born in 1902, a year before the Wright brothers' historic flight. In 1927, a man offered a $25,000 reward for the first person to fly from New York to Paris. Lindbergh **was** a pilot for the U.S. Mail Service at that time. He wanted to win the prize. He decided to try, and he won. He **was** the first person to fly across the Atlantic Ocean alone. His plane **was** in the air for 33 hours. The flight **was** 3,600 miles. There **were** thousands of people in New York to welcome him home. He **was** an American hero. He **was** only 25 years old.

Another famous American aviator **was** Amelia Earhart. In 1920, when she **was** 23 years old, she rode in a plane for the first time. As soon as the plane **was** in the air, she **was** sure that she wanted to be a pilot. She took flying lessons and soon bought her own plane. In 1932, she **was** the first woman to fly across the Atlantic Ocean alone. Americans **were** in love with Earhart. In 1937, she **was** ready for a bigger challenge. She wanted to fly around the world. She **wasn't** alone; she **was** with a navigator[1]. They disappeared somewhere in the Pacific Ocean. Maybe there **wasn't** enough fuel[2]. Maybe the weather conditions **were** bad. No one knows what happened to Earhart. It is still a mystery today.

---

[1] navigator: someone who guides a plane in the right direction
[2] fuel: gasoline

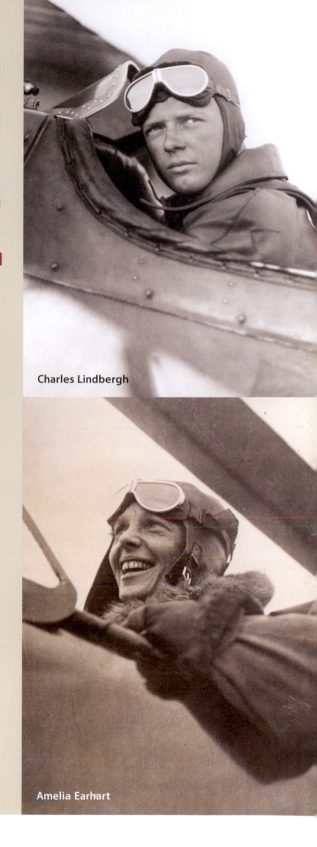

Charles Lindbergh

Amelia Earhart

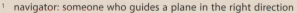

COMPREHENSION Based on the reading, write T for *true* or F for *false*.

1. _____ Charles Lindbergh was successful in his attempt to cross the Atlantic Ocean.

2. _____ Amelia Earhart was the first person to fly across the Atlantic Ocean.

3. _____ A navigator was with Earhart when she disappeared.

1. What are other possible explanations for the disappearance of Amelia Earhart?

2. Would you like to fly a plane? Why or why not?

7.3 The Simple Past of *Be*—Forms

AFFIRMATIVE STATEMENTS

SUBJECT	WAS/WERE	
I He/She/It Lindbergh	**was**	in New York.
We You They People	**were**	

NEGATIVE STATEMENTS

SUBJECT	WAS/WERE + NOT	
I He/She/It Earhart	**was not** **wasn't**	alone.
We You They People	**were not** **weren't**	

YES/NO QUESTIONS AND SHORT ANSWERS

WAS/WERE	SUBJECT		SHORT ANSWER
Was	I he she it	on an airplane?	Yes, you **were**. Yes, he **was**. No, she **wasn't**. Yes, it **was**.
Were	we you they		No, we **weren't**. Yes, I **was**. Yes, they **were**.

WH- QUESTIONS

WH- WORD	WAS/WERE WASN'T/WEREN'T	SUBJECT	
Why	**was** **wasn't**	I he/she/it	on an airplane?
	were **weren't**	we you they	

SUBJECT *WH-* QUESTIONS

WH- WORD	WAS/WERE	
Who	**was**	on the airplane?
How many people	**were**	on the airplane?
What	**was**	wrong with Earhart's airplane?

STATEMENTS, *YES/NO* QUESTIONS, AND *WH-* QUESTIONS

STATEMENT	YES/NO QUESTION	WH- QUESTION
Earhart **was** famous.	**Was** Earhart an inventor?	**Why was** Earhart famous?
The Wright brothers **were** Americans.	**Were** they from North Carolina?	**Where were** the Wright brothers from?
Newspapers **weren't** interested in the first airplanes.	**Were** newspapers interested in airplanes in 1909?	**Why weren't** they interested in airplanes in 1903?
Lindbergh **was** born in the 20th century.	**Was** Earhart born in the 20th century?	**When was** Earhart born?
Someone **was** with Earhart in 1937.	**Was** Lindbergh with Earhart?	**Who was** with Earhart?

EXERCISE 4 Complete the conversation between two friends with *was, wasn't, were,* or *weren't.*

A: _____Were_____ you interested in the article about Charles Lindbergh and Amelia Earhart?
1.

B: Yes, I _____ . They _____ very brave people.
2.   3.

A: I agree. At that time women _____ involved in professions like aviation.
4.

Many professions _____ only for men. But she believed that women and men
5.

_____ able to do the same things.
6.

B: _____ she married?
7.

A: Yes, she _____ .
8.

B: _____ her husband a pilot, too?
9.

A: No, he _____ .
10.

B: I _____ sad to read about her disappearance.
11.

A: I _____ , too. But she _____ happy in her profession. In fact,
12.   13.

she told her husband, "I want to do it because I want to do it."

B: What _____ the problem with her last flight?
14.

A: They _____ in the air for such a long time. Maybe there _____
15.   16.

enough fuel.

B: Why _____ there enough fuel?
17.

A: I'm not really sure.

7.4 The Simple Past of *Be*—Uses

EXAMPLES	EXPLANATION
Lindbergh **was brave**. Lindbergh **was an aviator**.	We use *be* with a description of the subject. We use *be* when we define or classify the subject or say what the subject is.
Lindbergh **was in Paris**.	We use *be* with the location of the subject.
Earhart **was from Kansas**.	We use *be* with the place of origin of the subject.
Earhart **was born** in 1897.	We use *be* with *born*.
Lindbergh **was 25 years old** in 1927.	We use *be* with ages.
There was a celebration of the 100th anniversary of flight in 2003.	We use *there was* to talk about the existence of a singular noun/noun phrase.
There were thousands of people in New York to welcome Lindbergh.	We use *there were* to talk about the existence of a plural noun/noun phrase.

EXERCISE 5 Complete the statements with *was, wasn't, were,* or *weren't*.

1. Lindbergh and Earhart _____ *were* _____ famous.

2. Lindbergh _____ an inventor.

3. The first airplane _____ in the air for 12 minutes.

4. Lindbergh and Earhart _____ American heroes.

5. Earhart's last flight _____ successful.

6. She _____ alone when her plane disappeared.

7. Earhart _____ the first woman to fly across the Atlantic Ocean.

8. She _____ born in the 20th century.

9. Lindbergh _____ 25 years old when he made his flight across the Atlantic.

10. There _____ any successful airplanes before the Wright Flyer.

EXERCISE 6 Read each statement. Then use the word(s) given to write a negative statement in the simple past.

1. The Wright brothers were inventors.

   (Earhart and Lindbergh) _Earhart and Lindbergh weren't inventors._

2. The train was a method of transportation in the early 1900s.

   (the airplane) _____

3. Earhart was from Kansas.

(Lindbergh) _____

4. Lindbergh was the first person to fly across the Atlantic Ocean alone.

(Earhart) _____

5. There were a lot of reporters at Kitty Hawk in 2003.

(in 1903) _____

6. Lindbergh was born in the 20th century.

(the Wright brothers) _____

EXERCISE 7 Read each statement. Then use the word(s) given to write a *yes/no* question in the simple past. Write a short answer for each question.

1. The Wright brothers were inventors.

(Lindbergh) _Was Lindbergh an inventor? No, he wasn't._____

2. The airplane was an important invention.

(the telephone) _____

3. There were telephones 100 years ago.

(airplanes) _____

4. Charles Lindbergh was adventurous.

(the Wright brothers) _____

5. Amelia Earhart was American.

(Lindbergh) _____

6. Travel by plane is common now.

(100 years ago) _____

7. I was interested in the story about the aviators.

(you) _____

EXERCISE 8 Read each statement. Write a *wh-* question in the simple past using the word(s) given. Then find a partner and ask and answer your questions.

1. Charles Lindbergh was famous. (why)

   A: Why was Charles Lindbergh famous?

   B: He was one of the first aviators.

2. Lindbergh was a hero. (why)

   A: _____

   B: _____

3. Lindbergh was American. (what nationality/Earhart)

   A: _____

   B: _____

4. Earhart was 34 years old when she crossed the ocean. (how old/Lindbergh)

   A: _____

   B: _____

5. Lindbergh was a famous aviator. (who/the Wright brothers)

   A: _____

   B: _____

6. Lindbergh was born in 1902. (when/Earhart)

   A: _____

   B: _____

7. The flight at Kitty Hawk in 2003 wasn't successful. (why)

   A: _____

   B: _____

The Father of
Modern Rocketry

Read the following article. Pay special attention to the words in bold. 🎧 7.4

When Robert Goddard **was** 17 years old, he **climbed** a cherry tree to cut its dead branches. He **looked** around himself and **imagined** going into space, maybe even to Mars. The year **was** 1899.

As a child, Goddard **loved** to read. He often **visited** the library to borrow books on physical sciences. He **was** a sick child and **didn't graduate** from high school until he **was** 21. He later **became** a physics professor at a university. In his free time, he **built** rockets and **took** them to a field, but they **didn't fly**.

In 1920, Goddard **wrote** an article about rocket travel. When the *New York Times* **saw** his article, a reporter **wrote** that Goddard **had** less knowledge about science than a high school student.

In 1926, Goddard **built** a 10-foot rocket, **put** it into an open car, and **drove** to a field on his aunt's nearby farm. He **lit** the fuse[1], and the rocket **went** into the sky. It **traveled** at 60 mph to an altitude[2] of 41 feet. Then it **fell** into the field. The flight **lasted** 2.5 seconds. The U.S. government **didn't show** much interest in Goddard's invention. To continue his experiments, Goddard **used** his own money and money from private foundations[3].

Over the years, his rockets **grew** to 18 feet and **flew** up to 9,000 feet. No one **made** fun of him after he **was** successful. In fact, he **became** known as the father of modern rocketry. He **wrote**, "The dream of yesterday is the hope of today, and the reality of tomorrow."

Goddard **didn't live** to see space flight. He **died** in 1945, but his work **didn't stop**. Scientists **continued** to build bigger and better rockets. In 1969, the American rocket *Apollo 11* **took** the first men to the moon. At that time, the *New York Times* **wrote** about its 1920 article: "The *Times* regrets the error."

Robert Goddard with one of his rocket designs in 1928

---

[1] fuse: a cord that, when lighted, carries a flame
[2] altitude: height
[3] foundation: an organization that provides money for projects

1. _____ Goddard used his aunt's farm to test his rockets.

2. _____ The first rocket was in the air for 60 seconds.

3. _____ The *New York Times* recognized Goddard's success many years later.

THINK ABOUT IT Discuss the questions with a partner or in a small group.

1. What kinds of activities did you enjoy when you were a child? Are they connected to your studies or your job as an adult?

2. What are some characteristics that extremely successful people share?

7.5 The Simple Past of Regular Verbs

We add *-ed* or *-d* to the base form of regular verbs to form the simple past.

EXAMPLES	BASE FORM	SIMPLE PAST FORM
Goddard **climbed** a tree.	climb	climb**ed**
He **looked** around him.	look	look**ed**
The rocket **traveled** for 2.5 seconds.	travel	travel**ed**
Some people **laughed** at his ideas.	laugh	laugh**ed**
Goddard **died** in 1945.	die	die**d**

EXERCISE 9 Underline the simple past verbs.

1. Goddard <u>climbed</u> a tree to cut its branches.

2. He loved to read.

3. He visited the library to get books about science.

4. He graduated from high school at the age of 21.

5. Goddard wanted to build rockets.

6. He experimented at his aunt's farm.

7. In 1926, one of Goddard's rockets lasted 2.5 seconds in the air.

8. The U.S. government ignored his work at first.

9. Some people laughed at his ideas.

10. He continued his work.

11. He died at the age of 63.

12. The *New York Times* regretted its error.

7.6 The Simple Past of Regular Verbs—Spelling

RULES	BASE FORM	SIMPLE PAST
We add -ed to the base form of most regular verbs.	start laugh	started laughed
When the base form ends in e, we add -d only.	die live	died lived
When the base form ends in a consonant + y, we change y to i and add -ed.	carry study	carried studied
When the base form ends in a vowel + y, we add -ed. We don't change the y.	stay enjoy	stayed enjoyed
When the base form of a one-syllable verb ends in a consonant-vowel-consonant (CVC), we repeat the final consonant and add -ed.	s t o p ↓ ↓ ↓ c v c h u g ↓ ↓ ↓ c v c	stopped hugged
When the base form ends in w or x, we don't repeat the final consonant.	show fix	showed fixed
When the base form of a two-syllable verb ends in a consonant-vowel-consonant, we repeat the final consonant and add -ed only if the last syllable is stressed.	refer	referred
When the last syllable of a two-syllable verb that ends in a consonant-vowel-consonant is not stressed, we don't repeat the final consonant.	open offer	opened offered

EXERCISE 10 Write the simple past form of each regular verb. In two-syllable verbs that end in consonant-vowel-consonant, the stressed syllable is underlined.

1. play   played
2. worry   worried
3. hope   _____
4. want   _____
5. like   _____
6. row   _____
7. look   _____
8. shop   _____
9. happen   _____
10. marry   _____

11. employ   _____
12. drag   _____
13. drop   _____
14. vote   _____
15. follow   _____
16. prefer   _____
17. tie   _____
18. mix   _____
19. admit   _____
20. propel   _____

7.7 The Simple Past of Regular Verbs—Pronunciation 🎧 7.5

RULES	EXAMPLES	
We pronounce -ed as /t/ after voiceless sounds: /p, k, f, s, ʃ, tʃ/.	jump—jumped cook—cooked cough—coughed	kiss—kissed wash—washed watch—watched
We pronounce -ed as /d/ after voiced sounds: /b, g, v, ð, z, ʒ, dʒ, m, n, ŋ, l, r/ and all vowel sounds.	rub—rubbed drag—dragged love—loved bathe—bathed use—used massage—massaged charge—charged	name—named learn—learned bang—banged call—called care—cared free—freed tie—tied
We pronounce -ed as /əd/ after /t/ or /d/ sounds.	wait—waited hate—hated	add—added decide—decided

EXERCISE 11 Find a partner. Take turns pronouncing the base form and the simple past form of each verb in Exercise 10.

EXERCISE 12 Complete each statement with the simple past form of a verb from the box.

believe	graduate	live	play	study	want
dream	like	open	receive✓	use	work

1. The Wright brothers _____received_____ a flying toy from their father.

2. They _____ with flying toys.

3. They _____ in Ohio.

4. They _____ about flying when they were children.

5. They _____ a lot about flight.

6. They _____ a bicycle shop in Dayton, Ohio.

7. Goddard _____ going to the library when he was young.

8. He _____ to study physical sciences.

9. He _____ from high school at the age of 21.

10. He _____ as a university professor.

11. He _____ in the possibility of going to the moon.

12. He _____ his aunt's farm to test his rockets.

7.8 The Simple Past of Irregular Verbs

Irregular verbs in the simple past do not end in -ed.

EXAMPLES	BASE FORM	SIMPLE PAST FORM
Goddard **built** rockets.	build	built
A newspaper **wrote** an article about him.	write	wrote

There are different ways to form the simple past of irregular verbs.

NO CHANGE IN FORM						
beat	cost	fit	hurt	put	set	split
bet	cut	hit	let	quit	shut	spread

CHANGE IN FORM			
feel—felt	mean—meant	dig—dug	sting—stung
keep—kept	sleep—slept	hang—hung	strike—struck
leave—left	sweep—swept	spin—spun	swing—swung
lose—lost	weep—wept	stick—stuck	win—won
awake—awoke	speak—spoke	begin—began	sing—sang
break—broke	steal—stole	drink—drank	sink—sank
choose—chose	wake—woke	ring—rang	spring—sprang
freeze—froze		shrink—shrank	swim—swam
bring—brought	fight—fought	blow—blew	grow—grew
buy—bought	teach—taught	draw—drew	know—knew
catch—caught	think—thought	fly—flew	throw—threw
arise—arose	rise—rose	bleed—bled	meet—met
drive—drove	shine—shone	feed—fed	read—read
ride—rode	write—wrote	lead—led	speed—sped
sell—sold	tell—told	find—found	wind—wound
mistake—mistook	take—took	lay—laid	say—said
shake—shook		pay—paid	
swear—swore	wear—wore	bite—bit	light—lit
tear—tore		hide—hid	slide—slid
become—became	forgive—forgave	fall—fell	run—ran
come—came	give—gave	hold—held	sit—sat
eat—ate	lie—lay	see—saw	
forget—forgot	shoot—shot	stand—stood	
get—got		understand—understood	
build—built	send—sent	be—was/were	have—had
lend—lent	spend—spent	do—did	hear—heard
		go—went	make—made

Pronunciation Notes:

1. *Meant* rhymes with *sent*.

2. The past form of *read* is pronounced like the color red.

3. *Said* rhymes with *bed*.

EXERCISE 13 Complete each statement with the simple past form of the verb given.

1. The Wright brothers' father _____*gave*_____ them a flying toy.
   _{give}

2. The brothers _____ a dream of flying.
   _{have}

3. They _____ interested in flying after seeing the toy.
   _{become}

4. They _____ many books about flight.
   _{read}

5. They_____ bicycles in Ohio.
   _{sell}

6. They _____ the first gas-powered airplane.
   _{build}

7. They_____ for the first time in 1903.
   _{fly}

8. Only a few people _____ the first flight.
   _{see}

9. Between 1903 and 1909, they _____ some changes to the airplane.
   _{make}

10. In 1909, they _____ their plane to the U.S. Army.
    _{sell}

11. The Wright brothers _____ celebrities when they returned to America in 1909.
    _{be}

12. The airplane was an important invention because it _____ people from different
    _{bring}

    places closer together.

13. Thousands of people _____ to North Carolina for the 100th anniversary of flight.
    _{go}

14. This time, the plane's wing _____ the ground, so the plane could not fly.
    _{hit}

EXERCISE 14 Complete each statement with the simple past form of a verb in the box.

be	drive	fly	see	think
become✓	fall	put	take	write

1. Goddard _____*became*_____ interested in rockets when he was a child.

2. He _____ a professor of physics.

3. People _____ that space travel was impossible.

4. Goddard _____ his first rocket in a car and _____ to his aunt's farm.

5. The rocket _____ for a couple of seconds, and then it _____ to the ground.

6. Goddard never _____ space flight.

7. The *New York Times* _____ about their mistake 49 years later.

8. *Apollo 11* _____ the first men to the moon in 1969.

7.9 Negative Statements with the Simple Past

RULES	EXAMPLES
We use *didn't (did not)* + the base form of the verb for regular and irregular verbs. This is the same for all subjects.	**REGULAR VERBS**
	You **didn't look** at the sky. We **didn't travel** to North Carolina. She **didn't return** to New York.
	IRREGULAR VERBS
	She **didn't have** an accident. He **didn't go** to Paris. It **didn't fly** for a long time.

Note:

Remember: The negative simple past forms of the verb *be* are *wasn't (was not)* and *weren't (were not)*.

EXERCISE 15 Complete each statement with the negative form of the underlined verb.

1. The Wright brothers <u>dreamed</u> about flying. They _____*didn't dream*_____ about rockets.

2. They <u>sold</u> bicycles. They _____ cars.

3. Their 1903 airplane <u>had</u> a pilot. It _____ wheels.

4. The Wright brothers <u>wanted</u> to show their airplane to the U.S. government. The government

   _____ to see it at first.

5. The Wright brothers <u>built</u> the first airplane. They _____ the first rocket.

6. Goddard <u>believed</u> in space flight. Other people _____ in space flight at that time.

7. Goddard <u>thought</u> his ideas were important. Other people _____ his ideas were

   important at first.

8. In 1920, a newspaper <u>wrote</u> that he was foolish. The newspaper _____ about the

   possibility of rocket travel.

9. In 1926, his rocket <u>flew</u>. Before that time, his rockets _____ .

10. The first rocket <u>stayed</u> in the air for 2.5 seconds. It _____ in the air for a long time.

11. Goddard <u>saw</u> his rockets fly. He _____ rockets go to the moon.

12. A rocket <u>went</u> to the moon in 1969. A rocket _____ to the moon during

    Goddard's lifetime.

13. Earhart <u>was</u> with someone when she disappeared. She _____ alone.

Sally Ride

Read the conversation between two friends. Pay special attention to the words in bold. 🎧 7.6

A: I watched an interesting documentary[1] about Sally Ride last night. She was amazing.

B: **Who was** Sally Ride?

A: She was the first female American astronaut to travel into outer space.

B: Is she alive now?

A: No. She was born in 1951 and died in 2012.

B: **Did** she always **want** to be an astronaut?

A: Actually, no, she **didn't**. As a child, she wanted to be a professional[2] tennis player.

B: **What changed** her mind?

A: She became very interested in math and science in college, at Stanford University. After getting her bachelor's degree in physics[3], she went on to get her Ph.D. in physics as well.

B: **How did** she **become** an astronaut?

A: That's an amazing story. In 1977 NASA put an ad in a newspaper. They wanted people to apply to become astronauts.

B: **How many** people **applied**?

A: Over 8,000.

B: **How many did** NASA **hire**?

---

[1] documentary: a movie or television program that tells the facts about actual people and events
[2] professional: paid to participate in a sport or activity
[3] physics: a science that focuses on matter and energy
[4] inducted: officially made a member of a group

A: Only 25. And Ride was one of them!

B: **When did** she **go** into space?

A: She went into space on June 18, 1983. She was a crew member on the Space Shuttle *Challenger*.

B: **How long did** she **stay** in space?

A: The flight lasted 147 hours.

B: **Did** she ever **go** back into space?

A: Yes, she **did**. She went into space on the *Challenger* for a second time in 1984.

B: **What did** she **do** after that?

A: After that, Dr. Ride became director of the Office of Exploration at NASA. She left NASA in 1987.

B: **What happened** next in her life?

A: She became a professor at the University of California. She also started a company called Sally Ride Science. It encouraged students—especially girls—to study math, science, and engineering.

B: **Did** she **get** any honors for her work?

A: Yes, she **did**! She was inducted[4] into the Astronaut Hall of Fame and the National Women's Hall of Fame. The post office created a Sally Ride stamp in 2018. There's even a spot on the moon named after her!

COMPREHENSION Based on the reading, write T for *true* or F for *false*.

1. _____ When she was a child, Sally Ride already wanted to be an astronaut.

2. _____ Sally Ride loved math and science classes.

3. _____ Sally Ride went into space twice.

THINK ABOUT IT Discuss the questions with a partner or in a small group.

1. What other "first women" do you know about?

2. What professions still have mostly men? What do you think is the reason for this?

7.10 Questions with the Simple Past

YES/NO QUESTIONS AND SHORT ANSWERS

DID	SUBJECT	BASE FORM		SHORT ANSWER
Did	I you he she it we they	fly	into space?	Yes, you **did**. No, I **didn't**. Yes, he **did**. No, she **didn't**. Yes, it **did**. No, we **didn't**. Yes, they **did**.

continued

WH- QUESTIONS

WH- WORD	*DID/DIDN'T*	SUBJECT	BASE FORM
Where When Why How	**did**	I you he she	**fly?**
Why	**didn't**	it we they	

SUBJECT *WH-* QUESTIONS

WH- WORD	VERB	
Who	**worked**	for Sally Ride?
How many people	**applied**	to be astronauts?
What	**happened**	to Earhart?

STATEMENTS, *YES/NO* QUESTIONS, SHORT ANSWERS, AND *WH-* QUESTIONS

STATEMENT	*YES/NO* QUESTION AND SHORT ANSWER	*WH-* QUESTION
Sally Ride **went** into space in 1983.	**Did** she **go** into space in 1994? Yes, she **did.**	**How many** times **did** she **go** into space?
She **directed** a company.	**Did** she **direct** NASA? No, she **didn't.**	**What** company **did** she **direct?**
The post office **made** a stamp for her.	**Did** the government **make** a movie about her? No, it **didn't.**	**Who made** a stamp for her?

Note:

Compare questions with *be* to other simple past questions.

> ***Was** she a good astronaut?*   ***Did** she **win** awards?*
>
> ***When was** she **born?***   ***When did** she **die?***

GRAMMAR IN USE

Short questions are common in speaking, especially to express surprise or doubt. In short questions, we use just a subject pronoun + auxiliary verb in sentence order. Use rising intonation at the end of short questions.

> A: *She was an astronaut.*   A: *She taught physics.*
>
> B: **She was?**   B: **She did?**

EXERCISE 16 Read each statement. Then complete the *yes/no* questions and short answers in the simple past. Use pronouns in your questions and answers.

1. **A:** Sally Ride wanted to be a professional tennis player.

   B: _____ _Did she want_ _____ to be an astronaut as a child?

   A: No, ___ _she didn't_ ___.

2. A: Ride worked as an astronaut for many years.

   B: _____ as a director of a company, too?

   A: Yes, _____ .

3. A: She directed a company called Sally Ride Science.

   B: _____ the U.S. space agency, NASA?

   A: No, _____ .

4. A: As an astronaut, Ride took trips into space.

   B: _____ many trips into space?

   A: No, _____ . She took only two trips.

5. A: Ride stayed in space for a long time.

   B: _____ in space for more than 100 hours?

   A: Yes, _____ .

6. A: After her career as an astronaut, Ride taught at the University of California.

   B: _____ math?

   A: No, _____ . She taught physics.

7. A: Ride received many honors for her work.

   B: _____ the Nobel Prize?

   A: No, _____ .

EXERCISE 17 Read each statement. Use the word(s) given to write a *yes/no* question and short answer in the simple past.

1. The Wright brothers had a dream.

   (Goddard) _Did Goddard have a dream?_

   (yes) _Yes, he did._

2. Wilbur Wright died in 1912.

   (in an airplane crash) _____

   (no) _____

3. The Wright brothers built an airplane.

   (Goddard) _____

   (no) _____

continued

4. Earhart loved to fly.

   (Lindbergh) _____

   (yes) _____

5. Lindbergh crossed the ocean.

   (Earhart) _____

   (yes) _____

6. Lindbergh worked for the U.S. Mail Service.

   (Earhart) _____

   (no) _____

7. Lindbergh was famous.

   (Earhart) _____

   (yes) _____

8. Lindbergh was born in the 20th century.

   (Earhart) _____

   (no) _____

9. People didn't believe the Wright brothers at first.

   people believe (Goddard) _____

   (no) _____

EXERCISE 18 Complete each question using the simple past. Use pronouns as needed.

1. **A:** Sally Ride was born in Los Angeles.

   B: When _____?

   A: In 1951.

2. **A:** Ride worked for NASA starting in 1978.

   B: How long _____ for NASA?

   A: For nine years.

3. **A:** She flew her first mission in 1983.

   B: When _____ her second mission?

   A: In 1984.

4. **A:** She didn't take a third flight.

   B: Why _____ a third flight?

   A: There was a terrible accident that stopped all space flights.

5. **A:** She served on a committee to find out what happened in the terrible accident.

   B: _____ on the committee?

   A: No, no other women served on the committee.

6. **A:** She told someone her idea about the cause of the accident.

   B: Who _____?

   A: She told her boss.

7. **A:** After she left NASA, Ride taught at a university.

   B: Where _____?

   A: She taught at the University of California at San Diego.

8. **A:** Ride also appeared in a television program called *Touched by an Angel*.

   B: Really? When _____ on television?

   A: In 1999.

9. **A:** In 2001, she started a company that designed educational programs.

   B: What kind of programs _____?

   A: It designed programs for elementary and middle school students.

10. **A:** Ride died in 2012.

    B: How _____?

    A: She died of cancer.

EXERCISE 19 Complete each question using the simple past.

1. **A:** What kind of engine ___did the first airplane have___?

    B: The first airplane had a gasoline engine.

2. **A:** Where _____ their plane?

    B: The Wright brothers built their plane in their bicycle shop.

3. **A:** Why _____ the first flight in 1903?

    B: Newspapers didn't report it because they didn't believe it.

4. **A:** Why _____ in the Wright brothers' airplane?

    B: The U.S. government wasn't interested because they didn't believe the Wright brothers.

5. **A:** Where _____?

    B: Lindbergh worked at the U.S. Mail Service.

6. **A:** Why _____ the ocean?

    B: He crossed the ocean to win prize money.

7. **A:** How much money _____?

    B: He won $25,000.

8. **A:** How old _____ when he crossed the ocean?

    B: Lindbergh was 25 years old when he crossed the ocean.

9. **A:** Where _____?

    B: Earhart was born in Kansas.

10. **A:** Where _____?

    B: Her plane disappeared in the Pacific Ocean.

11. **A:** What _____ to her plane?

    B: Nobody knows what happened to her plane.

12. **A:** Who _____ with Earhart?

    B: A navigator flew with Earhart.

13. **A:** When _____ on the moon?

    B: The first man walked on the moon in 1969.

ABOUT YOU Write questions in the simple past using the words given. Then find a partner and ask and answer your questions.

1. when/you/fly in a plane for the first time

   When did you fly in a plane for the first time?

2. who/be/with you

   _____

3. what/be/your first impression of flying

   _____

4. what/be/your longest trip

   _____

5. you/like the articles about aviation in this unit

   _____

6. which article/you/like the best

   _____

7. you/know about Robert Goddard before you read the story

   _____

8. you/know anything about Amelia Earhart before you read the story

   _____

9. you/see the first moon landing

   _____

FUN WITH GRAMMAR

Race to write. Your teacher will describe an important life event. As a class, ask questions to get more information about what happened, such as:

> *Who was with you? Why was that important? How did you feel?*

Then work with a partner to write as many details about the event as you can remember in two minutes. The team with the most accurate information wins.

SUMMARY OF UNIT 7

The Simple Past of *Be*

	WAS	WERE
AFFIRMATIVE STATEMENT	He **was** in Paris.	They **were** in Paris.
NEGATIVE STATEMENT	He **wasn't** in London.	They **weren't** in London.
YES/NO QUESTION	**Was** he in Rome?	**Were** they in Rome?
SHORT ANSWER	No, he **wasn't**.	Yes, they **were**.
WH- QUESTION	**When was** he in Paris?	**When were** they in Paris?
NEGATIVE WH- QUESTION	**Why wasn't** he in Rome?	**Why weren't** they in Rome?
SUBJECT WH- QUESTION	**Who was** in London?	**How many** people **were** in Paris?

The Simple Past of Other Verbs

	REGULAR VERB	IRREGULAR VERB
AFFIRMATIVE STATEMENT	They **worked** in a bike shop.	You **flew** to Florida.
NEGATIVE STATEMENT	They **didn't work** in a factory.	You **didn't fly** to New York.
YES/NO QUESTION	**Did** they **work** in Ohio?	**Did** you **fly** to Miami?
SHORT ANSWER	Yes, they **did**.	No, I **didn't**.
WH- QUESTION	**Where did** they **work**?	**Where did** you **fly**?
NEGATIVE WH- QUESTION	**Why didn't** they **work** in a factory?	**Why didn't** you **fly** to Miami?
SUBJECT WH- QUESTION	**Who worked** in a factory?	**How many** people **flew** to Miami?

Pronunciation of the Simple Past of Regular Verbs

RULES	EXAMPLES
We pronounce -*ed* as /t/ after voiceless sounds.	jumped, cooked, coughed, kissed, washed, watched
We pronounce -*ed* as /d/ after voiced sounds.	rubbed, dragged, loved, bathed, used, massaged, charged, named, learned, banged, called, cared, freed, tied
We pronounce -*ed* as /əd/ after /t/ or /d/ sounds.	waited, hated, added, decided

Uses of the Simple Past

USE	EXAMPLES
Single, short past actions	Lindbergh **flew** across the Atlantic Ocean.
Longer past actions	Lindbergh **worked** for the U.S. Mail Service.
Repeated past actions	Goddard **borrowed** books on physical sciences from the library.

REVIEW

Choose the correct word(s) to complete the conversation between two students.

A: You (*didn't come*/*wasn't come*/*didn't came*) to class last week. I (*was*/*were*/*did*) worried about you.
1.   2.

B: I (*didn't*/*wasn't*/*weren't*) in town.
3.

A: Where (*you go*/*was you go*/*did you go*)?
4.

B: I (*went*/*did go*/*was go*) to Washington, DC.
5.

A: (*Did you go*/*You did go*/*Did you went*) alone?
6.

B: No, I (*didn't*/*wasn't*/*not*). One of my brothers went with me.
7.

A: Which brother (*went*/*did go*/*did went*) with you?
8.

B: My brother Jackson.

A: (*You did drive*/*Did you drove*/*Did you drive*) there?
9.

B: No, we (*weren't*/*didn't*/*don't*). We (*flied*/*flew*/*fly*).
10.   11.

A: Washington isn't very far from here. Why (*you didn't drive*/*didn't you drive*/*didn't you drove*)?
12.

B: We (*finded*/*found*/*were find*) cheap airline tickets. Anyway, we (*didn't want*/*didn't wanted*/*weren't want*) to
13.   14.

have a car in Washington. Parking is expensive, and the streets are confusing. The subway system is very good.

We (*take*/*took*/*taked*) the subway everywhere.
15.

A: Where (*you stayed*/*did you stayed*/*did you stay*)?
16.

B: We (*stayed*/*staied*/*stayyed*) in a hotel.
17.

A: What (*did you do*/*did you did*/*you did*) in Washington?
18.

B: We (*visit*/*visitted*/*visited*) the government buildings, of course. But I (*did*/*was*/*were*) more interested in
19.   20.

the museums. I especially (*was loved*/*loved*/*did love*) the Air and Space Museum. We (*see*/*seen*/*saw*) the
21.   22.

Wright brothers' first airplane—the real one!

A: There (*was*/*had*/*were*) a lot of progress in flight in the 20th century.
23.

B: Yes. The first flight was in 1903. Only 66 years later, astronauts (*were*/*was*/*did*) on the moon.
24.

FROM GRAMMAR TO WRITING

PART 1 Editing Advice

1. Use the base form, not the past form, after *to*.

                    take
   I wanted to ~~took~~ flying lessons.

2. Use the base form after *did* or *didn't*.

                             finish
   Orville Wright didn't ~~finished~~ high school.

                    find
   Did they ~~found~~ Earhart's plane?

3. Use correct question formation.

                did Goddard invent
   When ~~Goddard invented~~ the rocket?

4. Use *be* with *born*. Don't add *-ed* to *born*. Don't use *be* with *died*.

                   was born
   Wilbur Wright ~~borned~~ in 1867. He ~~was~~ died in 1912.

5. Use the correct past form.

               built   was
   Goddard ~~builded~~ rockets. He ~~were~~ interested in engineering.

6. Use *be* with age.

                             was
   Sally Ride joined NASA when she ~~had~~ 27 years old.

7. Don't confuse *was* and *were*.

              were
   Where ~~was~~ you yesterday?

8. Don't use *did* in a subject *wh-* question.

              happened
   What ~~did happen~~ to Amelia Earhart?

PART 2 Editing Practice

Some of the shaded words and phrases have mistakes. Find the mistakes and correct them. If the shaded words are correct, write *C*.

                 had   C

A: Last week, we ~~have~~ an interesting homework assignment. We had to write about a famous person.
                    1.   **2.**

B: Who you wrote about?
          3.

A: I writed about Yuri Gagarin.
       4.

B: Who's that?

A: He was the first person in space.
       5.

B: Was he an American?
     6.

A: No, he didn't. He was Russian.

_{7.}   _{8.}

B: When he went into space?

          _{9.}

A: In 1961.

B: Did he went alone?

      _{10.}

A: Yes. But he wasn't the first living thing in space. There was dogs, chimpanzees, and even turtles

          _{11.}   _{12.}

in space before him.

B: Is Gagarin still alive?

A: No. He was died in 1968.

          _{13.}

B: When did he born?

          _{14.}

A: He borned in 1934. He had only 34 years old when he died in 1968. He didn't saw the moon

      _{15.}   _{16.}   _{17.}   _{18.}

landing. That was happened in 1969.

              _{19.}

B: How did Gagarin died? What was happened?

      _{20.}   _{21.}   _{22.}

A: He were in a plane crash.

      _{23.}

B: That's so sad.

A: Yes, it is.

WRITING TIP

When you write about a person's life, you generally begin with when they were born. Then you explain the major events of his or her life. If the person is not alive, you can conclude with when the person died.

Robert Henry Lawrence, Jr., was born on October 2, 1935. He was from Chicago, Illinois. Lawrence became the first African American astronaut in June 1967. He did not go into space though. Sadly, he died on December 8, 1967, in a plane crash.

PART 3 Write

Read the prompts. Choose one and write one paragraph about it.

1. Use the information from Part 2 to write a paragraph about Yuri Gagarin.
2. Choose another person from aviation or space exploration. Write a paragraph about what this person did.

PART 4 Edit

Reread the Summary of Unit 7 and the editing advice. Edit your writing from Part 3.

SHOPPING

Customers at a mall in Moscow, Russia

If you are not content today, there is nothing you can buy tomorrow to change that.

JOSHUA BECKER

A pop-up store is a temporary retail space, like this "igloo" in New York City. It attracts customers with new or limited-availability items.

SHOPPING In the Digital Age

Read the following article. Pay special attention to the words in bold. 🎧 8.1

Do you like **to shop** online? Or do you prefer **to go** into a store, **look** at a product, and **talk** to a salesperson? Maybe you like **to do** both. Smart shoppers know how **to use** different methods **to get** the best price. In order **to make** money, businesses need **to understand** the habits of today's shoppers.

One common strategy[1] is "showrooming." This means that customers go into a store, look at the product, talk to a salesperson, and then use their smartphones **to find** a better price. "Reverse showrooming" is another strategy: customers first go online **to do** research. It's easy **to compare** prices and then go into a store **to buy** the product that they found online. One thing is certain: shoppers are using many strategies **to get** the best price.

The number of online shoppers is rising, but not as fast as retailers[2] first thought. People still like **to go** into stores. Teens especially prefer **to shop** at the mall. Shopping for them is not about finding the best price; it's a social experience.

In order **to keep** customers, store managers need **to train** salespeople. In-store shoppers want salespeople **to give** them a lot of attention, **be** polite, and **know** the products well.

What products do shoppers like **to buy** online? The number one online purchase[3] is clothing. Customers often try on clothing in the store **to find** the right size and style. Then they find the cheapest price online.

Online shopping doesn't work for every product. People prefer **to shop** for food in a store. If you're buying a new car, it's important **to research** prices online, but it's still a good idea **to drive** the car. For some things, you still need **to go** into the store—for now.

---

[1] strategy: a plan to achieve a goal
[2] retailer: a company or store that sells products to the public
[3] a purchase: something you buy

COMPREHENSION Based on the reading, write T for *true* or F for *false*.

1. _____ Online shopping is growing faster than expected.

2. _____ Showrooming begins in a store and then continues online.

3. _____ For teens, shopping is often a social experience.

THINK ABOUT IT Discuss the questions with a partner or in a small group.

1. Where do you do most of your shopping: online or in stores? Explain.

2. Do you think in the future there will be no more stores? Why or why not?

8.1 Infinitives—Overview

An infinitive is *to* + the base form of a verb.

EXAMPLES	EXPLANATION
Do you **like to shop** online?	We use an infinitive after certain verbs.
It's **important to compare** prices.	We use an infinitive after certain expressions beginning with *it*.
Sales people are **ready to help** you.	We use an infinitive after certain adjectives.
Shoppers read reviews **to find** the best product.	We use an infinitive to show purpose.

Notes:

1. When we connect two or more infinitives in a list, we usually omit *to* on the second, third, etc., infinitive.

   You need **to go** into the mattress store, **lie** on the bed, and **see** how it feels.

2. An infinitive does not change form.

   He needs **to buy** a new car. (NOT: He needs to buys)

   He tried **to sell** his old car. (NOT: He tried to sold)

EXERCISE 1 Listen to the report. Then write T for *true*, F for *false*, or NS for *not stated*. 🎧 8.2

1. _____ You can get free samples of products at some stores.

2. _____ You must tip a salesperson who carries your purchases.

3. _____ Free samples are a better business strategy than special offers.

EXERCISE 2 Listen again. Fill in the blanks with the words you hear. 🎧 8.2

Businesses use several strategies _____*to get*_____ customers. One strategy is giving samples.
                                          1.

Shoppers like _____ a new product before buying it. Stores want you _____
                    2.   3.

the product, so they give you a sample.

Many stores have special offers each week. They know that if you are already in the store for the sale

item, it's convenient for you _____ other items there, too.
                                      4.

Another way to get a customer's attention is with good service. A salesperson may ask you, "Do you

want me _____ this to your car for you?" There's no extra charge for this service. It isn't
              5.

necessary _____ this person for the service.
                6.

There is so much competition between businesses. They need _____ all kinds of
                                                                          7.

strategies _____ our attention and encourage us _____ at their store.
                8.   9.

8.2 Verbs + Infinitives

EXAMPLES	EXPLANATION
I **need to buy** a new TV. I **want to get** a good price.	An infinitive can follow certain verbs.

We can use an infinitive after these verbs*:

begin	forget	love	promise
continue	hope	need	start
decide	know how	plan	try
expect	like	prefer	want

Pronunciation Notes:

1. In informal speech, we pronounce *want to* as /wɑnə/.
2. *To* can be pronounced differently depending on what word it follows.

> *I plan to buy a new smartphone.* (/tə/)
>
> *Try to get the best price.* (/də/)

*See Appendix I for more verbs followed by infinitives.

EXERCISE 3 Fill in the blanks with the infinitive form of the verbs from the box.

be	buy ✓	compare	get	read	shop	spend	wait

1. I want _____ to buy _____ a new TV.

2. I decided _____ about $500.

3. I need _____ prices online before going to the stores.

4. I want _____ the best price.

5. I like _____ about products before I decide.

6. I know how _____ a smart shopper.

7. I don't like _____ on Saturdays because the stores are crowded.

8. I prefer to shop in a store. I don't like _____ to get a product after I buy it.

ABOUT YOU Find a partner. Ask and answer *yes/no* questions using the words given. Use infinitives.

1. like/shop

   A: *Do you like to shop?*

   B: *Yes, I do.* OR *No, I don't.*

2. try/compare prices

3. plan/buy something new soon

4. prefer/shop alone

5. like/shop online

6. know how/use shopping apps

ABOUT YOU Find a partner. Ask and answer the questions.

1. When do you like to shop?

    A: *When do you like to shop?*

    B: *I like to shop on the weekend.*

2. What big item do you plan to buy soon?

3. Do you prefer to pay with a credit card, a debit card, or cash?

4. Where do you like to shop?

5. What do you need to know before making a big purchase?

8.3 *Be* + Adjective + Infinitive

EXAMPLES					EXPLANATION
Subject	*Be*	**Adjective**	**Infinitive**		We often use an infinitive after certain adjectives.
I	am	**ready**	**to talk**	to a salesperson.	
She	is	**happy**	**to help**	you.	

We can use an infinitive after these adjectives*:

afraid	happy	pleased	proud	sad
glad	lucky	prepared	ready	

*See Appendix I for more adjectives followed by infinitives.

EXERCISE 4 Fill in the blanks with the infinitive form of the verbs from the box.

buy ✓	do	help	make	use
bother	have	go	spend	

A: I need _____to buy_____ a new car. I'm not ready _____ a decision. I don't know what I
             1.   **2.**

  need _____ first. I'm afraid _____ a lot of money and maybe get a bad car.
         3.   **4.**

B: I can help you.

A: I don't want _____ you. I know you're very busy.
                          5.

B: I'm happy _____ you. There are websites that give information about new and used cars.
                      6.

  Let's look at my tablet. This site is free. Here's another good site, but it's not free.

A: Oh.

B: Don't worry. You can use this service for free at the library.

continued

A: Great. It's convenient for me _____ to the library. How can I compare cars

7.

on one of these sites?

B: It's easy _____ these sites. If you have a problem, ask the librarian for help.

8.

A: Thanks for all your advice. I'm lucky _____ you as a friend.

9.

8.4 *It* + *Be* + Adjective + (Noun +) Infinitive

EXAMPLES					EXPLANATION
It	*Be* (+ *Not*)	Adjective (+ Noun)	Infinitive		
It	is	**convenient**	**to use**	a shopping app.	We often use an infinitive after an expression with *it*.
It	isn't	**a good idea**	**to buy**	a bed online.	
It's easy **for me to use** a shopping app. It's hard **for my grandfather to shop** online.					We can add *for* + a person (noun or object pronoun) before the infinitive.

These are some common adjectives used in an expression with *it*:

convenient	difficult	expensive	hard	impossible	possible
dangerous	easy	fun	important	necessary	practical

ABOUT YOU Complete each statement about shopping experiences. Use *for* + a person, if you like. Then discuss your answers with a partner.

1. It's necessary _____ *for me to try on clothes before I buy them* _____ .

2. It's important _____ .

3. It's not convenient _____ .

4. It's convenient _____ .

5. It's impossible _____ .

6. It's difficult _____ .

7. It's not expensive _____ .

8. It isn't a good idea _____ .

8.5 Verb + Object + Infinitive

EXAMPLES					EXPLANATION
Subject	**Verb**	**Object**	**Infinitive**		
We	expect	the clerk	to know	about the product.	After *like, want, need, ask, expect,*
I	asked	her	to give	me information.	and *encourage,* we can use a noun
You	want	the employees	to be	polite.	or an object pronoun (*me, you,*
She	needs	them	to answer	her questions.	*him, her, it, us, them*) + an infinitive.

EXERCISE 5 Choose the correct word(s) to complete each conversation.

CONVERSATION 1: (between a salesman and a shopper)

A: Do you want (*me*/I) (*to help/help*) you find something?
          1.   2.

B: Yes. We could use your help. Our daughter asked (*we buy/us to buy*) her a new cell phone. We don't
                                                          3.

  know which plan to choose.

A: How much does she talk on the phone?

B: She never stops talking on the phone. I want (*her to use/that she use*) it just for important calls, but she
                                                4.

  chats and texts with her friends all the time.

A: Here's a plan I want (*you to consider/that you consider*). It has unlimited calls and texts.
                            5.

B: You don't understand. We want (*her/she*) to use the phone less, not more.
                                6.

CONVERSATION 2: (between two friends)

A: I'm going to buy a tablet on Saturday. I need (*that you/you to*) come with me.
                                            1.

B: Why? How do you want (*that I/me to*) help you?
                            2.

A: You just bought a new tablet, so you can give me advice.

CONVERSATION 3: (between a husband and wife at the supermarket)

A: Oh, look. There's free food over there. Do you want (*me to get/I get*) you a little hotdog?
                                                        1.

B: No. They just encourage (*us/we*) to spend our money on things we don't need.
                              2.

CONVERSATION 4: (between a supermarket clerk and a customer)

A: You have a lot of bags. Do you want (*me/I*) (*to help/helping*) you take them to your car?
                                      1.   2.

B: Thanks. Do I need (*pay/to pay*) for this service?
                        3.

A: No, of course not. We're happy (*to help/help*) our customers.
                                4.

EXERCISE 6 Complete the conversation between two brothers. Fill in the blanks with the first verb given, an object pronoun, and then the second verb given.

A: Mom and Dad say I spend too much money. They _____*expect me to save*_____ my money
1. expect/save

for the future. I _____ me alone.
2. want/leave

B: You do? I thought you _____ you a car.
3. wanted/buy

A: Well, I do. You know how much I hate to take the bus. I _____ to them
4. want/talk

for me. Tell them I need a car.

B: I'm not going to do that. They're trying to _____ more responsible.
5. encourage/be

A: I *am* responsible.

B: No, you're not. Remember when you told Mom and Dad you wanted a new tablet? You

_____ one for you. There was nothing wrong with your old one.
6. expected/buy

And remember when you lost your cell phone? You told Dad because you

_____ you a new one.
7. wanted/buy

A: Well, I'm still in school, and I don't have much money.

B: Mom and Dad _____ and start to take responsibility for yourself.
8. expect/graduate

You buy too much stuff.

A: No, I don't. By the way, did I tell you I broke the screen on my cell phone?

8.6 Infinitives to Show Purpose

EXAMPLES	EXPLANATION
You need to pay **in order to use** this website. He used a shopping app **to find** a better price.	We can use infinitives to show purpose. To make it very clear we are expressing purpose, we sometimes add *in order*.
In order to save money, I use coupons. **To compare prices,** I use the Internet.	The infinitive phrase can come at the beginning of a sentence. If so, we use a comma after the infinitive phrase.

> **GRAMMAR IN USE**
>
> To express purpose, *in order to* is more formal than *to*. We use it more in writing than in speaking. In speaking, we usually use *to*.
>
> *I'm going to the store **to get** some bread.*
>
> *He got a second job **to pay** the bills.*

EXERCISE 7 Complete the conversation between two friends. Fill in the blanks with the infinitive form of the verbs from the box.

change	compare	give	learn	look for	print	take ✓

A: Do you want to see my new camera?

B: Sure. Does it take good pictures?

A: Absolutely. I use this camera _____to take_____ most of my pictures.
          1.

B: I just use my smartphone.

A: This camera takes better pictures than a smartphone.

B: Was it expensive?

A: Not really. I went online _____ prices. Then I went to several stores in the city
                                  2.

_____ the best price.
3.

B: Do you ever make prints of your pictures?

A: Sometimes. I buy high-quality paper _____ photos for my album. Sometimes I make little
                                            4.

books of my vacations.

B: Is it hard to use the camera?

A: At first I had to read the manual carefully _____ how to take good pictures. But now it's
                                                  5.

easy. I'll take a picture of you. Smile.

B: Let me see it. My eyes are closed in the picture. Will you take another picture of me?

A: OK. This one's better.

B: I don't like the background. It's too dark.

A: I can use a photo-editing program _____ the color.
                                         6.

B: Can you use the program _____ me a brighter smile?
                               7.

EXERCISE 8 Fill in the blanks to make true statements. Then find a partner and discuss your answers.

1. To take a good selfie, _you need good lighting_____.

2. To get a good price, _____.

3. In order to buy a car, _____.

Are Free Trials Really FREE?

Read the following article. Pay special attention to the words in bold. 🎧 8.3

You're surfing the Internet[1] and see an offer for a free trial for a product or service. It **might be** an offer for free magazines. Or it **may be** a subscription[2] to a music app. You **may** already **have** a free music app, but you **have to listen** to a lot of ads. With a paid service, you **don't have to listen** to ads. You **can** even **download** music and **listen** to it offline.

Should you **accept** the offer? If it's free, what **can** you **lose**? Try it. You **might like** it. Right? Well, it **might not be** such a good deal after all. Why not?

First, you **have to give** the company your email address. The company **might sell** your email address to other companies. You **may start** to get a lot of unwanted ads.

Second, it's easy to start a free trial, but it's hard to cancel[3] the service when the trial period is over. You call the phone number on the website (if you **can find** it!), and someone tells you, "You **can't cancel** by phone. You **have to cancel** online."

Why **must** they **make** it so hard to cancel? Think about it—why **should** they **make** it easy? Your free trial is now a charge to your credit card. You **might not notice** the charge until you get your next bill. Before you sign up for a free trial, you **should read** the cancellation policy[4]. It **might be** in very small writing. You **should mark** your calendar to cancel before the trial period ends.

Here's the best advice: if you don't need the service or product, don't take it just because it's free. Free trials **can** sometimes **cost** you a lot of money.

---

[1] to surf the Internet: to search casually for information online
[2] subscription: an agreement to buy a product or service for a certain amount of time
[3] to cancel: to stop something
[4] cancellation policy: the rules about canceling something

COMPREHENSION Based on the reading, write T for *true* or F for *false*.

1. _____ A paid subscription to a music app gives you service without ads.

2. _____ It is sometimes hard for you to cancel a free trial.

3. _____ Online companies can make money when they have your email address.

THINK ABOUT IT Discuss the questions with a partner or in a small group.

1. Did you ever accept a free trial? If yes, describe your experience. If not, why not?

2. Do you think free trials are a good business strategy? Explain.

8.7 Modals and Phrasal Modals—Overview

EXAMPLES	EXPLANATION
You **can start** a free trial easily. You **should read** the cancellation policy.	The base form of the verb follows a modal. Don't use an infinitive after a modal.
The free trial **might not** be a good idea. You **cannot** cancel this subscription online.	To form the negative, we put *not* after the modal. We write the negative of *can* as one word: *cannot*.
I **can't** find the phone number on the website. You **shouldn't** use a debit card for an online purchase.	We can form a contraction for *cannot* (*can't*), *should not* (*shouldn't*), *must not* (*mustn't*), and *would not* (*wouldn't*). There is no contraction for *may not* and *might not*.

Note:

Notice these patterns with a modal:

AFFIRMATIVE STATEMENT:	*We **can cancel** online.*
NEGATIVE STATEMENT:	*We **can't cancel** by phone.*
YES/NO QUESTION:	***Can** we **cancel** by email?*
SHORT ANSWER:	*No, you **can't**.*
WH- QUESTION:	*How **can** we **cancel**?*
NEGATIVE WH- QUESTION:	*Why **can't** we **cancel** by phone?*
SUBJECT WH- QUESTION:	***Who can cancel** this?*

Phrasal modals also take the base form of a verb.

PHRASAL MODAL	EXAMPLES
have to be able to be allowed to	You **have to cancel** by Friday. I **am not able to understand** the cancellation policy. The company **is allowed to sell** your email address.

EXERCISE 9 Listen to the report. Then write T for *true*, F for *false*, or NS for *not stated*. 🎧 8.4

1. _____ You can't use a coupon on a sale item.

2. _____ Stores usually have a limit on the number of items you can buy at a special price.

3. _____ A rain check lets customers buy products at the sale price before the sale starts.

EXERCISE 10 Listen again. Fill in the blanks with the words you hear. 🎧 8.4

Manufacturers often send coupons to shoppers to encourage them to buy a new product. If you receive

a coupon for a new kind of toothpaste, you _____ want to try it. Coupons have an expiration
1.

date. You _____ pay attention to this date because you _____ use the coupon
2.   3.

after this date.

Stores have weekly specials, but there's usually a limit. You _____ buy more than the
4.

limit. If you see a sign that says, "3 for $5," you _____ buy three items to get the special
5.

price. You _____ buy just one or two.
6.

What _____ you do if a store has a special, but you _____ find the item on
7.   8.

the shelf? If the item is sold out, you _____ go to the customer service desk and ask for a
9.

"rain check." A rain check allows you to buy this item at the sale price even after the sale is over. A rain

check has an expiration date. You _____ use the rain check by this date.
10.

If you see a sign that says "rebate," this means that you _____ get money back
11.

from the manufacturer. You _____ mail the receipt to the manufacturer. Also, you
12.

_____ fill out a small form. It _____ take 6 to 8 weeks to get your money.
13.   14.

You _____ keep a copy of the receipt.
15.

8.8 *Can, Be Able To, Be Allowed To*

EXAMPLES	EXPLANATION
Can you **find** the phone number of this website? I'm **not able to find** the phone number.	We use *can* or *be able to* for ability.
The offer says "free trial." What **can** I **lose**? Free trials **can** sometimes **cost** money.	We use *can* for possibility.
Can I **download** music for free? **Are** we **allowed to sample** the food? The sign for this item says "Limit two." You **can't buy** more than that.	We use *can* or *be allowed to* for permission. The negative shows prohibition.

Pronunciation Notes:

1. We usually pronounce *can* as /kən/.

   *I **can** go tomorrow. (/kən/)*

2. We usually pronounce *can't* as /kænt/. The stress is stronger than in *can*. Sometimes it is hard to hear the *t* in *can't*. The vowel sound and the word stress help us hear the difference between *can* and *can't*.

   *I **can** go today. (/kən/)*

   *I **can't** go today. (/kænt/)*

3. In a short answer, we pronounce *can* as /kæn/ and *can't* as /kænt/.

   *Can you help me? Yes, I **can**. (/kæn/)*

   *Can I pay by check? No, you **can't**. (/kænt/)*

GRAMMAR IN USE

In informal and everyday speech, we use *can I* to ask permission.

   ***Can I** come in?*

In formal situations, we use *may I*.

   ***May I** come in?*

ABOUT YOU These statements are true for most U.S. supermarkets. Check (√) the ones that are true for supermarkets in your country. Then find a partner and discuss your answers.

1. _____ You can use coupons.

2. _____ You can sometimes buy two items for the price of one.

3. _____ You can get a rain check.

4. _____ You're allowed to pay with a check.

5. _____ You're allowed to return an item if you're not happy with it.

6. _____ Small children can sit in a shopping cart.

7. _____ If you have a small number of items, you can go to a special checkout lane.

8. _____ You can ask someone to help you take your bags to your car.

9. _____ You're sometimes able to get free samples.

EXERCISE 11 Complete the conversation between two friends. Fill in the blanks with the phrases from the box.

'm not able to finish	can give	can say
're not allowed to apply	can help ✓	can't wait

A: I need some help with this website.

B: I _____ can help _____ you. What's the problem?
                      1.

A: I _____ the registration for this free trial. It's for a magazine. It's a
                              2.

sports magazine, and I love sports.

B: I have a subscription to this magazine. I _____ you my magazine in about a week.
                                                            3.

A: I _____ a week. The sports news will be old.
                4.

B: OK. Let me see what we need to do. Oh, I see the problem. You _____
                                                                              5.

for this offer. It says that it's only for people over the age of 18. You're 17, right?

A: I _____ that I'm 18.
                6.

B: I don't think that's a good idea.

8.9 Should

We use *should* for advice.

EXAMPLES	EXPLANATION
You **should compare** prices before you buy.	*should* = It's a good idea.
You **shouldn't buy** things you don't need.	*shouldn't* = It's not a good idea.

ABOUT YOU If someone from another country is going to live in the United States, what advice would you give him or her about shopping? Work with a partner to write sentences of advice. Use *should*.

1. You should shop for summer clothes in July and August. Summer clothes are
   cheapest at that time.

2. _____

   _____

3. _____

   _____

EXERCISE 12 Complete the conversation between a husband and wife at the supermarket. Fill in the blanks with the phrases from the box.

shouldn't buy	should use	shouldn't eat	should look at	should take
should be	should we buy ✓	should come	should we pay	should bring

A: _____Should we buy_____ ice cream? It's on sale.
1.

B: It's a hot day. And we have to stop at the post office before we go home.

We _____ it today. It'll melt.
2.

A: How about candy for the kids? They always ask us for candy.

B: That's not a good idea. They _____ so much candy. Where's our shopping
3.

list? We _____ our list and not buy things we don't need. We
4.

_____ careful about how we spend our money.
5.

A: You're right. OK. Milk is on our list.

B: You _____ the expiration date. This milk carton has tomorrow's date. You
6.

_____ milk from the back row. It's usually fresher.
7.

A: Really?

B: You almost never come shopping with me. You _____ with me more often.
8.

You can learn to be a better shopper.

A: You're right. Look. That sign says, "Bring your own bags. Get 10¢ for each bag." Next time,

we _____ our own bags. You see? I'm learning.
9.

B: Great. _____ with a credit card or use cash?
10.

A: I've got enough cash. Let's use cash.

8.10 *Must* and *Have To*

We use *must* and *have to* for necessity.

EXAMPLES	EXPLANATION
You **must cancel** your free trial by Friday. To get a rebate, you **must send** the receipt.	*Must* has a very official, formal tone.
When you sign up for a free trial, you **have to use** your credit card or debit card.	*Have to* is less formal than *must*.

EXERCISE 13 Fill in the blanks with the phrases from the box.

has to go	must show	have to return ✓
must send	have to buy	have to use

1. Eggs are on sale for $2.19 a dozen, "Limit two." I have three cartons of eggs. I __have to return__

   one of the cartons.

2. I have a coupon for cereal. The expiration date is tomorrow. I _____ it by tomorrow,

   or I won't get the discount.

3. The coupon for cereal says "Buy 2, get 50¢ off." Do I _____ two in order to get the discount?

4. She has a rebate application. She _____ the receipt to the manufacturer.

5. He wants to pay by check. The cashier asks for his driver's license. He _____ his

   driver's license.

6. She has 26 items in her shopping cart. She can't go to a lane that says "10 items or fewer."

   She _____ to another lane.

8.11 *Not Have To* and *Must Not*

EXAMPLES	EXPLANATION
To get a rebate, you **must mail** in a receipt. To get a rebate, you **have to mail** in a receipt.	In affirmative statements, *have to* and *must* are very similar in meaning. *Must* is more formal.
Stores **must not sell** an item after the expiration date.	In negative statements, *must not* shows that something is prohibited.
I usually shop online. I **don't have to go** into a store.	*Don't have to* shows that something is not necessary.

Note:

Must not is very formal. Informally, we use *can't*.

> Stores **can't sell** an item after the expiration date.

EXERCISE 14 Fill in the blanks with the correct verbs from the box. You can use some verbs more than once.

buy	carry	go	pay	take	bring

1. If you sample a product, you don't have to _____*buy*_____ it. But if you decide to buy it, you will usually get a coupon.

2. If you have just a few items, you don't have to _____ a shopping cart. You can use a basket.

3. At some supermarkets, you don't have to _____ your bags home yourself. Someone from the supermarket will deliver them to your home.

4. I don't have to _____ to the store to get information on a product. I can get most information on my phone.

5. When you're leaving a supermarket, you don't have to _____ your bags to your car. A sales assistant can do it for you.

6. I don't have to _____ with cash. I can use my credit card.

7. I don't have to _____ into a store to buy electronics. But I have to shop in a store for certain items, like a car.

8.12 *May, Might,* and *Will*

EXAMPLES	EXPLANATION
A free trial **may cost** a lot of money. I have a coupon for a new toothpaste, so I **might try** it.	*May* and *might* have the same meaning. They show possibility for the future.
If you're a careful shopper, you **will save** money.	*Will* shows certainty about the future.

Note:
Compare the adverb *maybe* with *may* or *might* modals.

Maybe my friend **will buy** a new tablet.

My friend **may buy** a new tablet.

My friend **might buy** a new tablet.

EXERCISE 15 Fill in the blanks with the phrases from the box. More than one answer may be possible.

will get	might want ✓	will receive
might not be	may be	may try

1. Meg needs to go shopping. She's not sure what her kids want. They ___might want___ to try

   a new kind of cereal.

2. She's not sure if she should buy the small or the large size of cereal. The large size _____

   cheaper.

3. The store sold out of all the coffee that was on sale. The clerk said, "We _____

   more tomorrow."

4. The milk has an expiration date of June 27. Today is June 27. She's not going to buy the milk because

   it _____ good.

5. She's not sure what kind of toothpaste she should buy. She might buy the one she usually buys,

   or she _____ a new kind.

6. If she requests rebates through an app today, she _____ money back in 48 hours.

EXERCISE 16 Complete each statement. Write what *may* or *might* happen. Use *will* if you think the result
is certain. Find a partner and compare your answers.

1. If you shop online, _you might find a better price_____.

2. If you go into a store and talk to a salesperson, _____

   _____.

3. If you buy shoes online, _____

   _____.

4. If you try a free sample in a supermarket, _____

   _____.

5. If you bring your own bags to a supermarket, _____

   _____.

6. If you don't cancel a free trial on time, _____

   _____.

SHOPPING TIPS

Read the following article. Pay special attention to the words in bold. 🎧 8.5

Here are some shopping tips to help you make smart choices and save money:

1. If you have a favorite store, **search** online for store coupons. **Google** the name of the store and the word *coupon*. You can print the coupon or save it on your smartphone.

2. We often see sales such as "Buy one, get one free." **Ask** yourself, "Do I really need this item?" **Don't buy** something just because it's on sale.

3. **Ask** about the return policy. Can you return the item? If so, what is the time limit for a return?

4. If you receive a gift card, **use** it as soon as you can. Some gift cards have an expiration date.

5. **Shop** for groceries with a list. You'll save money if you use your list. **Don't shop** when you're hungry. Hungry shoppers often buy a lot of junk food[1].

6. If possible, **don't take** small children to a store where they can see candy or toys. Kids often say, "**Buy** me this; **buy** me that."

7. If you shop online, **ask** about the refund[2] policy.

8. If you pay with a credit card, **read** your bill as soon as you receive it. **Look** for charges you don't recognize.

9. **Look** for discounts. Teachers get discounts at some stores. College students and senior citizens often get discounts.

---

[1] junk food: food that is bad for you
[2] refund: money returned to the customer

COMPREHENSION Based on the reading, write T for *true* or F for *false*.

1. _____ You can find the coupons for some stores online.

2. _____ Some stores give discounts to students.

3. _____ Gift cards never expire.

THINK ABOUT IT Discuss the questions with a partner or in a small group.

1. How do you shop for groceries? Do you use a list? Do you compare prices?

2. What is one more piece of shopping advice?

8.13 Imperatives

EXAMPLES	EXPLANATION
Use a gift card right away. **Don't shop** for food when you're hungry.	The imperative is the base form of the verb. For a negative, we put *don't* before the verb. The full form, *do not*, is not common in conversation.
Search for *coupon* and the name of a store on the Internet. **Ask** about the refund policy. **Wait** in line! **Do** your best.	We use the imperative for: • instructions • suggestions • demands • encouragement

Notes:

1. We can put *always* or *never* before an imperative.

   Always take *a list with you.* ***Never shop*** *for groceries when you're hungry.*

2. The subject of an imperative is *you*, but we don't include *you* in the sentence.

GRAMMAR IN USE

We use the imperative in certain social expressions. These can be used when you are talking to one person or to more than one person.

Have *a nice day.*	***Be*** *careful.*
Take *care.*	***Have*** *fun.*
Stay *safe.*	***Sleep*** *well.*

EXERCISE 17 Fill in the blanks with the correct words from the box.

ask	don't buy	don't lose	take
compare ✓	don't forget	find	train

1. Before you buy an electronic device, _____ *compare* _____ prices online.

2. If you go to a store, _____ a salesperson who knows about the product.

3. _____ a lot of questions.

4. _____ a car without driving it first.

5. _____ your receipt. If you need to return an item, you may need your receipt.

6. Always _____ your own bags to a supermarket. It's good for the environment.

7. If you do a free trial, _____ to cancel before the end date.

8. If you are a store manager, _____ your salespeople well.

The Difficult Return

Read the following conversation between a customer service representative (A) and a customer (B) in a store. Pay special attention to the words in bold. 🎧 8.6

A: **Can** I help you?

B: **I'd like** to return a pair of shoes.

A: Of course.

B: Finally! I was here on Monday, but the customer service window was closed. Then I was here on Tuesday, but the line was too long, so I went home. And just now I waited in line for 20 minutes!

A: Oh, I'm so sorry. **Let's** take care of this right now.

B: Thank you!

A: Is there a problem with the shoes?

B: No, they're just too big.

A: **Could** I see your receipt, please?

B: Yes. Here it is.

A: Great. **Would** you **like** the refund on your credit card?

B: Yes, I would. Thanks.

A: **May** I have the shoes? I need to scan them.

B: Sure.

A: (The salesperson scans the shoes.) Oh.

B: Is there a problem?

A: I'm afraid there is. These are children's shoes.

B: Yes, they are. I bought them for my daughter. But they're too big for her.

A: I'm really sorry. But I can't handle refunds for children's shoes. They need to be returned to the children's department.

B: Are you serious[1]?

A: I am. I'm sorry. **Would** you **like** directions to the children's return desk?

B: No. I'm giving up on making this return. The shoes will fit my daughter eventually[2].

_____

[1] serious: not joking
[2] eventually: at some time in the future

COMPREHENSION Based on the conversation, write T for *true* or F for *false*.

1. _____ The customer wants to return a pair of shoes.

2. _____ The shoes were for the customer's husband.

3. _____ The customer returned the shoes and got a refund.

Discuss the questions with a partner or in a small group.

1. Did you ever return something you bought? Why? Describe your experience.

2. What do you think is a good reason for a store not to accept a returned item?

8.14 Modals and Other Expressions for Politeness

EXAMPLES	EXPLANATION
Would Can } you **cash** my check, please? Could	We use *would, can,* and *could* to make a request. We do not use the imperative, as in "Cash my check" to make requests. It is impolite.
May Could } I **use** your pen, please? Can	We use *may, could,* and *can* to ask for permission. We do not use the imperative as in, "Give me your pen" to ask for permission. It is impolite.
I **would like to cash** a check. **Would** you **like to use** my pen?	*Would like* has the same meaning as *want. Would like* is more polite than *want.* It is followed by the infinitive form of a verb.
I**'d like to cash** a check. He**'d like to buy** stamps.	The contraction with *would* after a pronoun is *'d.*
Why don't you fill out another form?	We use *Why don't you . . . ?* to offer a suggestion.
Why don't we walk to the supermarket? **Let's walk** to the supermarket. **Let's not take** the car.	We use *Why don't we . . . ?* or *Let's (not)* to make a suggestion that includes the speaker.

GRAMMAR IN USE

People in customer service use these expressions to offer help:

May I help you?

Can I help you?

Typical answers are:

Yes, I'd like . . . /Sure.

No, I'm fine./No, I'm just looking.

EXERCISE 18 Complete the conversation between a salesperson (A) and a customer (B) in an electronics store. Choose the correct words. If both answers are correct, circle both choices.

A: (May I/Would I) help you?
        1.

B: Yes. (*I'd want/I'd like*) to buy a new computer. (*May you/Could you*) show me some under $600?
              2.   3.

A: (*Would you like/Do you like*) to see the laptops or the desktops?
              4.

B: (*Can you/Would you*) show me the laptops, please?
5.

A: (*Let's/Why don't we*) go to the next aisle. Our laptops are over there. How do you plan to use
6.

your computer?

B: I like to play games and watch movies.

A: This computer is great for games.

B: (*Could you/May you*) tell me the price?
7.

A: We have a great deal on this one. It's $599.99. If you buy it this week, you can get a $100 rebate from the

manufacturer.

B: (*Can I/Would I*) take it home and try it out?
8.

A: That's not a problem. If you're not happy with it, you can return it within 14 days and get a full refund.

B: OK. I'll take it.

A: That'll be $635.99 with tax. (*Do you want/Would you like*) to buy a service contract?
9.

B: What's that?

A: If you have any problems with the computer within the next two years, we will replace it for free. The

contract costs $129.99.

B: Hmmm. I don't know.

A: (*Why don't you think about it?/Let's think about it.*) You have 10 days to buy it. We have information
10.

in this brochure about the service contract.

B: Thanks.

FUN WITH GRAMMAR

Race to write. Form two teams. Each team picks a topic from the list below. You have 5 minutes to write rules that explain how to do this thing in the United States and/or in your home country. Use modals and imperatives. The team who uses the most modals and imperatives wins.

Topics:

- Tipping
- Making a dinner reservation
- Requesting more time for an assignment
- Returning an item you bought online
- Buying a house
- Doing a group project

In the United States, you should tip at a restaurant.
Don't tip at restaurants in my country.

SUMMARY OF UNIT 8

Infinitives

After certain verbs	Do you **like to shop**?
After expressions with *it*	**It's important to save** the receipt.
After adjectives	The sales clerk is **happy to help** you.
After certain verbs + object nouns or pronouns	I **want you to show** me your laptops.
To express purpose	We use coupons **to save** money.

Modals

can	The clerk **can give** you information.	Ability
	You **can shop** online.	Possibility
	You **can borrow** my tablet.	Permission
	Can I **cash** a check here?	Permission request
can't	You **can't park** here. It's a bus stop.	Prohibition
	I **can't help** you now. I'm busy.	Inability
should	You **should compare** prices.	A good idea
shouldn't	You **shouldn't shop** when you're tired.	Not a good idea
may	**May** I **borrow** your pen?	Permission request
	I **may buy** a new car.	Possibility
may not	You **may not understand** the instructions.	Possibility
might	A "free" trial **might cost** a lot of money.	Possibility
might not	You **might not remember** to cancel.	Possibility
must	You **must cancel** your trial by Friday.	Necessity
must not	Stores **must not sell** food after the expiration date.	Prohibition
would	**Would** you **help** me shop for a tablet?	Request
would like	I **would like to buy** the newest model.	Want
could	**Could** you **help** me shop for a tablet?	Request

Phrasal Modals

have to	She **has to buy** a new computer.	Necessity
not have to	She **doesn't have to buy** the most expensive model.	Lack of necessity
be allowed to	You**'re allowed to take** a shopping cart to your car.	Permission
not be allowed to	We**'re not allowed to sit** on the grass.	Prohibition
be able to	**Are** you **able to understand** the warranty?	Ability

Imperatives

Save your money.	**Don't buy** another tablet.

Suggestions

let's (not)	**Let's compare** prices online.	**Let's not waste** our money.
why don't we/you	**Why don't we compare** prices?	**Why don't you use** a shopping app?

REVIEW

Choose the correct word(s) to complete the essay. If both answers are correct, circle both choices.

I want (*get*/*to get*) the best price when I shop. I know you do, too. So I (*would*/*'d*) like you
   1.   2.
(*follow*/*to follow*) my advice.
   3.

First, (*is*/*it's*) important (*compare*/*to compare*) prices. If you see something you like at a store,
   4.   5.
(*you get*/*get*) the information about the product. If you have a camera on your phone, (*is*/*it's*) a good idea
   6.   7.
(*take*/*to take*) a picture of the tag (*for having*/*to have*) all the information about it. You
   8.   9.
(*don't have to*/*shouldn't*) go from store to store. You can (*to go*/*go*) online and look for this item from
   10.   11.
another seller. You (*may*/*might*) find a better price.
   12.

If you like the store where you first saw the item, you can go back and talk to a salesperson about your

research. Tell him that you want (*that he match*/*him to match*) the price.
                                       13.

You (*should*/*must*) read sales ads carefully. You (*must*/*might*) find that the item is not available at all
   14.   15.
stores. Some people like (*call*/*to call*) first (*to*/*for*) be sure that the item is at the store. Nowadays, (*it's*/*is*)
   16.   17.   18.
difficult (*to get*/*for get*) a real person on the telephone. Often we (*have to wait*/*should wait*) a long time
   19.   20.
before a person picks up our call. Yesterday I made a call. It was frustrating (*to wait*/*waited*) on the phone
                                                                                    21.
for such a long time, but it was faster than going to the store.

When you decide on an item, you (*have to*/*should*) ask about the price policy. If the item goes on sale
                                       22.
in the next few weeks at this company or another company, (*can you*/*you can*) bring in your receipt and get
                                                              23.
the lower price?

Be careful of "Buy one, get one free" offers. They sound good, but the store (*wants that we*/*wants us to*)
                                                                                    24.
buy something we (*might not*/*must not*) even need.
                     25.

I hope you follow my advice. I (*would*/*might*) like you (*to learn*/*learn*) from my experience.
                                   26.   27.

FROM GRAMMAR TO WRITING

PART 1 Editing Advice

1. Don't use *to* after a modal.

   I should ~~to~~ buy a new computer.

2. Don't forget *to* for an infinitive.

   Do you like ^to^ shop?

   It's important ^to^ save your receipt.

3. Use the base form in an infinitive.

   I tried to ~~found~~ find a good price.

4. Don't forget *it* in certain expressions.

   It's
   ~~Is~~ important to be a careful shopper.

5. Use *to,* not *for,* to show purpose.

   I went online ~~for~~ to compare prices.

6. Use the object pronoun and an infinitive after *want, expect, need, ask,* etc.

   I want ~~that he~~ him to explain the product to me.

7. Don't use *you* with an imperative.

   ~~You bring~~ Bring a list to the grocery store.

PART 2 Editing Practice

Read the following email to a friend. Some of the shaded words and phrases have mistakes. Find the mistakes and correct them. If the shaded words are correct, write C.

Hi Dave,

Recently I bought a new tablet, and I wanted to ~~got~~ get the best price. Now you want I help you
1. (C)   2. (get)   3.

buy a new TV.

I want you be a good shopper. First, do the research. Is important to compare prices at different stores.
4.   5.   6.

Buy the Sunday newspaper for look at ads.
7.

You can to look for prices online, too. Remember that if you buy something online, you sometimes
8.

have to pay for shipping, too. Go to the stores and try use the product. It might look good online, but you
9.   10.   11.

need to see it and try it out. It's not always easy make a decision. But if you follow this advice, you can be a
12.   13.   14.

smart shopper. Let me know if you need help with something else. I'm always happy help you.
15.

When you can help me with my school paper? I want you help me check the grammar.
16.   17.

Take care,
Toni

WRITING TIP

When you present an idea, you should follow it up with a reason and/or example. This makes your writing stronger. Your reason or example can be based on facts or personal experience. In an example response to the first prompt below, the writer uses both a reason and example to support why coupons could help someone save money on groceries.

> *There are a lot of ways to save money. To save money on food, use coupons at the grocery store. You can get a lower price or sometimes get two items for the price of one. Last week, I was able to get two boxes of my favorite cereal for the price of one, so I won't need to buy cereal again this week.*

PART 3 Write

Read the prompts. Choose one and write one paragraph about it.

1. Write advice to a friend who wants to save money. How can your friend save money on food, clothes, and other items? What are some things your friend should not spend money on?
2. Write advice to a friend who wants to have a better experience shopping for food. What is the best time to go grocery shopping? Should your friend always go to the same store? Should your friend take a list? Should your friend go alone?

PART 4 Edit

Reread the Summary of Unit 8 and the editing advice. Edit your writing from Part 3.

People on green mats participate in a large group yoga class in Times Square in New York City, USA.

Healthy Living

Take care of your body. It's the
only place you have to live.

JIM ROHN

TIRED
of Being Tired

Read the following article. Pay special attention to the words in bold. 🎧 9.1

Ella is exhausted[1]. She can hardly keep her **eyes** open. But it's only two o'clock in the **afternoon**, and she is at **work**. How will she get through the **day**? Ella feels this tired every **day**, and she doesn't know why.

Ella isn't alone. According to **research**, 15.3 percent of **women** and 10.15 percent of **men** in the United States often feel exhausted. Are you one of these **people**? Here are some possible **causes**, and some **solutions**[2].

Sometimes the **problem** is simply **lack** of **sleep**. One in three **adults** in America do not get enough **sleep**. Do you have trouble getting seven **hours of sleep**? Follow these **tips**: Don't take **naps** during the **day**. Don't drink more than two **cups of coffee** a day, or any **coffee** after **noon**. Make sure your **bedroom** is dark and quiet. Don't look at your **phone** or **tablet** in **bed**.

Diet can also affect your **energy**. Try to cut down on **sugar** and **fats**. Do you really need that **teaspoon of honey** in your **tea**? Or that extra **scoop of ice cream**? Never skip **breakfast**. That **bowl of oatmeal** and **cup of fruit** will give you **energy** all **morning** long. Also, your **body** needs **water**. Try to drink eight **glasses of water** each **day**.

And finally, ask yourself: Do I get enough **exercise**? When you are tired, you may want to relax on the **couch**. But that only makes you more tired. Just 20 **minutes of exercise** three **times a week** can improve your **energy**. As your **sleep**, **diet**, and **exercise** improve, you may be surprised to see how much your **energy** does as well!

---

[1] exhausted: very tired
[2] solutions: things that are used or done to deal with a problem

A woman trail running in Inyo County, California, USA

COMPREHENSION Based on the reading, write T for *true* or F for *false*.

1. _____ One third of Americans don't get enough sleep.

2. _____ Breakfast is an important meal.

3. _____ Reading your tablet in bed can help you sleep better.

THINK ABOUT IT Discuss the questions with a partner or in a small group.

1. The reading gives advice for a healthy lifestyle. Which suggestion do you think is the most important? Why?

2. Describe your lifestyle. Is it healthy?

9.1 Count and Noncount Nouns—An Overview

EXAMPLES	EXPLANATION
I eat **an apple** every day. She eats **two eggs** for breakfast.	We use a count noun in the singular form or plural form. We can put *a, an,* or a number before a count noun.
Do you eat **meat**? I like to eat **corn** in the summer.	We use a noncount noun in the singular form only. We don't put *a, an,* or a number before a noncount noun.

EXERCISE 1 Listen to the report. Then write T for *true*, F for *false*, or NS for *not stated*. 🎧 9.2

1. _____ The fat in olive oil is healthy.

2. _____ All carbs are the same.

3. _____ Eating too much protein can cause health problems.

EXERCISE 2 Listen again. Fill in the blanks with the words you hear. 🎧 9.2

Packaged _____ at the supermarket have a lot of nutrition facts. This
                          1.

_____ can help you make healthy _____ . But it can also be confusing.
2.   **3.**

Let's look at some of the categories on a package of _____ .
                                                              4.

- SERVING SIZE. If the package says "serving size: ½ cup" and you use a whole cup, double

  the _____ .
           5.

- CALORIES. This section also shows the number of calories from _____ .
                                                                            6.

- FAT. Not all _____ are the same. The fat in _____ , olive _____ ,
                      7.   **8.**   **9.**

  and _____ is healthy. Many _____ , potato _____ , and other
           10.   **11.**   **12.**

  _____ contain unhealthy fats.
         13.

continued

- SODIUM. Limit your intake of _____. It can raise your blood pressure.

  14.

- CARBOHYDRATES. Carbs give us energy. But there are good carbs and bad carbs. Healthy carbs come

  from _____, _____, _____, and whole _____.

  15.   16.   17.   18.

  Brown _____ is healthier than white rice. Avoid _____ and _____

  19.   20.   21.

  made from white _____. _____ is a bad carb. It provides empty calories and

  22.   23.

  can lead to type 2 diabetes. _____ also has sugar, but it has _____ and

  24.   25.

  _____, too.

  26.

- PROTEIN. _____, _____, _____, and _____

  27.   28.   29.   30.

  are healthy sources of protein. Limit red _____.

  31.

9.2 Groups of Noncount Nouns

GROUP A: NOUNS THAT HAVE NO DISTINCT, SEPARATE PARTS (WE LOOK AT THE WHOLE)				
air	cheese	honey	oil	soup
blood	coffee	juice	paper	tea
bread	dirt	meat	rain	water
butter	fat	milk	soil	yogurt

GROUP B: NOUNS THAT HAVE PARTS TOO SMALL OR INSIGNIFICANT TO COUNT							
grass	hair	popcorn	rice	salt	sand	snow	sugar

GROUP C: NOUNS THAT ARE CATEGORIES OF THINGS (THE MEMBERS OF THE GROUP ARE NOT THE SAME)	
candy (candy bars, chocolates, mints)	jewelry (necklaces, bracelets, rings)
clothing (sweaters, pants, dresses)	mail (letters, packages, postcards)
fruit (apples, peaches, pears)	money or cash (nickels, dimes, dollars)
furniture (chairs, tables, beds)	poultry (chickens, ducks, turkeys)
homework (essays, exercises, readings)	produce (oranges, apples, corn)

GROUP D: NOUNS THAT ARE ABSTRACTIONS				
advice	experience	health	love	patience
art	friendship	information	luck	pollution
beauty	fun	intelligence	music	truth
education	happiness	knowledge	noise	work

GROUP E: SOME FRUITS AND VEGETABLES				
asparagus	cabbage	celery	grapefruit	lettuce
broccoli	cauliflower	corn	kale	spinach

Notes:

1. Some nouns work as both count and noncount nouns.

    *We ate **chicken** for dinner. (chicken = food)*

    *He has 100 **chickens** on his farm. (chickens = live animals)*

2. *Food, fruit, juice,* and *fat* can be count or noncount nouns. As count nouns, they refer to categories or kinds.

    *Eggs and cheese are **foods** that contain cholesterol. (foods = kinds of food)*

    *Lemons and oranges are **fruits** that contain vitamin C. (fruits = kinds of fruit)*

3. When we refer to part of a food, it's a noncount noun. When we refer to the whole, it's a count noun.

    *We baked two **pies**. We ate some **pie** for dessert.*

    *I bought two large **watermelons**. We ate some **watermelon** after dinner.*

EXERCISE 3 Categorize each noun as count or noncount. Some words may fit both groups.

information ✓	chemical	choice ✓	advice	bean	salt	sugar	rice	egg
ingredient	homework	snack	bread	pasta	fruit	meat	dirt	fat
vegetable	cookie	health	peach	work	soil	seed	nut	oil

COUNT NOUNS	NONCOUNT NOUNS
choice	information

EXERCISE 4 Fill in the blanks with the noncount nouns from the box.

advice	coffee	milk ✓	salt
candy	information	olive oil	sugar

1. Babies need to drink a lot of _____ milk _____, but adults don't.

2. Children like to eat _____, but it's not good for them. It has a lot of sugar.

3. A lot of people drink _____ in the morning.

4. _____ is a source of good fat.

5. Potato chips contain a lot of _____.

6. Soda and candy contain a lot of _____.

7. You can get _____ about nutrition from a food package.

8. Ask your doctor for _____ about a healthy diet.

EXERCISE 5 A nutritionist (A) is talking to a patient (B) about the patient's eating habits. Fill in the blanks with the singular form of the words given for noncount nouns and the plural form for count nouns.

A: You should eat _____ vegetables _____ every day.
                  1. vegetable

B: I eat veggies. I especially love _____.
                                      2. potato

A: That's not good. They can raise your blood sugar level. It's almost like eating _____.
                                                          3. sugar

B: Really? I didn't know that.

A: French _____ are especially bad for you. They contain unhealthy fats, which affect your
              4. fry

   _____. It's better to eat _____, _____, _____,
      5. cholesterol   **6.** carrot   **7.** broccoli   **8.** spinach

   and _____. Do you eat enough _____?
        9. pea   **10.** fruit

B: Yes. I especially love _____, _____, and _____.
                    11. banana   **12.** strawberry   **13.** cherry

   I also drink a lot of _____ and eat a lot of _____. These are good sources of
                14. milk   **15.** yogurt

   calcium, right?

A: Yes. But it's not clear how much dairy we need. Other sources of calcium are white _____,
                                16. bean

   _____, and _____.
      17. almond   **18.** orange

B: I take a lot of _____ and _____. That's good, right?
               19. vitamin   **20.** mineral

A: Yes. But the best source is from _____, not from _____.
                         21. food   **22.** pill

ABOUT YOU Read the list below. Which items do you like? How much of each did you eat yesterday? Then find a partner and discuss.

red meat	fruit	water
poultry	vegetables	bread
fish	dairy	sugar

9.3 Units of Measure with Noncount Nouns

We don't use *a/an* or a number before a noncount noun. We use a unit of measure that we can count—for example, two *glasses* of milk. We measure by:

CONTAINER	PORTION	MEASUREMENT	SHAPE OR WHOLE PIECE	OTHER
a bottle of water	a slice/piece of	a spoonful of sugar	a loaf of bread	a piece of mail
a carton of milk	bread	a teaspoon of salt	an ear of corn	a piece of furniture
a bag of flour	a slice/piece of	a cup of oil	a piece of fruit	a piece of advice
a bag of rice	meat	a pound/kilo of meat	a head of lettuce	a piece of information
a can of soda	a slice/piece of cake	a gallon of milk	a bar of soap	a work of art
a cup of coffee	a slice/piece of	a pint of ice cream		a piece of paper
a glass of juice	pizza	a scoop of ice cream		
a bowl of soup	a piece of candy			
a tube of toothpaste				

Note:

We can use *a serving of* for almost any food.

> How many **servings of** fruit did you have today?

EXERCISE 6 Fill in the blanks with a logical unit of measure for the noncount nouns. More than one answer is possible.

1. She drank two _____ cups of _____ coffee.

2. She ate a _____ meat.

3. She bought two _____ meat.

4. She bought a _____ bread.

5. She ate two _____ bread.

6. She bought a _____ rice.

7. She ate a _____ rice.

8. She put one _____ sugar in her coffee.

9. She ate a _____ soup.

10. She ate two _____ corn.

GRAMMAR IN USE

When you are ordering in a restaurant, you can use count nouns with drinks.

> *Can you bring us three **waters**?*
> *I'd like two **iced teas**, please.*

Count and Noncount Nouns, Quantity Words and Phrases **217**

The Importance of WATER

Read the following article. Pay special attention to the words in bold. 🎧 9.3

How **much** water should you drink? Four glasses a day? Eight glasses a day? There's **no** easy answer to that question. You sometimes hear, "Drink eight 8-ounce glasses of water every day." We probably need the equivalent[1] of eight glasses of fluid[2] a day. We get **some** water from the food we eat. Watermelon, for example, is 90 percent water. If you drink milk, juice, soda, tea, or coffee, you're also getting water from these sources. Be careful with soda and **some** juices. They can contain **a lot of** sugar, which isn't good for you. The best source of water is water!

Water makes up about 60 percent of your body weight. **Many** factors determine your need for water: your health, your physical activity, and even where you live.

When you're sick, you need to drink plenty of fluids. Having a fever, vomiting, or even taking medicine for a cold can cause you to lose some fluids from your body. Drinking water will keep you hydrated[3].

Physically active people lose **a lot of** water through sweat. They also lose sodium. **Some** athletes use sports drinks because they contain not only water but also sodium. The problem with **some** commercial sports drinks is that they contain **a lot of** sugar. There are **a few** alternatives[4] to sports drinks: coconut water, chocolate milk, and watermelon juice. However, for most people, water is the best option.

Do you live in a hot or humid climate? Then you probably lose water through sweat. Do you live in a cold climate? Then your house is probably heated in the winter. Heated air dries your skin, so you need **some** water to replace what you lose.

A lot of people use bottled water. However, there isn't **much** proof[5] that bottled water is better than tap water. One thing is for sure: drinking water is important.

---

1 equivalent: same amount as
2 fluid: liquid
3 hydrated: having enough water or other liquid in your body
4 alternative: another choice
5 proof: evidence that something is true

A boy drinks water during a training session at the Guangzhou R&F Football Academy in Meizhou in southern China's Guangdong province.

COMPREHENSION Based on the reading, write T for *true* or F for *false*.

1. _____ Everyone needs eight glasses of water a day.

2. _____ If you live in a hot, humid climate, you lose water through sweat.

3. _____ People who run marathons need to replace not only water but sodium, too.

THINK ABOUT IT Discuss the questions with a partner or in a small group.

1. Why do you think that sports drinks are popular?

2. How much liquid do you drink every day? Think about all the sources of liquid in the reading.

9.4 *Many, Much,* and *A Lot of* with Large Quantities

We use *many* with count nouns. We use *much* with noncount nouns. We use *a lot of* with both count and noncount nouns.

	COUNT	NONCOUNT
AFFIRMATIVE STATEMENT	**Many people** use bottled water. **A lot of people** use bottled water.	I drink **a lot of water**.
NEGATIVE STATEMENT	Broccoli doesn't have **many calories**. Broccoli doesn't have **a lot of calories**.	He doesn't drink **much coffee**. He doesn't drink **a lot of coffee**.
QUESTION	Did you buy **many oranges**? Did you buy **a lot of oranges**? **How many oranges** did you buy?	Does he drink **much water**? Does he drink **a lot of water**? **How much water** does he drink?

Notes:

1. We don't usually use *much* in affirmative statements. We use *a lot of* in affirmative statements.
2. We can omit the noun after quantity words.
   > I don't drink **much coffee**. Do you drink **much**?
3. When the noun is omitted, we use *a lot* not *a lot of*.
   > I drink **a lot of water**, but she doesn't drink **a lot**.

EXERCISE 7 Fill in the blanks with *much, many, a lot of,* or *a lot*. More than one answer may be possible.

1. Athletes need to drink _____*a lot of*_____ water.

2. _____ people carry a water bottle with them.

3. Children usually drink _____ milk, but adults don't drink _____.

4. There are _____ sports drinks in the supermarket.

5. I drink _____ coffee in the morning, but I don't drink _____ in the afternoon.

6. Is there _____ water in spinach?

7. How _____ glasses of water did you drink today?

8. How _____ fruit did you eat today?

continued

9. I have _____ recipes for healthy meals.

10. It isn't good to eat _____ candy.

9.5 *A Few* and *A Little* with Small Quantities

We use *a few* with count nouns. We use *a little* with noncount nouns.

COUNT	NONCOUNT
I ate **a few raisins**.	He put **a little sugar** in the tea.
She keeps **a few bottles** of water in her car.	Do you want **a little milk** in your coffee?

EXERCISE 8 Fill in the blanks with *a few* or *a little*.

1. It's important to eat _____*a little*_____ fruit every day.

2. It's important to eat _____ pieces of fruit every day.

3. I use _____ milk in my coffee.

4. Do you want _____ sugar in your coffee?

5. We put _____ carrots in the soup.

6. We put _____ celery in the soup.

7. We put _____ salt in the soup.

8. After I exercise, I drink _____ glasses of water.

9. Eat _____ raisins after you exercise.

9.6 *A/An, Some, No,* and *Any*

	SINGULAR COUNT	PLURAL COUNT	NONCOUNT
AFFIRMATIVE STATEMENT	I ate **a peach**. I ate **an apple**.	I ate **some peaches**. I ate **some apples**.	I drank **some water**.
QUESTION	Do you want **a banana**?	Do you want **any raisins**? Do you want **some grapes**?	Did you put **any salt** in the soup? Did you put **some oil** in the soup?
NEGATIVE STATEMENT	I didn't buy **a watermelon**.	There **aren't any potatoes** in the soup. There **are no potatoes** in the soup.	There **isn't any salt** in the soup. There **is no salt** in the soup.

Notes:

1. We can use *any* or *some* for questions with plural count nouns and noncount nouns.

2. We use *any* after a negative verb. We use *no* after an affirmative verb.

   *I **didn't eat any** raisins.* OR *I **ate no** raisins.* NOT: *I **didn't eat no** raisins.*

EXERCISE 9 Fill in the blanks with *a, an, some, no,* or *any*. More than one answer may be possible.

1. I ate _____*an*_____ apple.

2. Did you buy _____ bananas?

3. I didn't buy _____ potatoes.

4. Did you eat _____ piece of fruit today?

5. I didn't put _____ beans in the soup.

6. There are _____ apples in the refrigerator. I bought them yesterday.

7. There are _____ grapes in the refrigerator. We need to buy some.

8. Do you want _____ orange?

9. Do you want _____ cherries?

10. I ate _____ rice.

11. I didn't eat _____ strawberries.

12. There's _____ milk in my coffee. I drink it black.

EXERCISE 10 Fill in the blanks with *a lot of, much, many, some, a little, any,* or *no*. More than one answer may be possible.

1. Eggs have _____*a lot of*_____ cholesterol.

2. You shouldn't eat so much red meat because it has _____ fat.

3. Only animal products contain cholesterol. There is _____ cholesterol in fruit.

4. Diet sodas use a sugar substitute. They don't have _____ sugar.

5. There is _____ sugar in a cracker, but not much.

6. Plain popcorn is healthy, but popcorn with butter has _____ fat.

7. Coffee has caffeine. Tea has _____ caffeine, too, but not as much as coffee.

8. She doesn't drink _____ tea. She usually drinks coffee.

9. I usually put _____ butter on a slice of bread.

10. I put _____ milk in my coffee. Do you want _____ milk for your coffee?

11. My sister is a vegetarian. She doesn't eat _____ meat.

12. Does the cake have _____ sugar?

13. How _____ apples did you use for the apple pie?

ABOUT YOU Find a partner. Ask and answer questions about what you eat and drink. Ask questions with *much*. Use quantity words in your answers.

1. eat/candy

   A: *Do you eat much candy?*

   B: *No. I don't eat any candy.*

2. drink/orange juice

3. eat/rice

4. drink/milk

5. eat/fish

6. eat/chicken

7. eat/bread

8. drink/water

9. eat/cheese

10. drink/coffee

11. drink/tea

12. eat/fruit

13. drink/soda

EXERCISE 11 Complete the conversation between a husband (A) and wife (B). Choose the correct word(s). If both answers are correct, circle both choices.

A: Where were you today? I called you (*much/many*) times, but I just got your voice mail. I left
                                                                    1.

   (*much/a lot of*) messages. I started to get worried about you.
         2.

B: Sorry. I forgot to take my cell phone. I went to the supermarket today. I bought (*a few/a little*) things.
                                                                                                    3.

A: What did you buy?

B: There was a sale on coffee, so I bought (*a lot of/much*) coffee. I didn't buy (*any/no*) strawberries because
                                                      4.   **5.**

   the price was too high. I bought (*some/any*) grapes instead. And I bought (*a/any*) watermelon, too.
                                            6.   **7.**

A: How (*much/many*) money did you spend?
              8.

B: I spent (*much/a lot of*) money because of the coffee. I bought five one-pound bags.
               9.

A: It took you a long time.

B: Yes. There were (*a lot of/many*) people in the store. And there was (*a lot of/much*) traffic.
                          10.   **11.**

A: There's not (*much/many*) time to cook dinner.
                    12.

B: Maybe you can cook today and let me rest.

A: I don't have (*any/no*) time. I have (*a lot of/a lot*) work to do. I have to finish a report.
                    13.   **14.**

B: Maybe we should just order a pizza tonight.

A: Good idea. Cooking is (*a lot of/much*) trouble.
15.

EXERCISE 12 Complete the conversation between a server (A) and two customers (B) and (C). Fill in the blanks with an appropriate quantity word or unit of measure. More than one answer may be possible.

A: We have _____*some*_____ specials today. Would you like to hear about them?
1.

B: No, thank you. For now, we'd each like _____ coffee, please.
2.

A: Do you want _____ cream for your coffee?
3.

B: Yes. I'd like _____ cream.
4.

C: I don't need _____ cream. I like my coffee black.
5.

A: Are you ready to order now?

continued

A waitress pours a cup of coffee at the Palace Diner in Biddeford, Maine, USA.

C: We need _____ more time to decide.
6.

A few minutes later:

A: Can I take your order now?

B: Yes. I'd like the scrambled eggs and a _____ toast. I'd also like _____
7.   8.

orange juice.

A: Do you want _____ butter or jam with your toast?
9.

B: No, thanks.

A: And you, sir?

C: I'd like _____ pancakes.
10.

A: Do you want _____ syrup with your pancakes?
11.

C: Yes, please.

Later:

A: Would you like _____ dessert?
12.

C: What do you have?

A: We have a fresh cherry pie. We have a special today: a _____ pie with a
13.

_____ of ice cream for only $1.99.
14.

B: We're trying to lose weight. Do you have _____ other choices?
15.

A: We have _____ fresh fruit.
16.

C: That sounds good. Please bring us one _____ of fruit and two forks.
17.

We can share. And we'd like _____ more coffee, please.
18.

After the customers finish eating:

A: Would you like anything else?

B: Just the check. I don't have _____ cash with me. Can I pay with a credit card?
19.

A: Of course.

FUN WITH GRAMMAR

Role-play in a restaurant. Work in pairs. Create a short conversation like the one in Exercise 12. One person is a waiter, and the other person orders food. Act out your conversation in front of the class. Take turns presenting your conversations.

An Okinawan woman inspects a handful of edible seaweed.

Eat Less,
Live Longer

Read the following article. Pay special attention to the words in bold. 🎧 9.4

More than 70 percent of Americans are overweight. The typical American consumes[1] **too many** calories and **too much** fat and doesn't get enough exercise. Many American children are overweight, too. About 30 percent of two- to five-year-olds and 35 percent of school-age children are overweight or obese[2] in the United States. Children spend **too many** hours watching TV and not enough time getting exercise. They see **too many** commercials for food products every day. Over 90 percent of food commercials during children's TV shows are for foods that have **a lot of** fat, sugar, or sodium.

Eating fewer calories can help us live longer. Doctors studied people on the Japanese island of Okinawa. Okinawans eat 40 percent less than the typical American. The Okinawan diet is low in calories and salt. Okinawans also eat **a lot of** fruit, vegetables, and fish and drink **a lot of** green tea and water. Many Okinawans in their eighties have excellent health. Okinawa has **a lot of** people over the age of 100. However, as younger Okinawans start to eat like Westerners, they will probably have much shorter lives than their grandparents.

How can we live longer and healthier lives? The answer is simple: eat less and exercise more.

---

[1] to consume: to eat or drink
[2] obese: very overweight

Based on the reading, write T for *true* or F for *false*.

1. _____ The majority of Americans are overweight.

2. _____ There are a lot of commercials for food during children's TV shows.

3. _____ Okinawans have a lot of salt in their diet.

THINK ABOUT IT Discuss the questions with a partner or in a small group.

1. Why do you think Okinawans follow this diet?

2. Would you follow this diet? Why or why not?

9.7 *A Lot Of* and *Too Much/Too Many*

EXAMPLES	EXPLANATION
There are **a lot of healthy older people** in Okinawa. I don't eat **a lot**.	We use *a lot (of)* to show a large quantity. It is a neutral term. Use *a lot of* + noun. Use *a lot* without a noun.
I ate **too many cookies**. Now I don't feel well. If you drink **too much coffee**, you won't sleep tonight.	*Too much* and *too many* show that a quantity is excessive and causes a problem. We use *too many* with count nouns. We use *too much* with noncount nouns.
If you **eat too much**, you will gain weight.	We use *too much* after a verb.
The potatoes are **too salty**. I can't eat them. Please walk faster. You walk **too slowly**.	We use *too* with adjectives and adverbs.

GRAMMAR IN USE

We often use *too, too much,* and *too many* to complain about something.

> This tea has **too much** sugar in it. I can't drink it.

> It's **too expensive**.

EXERCISE 13 Choose the correct word(s) in the conversation between a mother (A) and her son (B).

A: I'm worried about you. You spend too (*much/many*) hours watching TV. And you eat too (*much/many*)

                                      1.   **2.**

junk food and don't get enough exercise.

B: Mom, I know I watch (*a lot of/a lot*) TV, but I learn (*a lot of/a lot*) from TV.

                            3.   **4.**

A: No, you don't. Sometimes you have (*a lot of/too much*) homework, but you watch TV. I'm going to make

                                                5.

a rule: no TV until you finish your homework.

B: Oh, Mom. You have too (*much/many*) rules.

                                    6.

A: There are (*a lot of/too many*) things to do besides watching TV. Why don't you go outside

                            7.

and play? When I was your age, we played outside.

B: "When I was your age." Not again. You always say that.

A: Well, it's true. We had (*too much/a lot of*) fun playing outside. I didn't have (*a lot of/too much*) toys when

8.
9.

I was your age. Also, we helped our parents (*a lot/too much*) after school.

10.

B: My friend Josh cleans the basement and takes out the garbage. His mom pays him (*too much/a lot of*)

11.

money for doing those things.

A: You're not Josh, and I'm not Josh's mother. I'm not going to pay you for things you should do.

B: OK. Just tell me what to do, and I'll do it.

A: There are (*a lot of/too much*) leaves in the yard. Why don't you put them in garbage bags?

12.

ABOUT YOU Fill in the blanks to make true statements about yourself. Then find a partner and discuss your answers.

1. I sometimes eat too much _____ .

2. I sometimes drink too much _____ .

3. I sometimes spend too many hours on _____ .

EXERCISE 14 A group of students is complaining about the school cafeteria. They are giving reasons why they don't want to eat there. Fill in the blanks with *too, too much,* or *too many*.

1. The food is _____*too*_____ greasy.

2. There are _____ students there.

3. The lines move _____ slowly.

4. The food is _____ expensive.

5. There's _____ noise.

6. They put _____ salt in the food.

EXERCISE 15 Fill in the blanks with *too, too much,* or *too many* if a problem is presented. Use *a lot (of)* if a problem is not presented.

1. Strawberries are _____*too*_____ expensive this week. Let's not buy them.

2. Some kids spend _____ time watching TV. They don't get enough exercise.

3. Oranges have _____ vitamin C.

continued

4. I don't eat potato chips. They have _____ calories and _____ fat.

5. Babies drink _____ milk.

6. If you drink _____ coffee, you won't sleep.

7. If you exercise, you need to drink _____ water.

8. I exercised _____, and now I feel much better.

9. _____ older Okinawans are very healthy.

EXERCISE 16 Complete the conversation between a doctor (A) and a patient (B). Fill in the blanks with an appropriate quantity word or unit of measure. More than one answer may be possible.

A: Your lab results show that your cholesterol level is high. Also your blood pressure is

_____*too*_____ high. Do you use _____ salt on your food?
      1.   **2.**

B: Yes, Doctor. I love salt. I eat _____ potato chips and popcorn.
                            3.

A: That's not good. What else do you usually eat?

B: For breakfast I usually have _____ coffee and a doughnut. I don't have
                              4.

_____ time for lunch, so I eat _____ cookies and drink
    5.   **6.**

_____ soda while I'm working. I'm so busy that I have _____ time to
    7.   **8.**

cook at all. So for dinner, I usually stop at a fast-food place and get a burger and fries.

A: That's a terrible diet! How _____ exercise do you get?
                            9.

B: I never exercise. I don't have _____ time at all. I own my own business, and I have
                              10.

_____ work. Sometimes I work 80 hours a week.
    11.

A: I'm going to give you an important _____ advice. You're going to have to change
                            12.

your lifestyle.

B: I'm _____ old to change my habits.
      13.

A: That's not true. I'm going to give you a booklet about staying healthy. It has _____
                              14.

information that will teach you about diet and exercise. Please read it and come back in three months.

ABOUT YOU Write three sentences of advice about being healthy. Use quantity words and units of measure. Then find a partner and compare your sentences.

1. _____

_____

2. _____

_____

3. _____

_____

FUN WITH GRAMMAR

Compete to make a unique shopping list. Work with a partner to create a list of 10 items to buy at the grocery store. Include quantities or units of measure for each (for example: *a loaf of bread, a gallon of milk*). Share your lists as a class. If another pair has the same thing, cross it off the list. The pair with the most items remaining at the end wins.

A cashier rings up groceries in Brooklyn, New York, USA.

SUMMARY OF UNIT 9

Quantity Words and Phrases with Count and Noncount Nouns

QUANTITY WORDS AND PHRASES	SINGULAR COUNT EXAMPLE: *APPLE*	PLURAL COUNT EXAMPLE: *GRAPES*	NONCOUNT EXAMPLE: *MILK*
a/an	✓		
one	✓		
two, three, etc.		✓	
some (with affirmative statements and questions)		✓	✓
any (with negative statements and questions)		✓	✓
no	✓	✓	✓
a lot of		✓	✓
much (with negative statements and questions)			✓
many		✓	
a little			✓
a few		✓	

Groups of Noncount Nouns

GROUP A: NOUNS THAT HAVE NO DISTINCT, SEPARATE PARTS				
air	cheese	honey	oil	soup
blood	coffee	juice	paper	tea
bread	dirt	meat	rain	water
butter	fat	milk	soil	yogurt

GROUP B: NOUNS THAT HAVE PARTS TOO SMALL OR INSIGNIFICANT TO COUNT						
grass	hair	popcorn	rice	salt	sand	snow	sugar

GROUP C: NOUNS THAT ARE CATEGORIES OF THINGS				
candy	clothing	fruit	furniture	homework
jewelry	mail	money/cash	poultry	produce

GROUP D: NOUNS THAT ARE ABSTRACTIONS				
advice	experience	health	love	patience
art	friendship	information	luck	pollution
beauty	fun	intelligence	music	truth
education	happiness	knowledge	noise	work

GROUP E: SOME FRUITS AND VEGETABLES				
asparagus	cabbage	celery	grapefruit	lettuce
broccoli	cauliflower	corn	kale	spinach

Units of Measure with Noncount Nouns

CONTAINER	PORTION	MEASUREMENT	SHAPE OR WHOLE PIECE	OTHER
a bottle of water	a slice/piece of bread	a spoonful of sugar	a loaf of bread	a piece of mail
a carton of milk	a slice/piece of meat	a teaspoon of salt	an ear of corn	a piece of furniture
a bag of flour	a slice/piece of cake	a cup of flour	a piece of fruit	a piece of advice
a bag of rice	a slice/piece of pizza	a pound/kilo of meat	a head of lettuce	a piece of information
a can of soda	a piece of candy	a gallon of milk	a bar of soap	a work of art
a cup of coffee		a pint of ice cream		a piece of paper
a glass of juice		a scoop of ice cream		
a bowl of soup				
a tube of toothpaste				

REVIEW

Choose the correct word(s) to complete the essay.

I had (*some*/*any*/*a little*) problems when I first came to the United States. First, I didn't have
    1.

(*much*/*a*/*some*) money. (*A few*/*A little*/*A few of*) friends of mine lent me (*some*/*a*/*any*) money, but I didn't
  2.   **3.**   **4.**

feel good about borrowing it.

Second, I couldn't find (*a*/*an*/*no*) apartment. I went to see (*some*/*a little*/*an*) apartments, but I couldn't
          5.   **6.**

afford (*not any*/*any*/*none*) of them. For (*a little*/*a few of*/*a few*) months, I had to live with my uncle's family,
    7.   **8.**

but the situation wasn't good.

Third, I started to study English, but I soon found (*a*/*any*/*some*) job and had (*no*/*any*/*not any*) time to
              9.   **10.**

study. I worked (*a lot of*/*too much*/*a lot*) and earned enough for my apartment and other expenses, but I
          11.

didn't have (*no*/*any*/*some*) free time.
    12.

Fourth, I gained weight. I started eating (*much*/*many*/*a lot of*) junk food. I knew I should eat a healthier
          13.

diet, but I didn't have time to cook. In the morning, I drank (*a cup of coffee*/*a cup coffee*/*cup of coffee*) and
          14.

ran out the door. I knew I should get (*some*/*much*/*a few*) exercise every day, but I just didn't have the time.
          15.

I had (*too much*/*too many*/*a lot*) things to do.
    16.

Little by little my life is starting to improve. I'm saving (*a few*/*a little*/*a*) money and starting to
          17.

eat better.

FROM GRAMMAR TO WRITING

PART 1 Editing Advice

1. Don't put *a* or *an* before a noncount noun.

   My doctor gave me ~~an~~ *some* advice about nutrition.

2. Don't use the plural form with noncount nouns.

   He drank three ~~waters~~ *glasses of water* today.

3. Don't use a double negative.

   He doesn't have ~~no~~ *any* time for breakfast. OR He has no time for breakfast.

4. Don't use *much* with an affirmative statement.

   We prepared ~~much~~ *a lot of* soup.

5. Don't use *a* or *an* before a plural noun.

   He ate ~~a~~ potato chips with his sandwich.

6. Use the plural form with plural count nouns.

   He ate a lot of grape*s*.

7. Omit *of* after *a lot* when the noun is omitted.

   I drank a lot of water yesterday, but I didn't drink a lot ~~of~~ today.

8. Use *of* with a unit of measure.

   I ate two pieces *of* bread.

9. Don't use *of* after *many, much, a few,* or *a little* if a noun follows directly.

   He put a little ~~of~~ milk in his coffee.

10. Only use *too/too much/too many* if there is a problem.

    My grandfather is ~~too~~ *very* healthy. He gets ~~too much~~ *a lot of* exercise.

11. Don't use *too much* before an adjective or an adverb. Use *too*.

    I can't exercise today. I'm too ~~much~~ tired.

    You're walking too ~~much~~ slowly.

PART 2 Editing Practice

Some of the shaded words and phrases have mistakes. Find the mistakes and correct them. If the shaded words are correct, write C.

My parents gave me ~~a~~ good advice: stay healthy. They told me to get good nutrition (C) and to exercise
1.   2.

every day. My parents follow their own advice, and, as a result, they're too healthy.
3.

I try to follow their advices, but sometimes I can't. I'm very busy, and sometimes I don't have no
4.   5.

time for exercise. When I was in high school, I had a lot of free time, but now I don't have a lot of. So for
6.

breakfast, I just have a cup coffee with a little of sugar and two pieces of toast.
7.   8.   9.

I have a lot of friend at college, and we often go out to eat after class. They always want to go to a fast
10.   11.

food places. I know the food is too much greasy. When I suggest healthier restaurants, they say they're
12.

too expensive. When I get home from work at night, I just heat up a frozen dinner. I know this is not
13.

healthy, but what can I do?

WRITING TIP

When you write about daily habits or schedules, organize your ideas in order by time (chronological order). For the first prompt below, describe your breakfast habits first, followed by lunch and then dinner habits. Add in any snacking habits in the appropriate places.

PART 3 Write

Read the prompts. Choose one and write one paragraph about it.

1. Describe your eating habits in a typical day.
2. Describe food and eating habits in your native country or culture. What is a typical breakfast, lunch, and dinner? What times do people eat? Do people generally eat a healthy diet?

PART 4 Edit

Reread the Summary of Unit 9 and the editing advice. Edit your writing from Part 3.

GREAT WOMEN

A portrait of a firefighter in Columbus, Ohio, USA

What you do makes a difference, and you have to decide what kind of difference you want to make.

JANE GOODALL

Helen Keller

Do you know of anyone with a disability[1] who did **remarkable** things? Helen Keller is a **good** example. She was an **amazing** woman.

Helen Keller was a **healthy** baby. But when she was 19 months old, she had a **sudden** fever[2]. The fever disappeared, but she became **blind** and **deaf**. Because she couldn't hear, it was **difficult** for her to learn to speak. As she grew, she was **angry** and **frustrated**[3] because she couldn't understand or communicate. She became **wild**, throwing things and kicking and biting.

When Helen was seven years old, a teacher, Anne Sullivan, came to live with Helen's family. First, Anne taught Helen how to talk with her fingers. Helen was **excited** when she realized that things had names. Then Anne taught Helen to read using braille[4]. Helen learned these skills **quickly**. However, learning to speak was harder. Anne continued to teach Helen **patiently**. Finally, when Helen was 10 years old, she could speak **clearly** enough for people to understand her.

Helen was very **intelligent**. She went to a school for **blind** students, where she did very **well**. Then she went to college, where she graduated with honors[5] when she was 24 years old. Helen traveled all over the United States, Europe, and Asia with Anne to raise money to build schools for **blind** people. Her **main** message was that **disabled** people are like everybody else. They want to live life **fully** and **naturally**. Helen wanted all people to be treated **equally**.

Anne Sullivan "talking" to Helen Keller using her fingers

---

[1] disability: a physical or mental limitation
[2] fever: a body temperature that is higher than normal
[3] frustrated: angry at being unable to do something
[4] braille: a form of written language in which characters are represented by patterns of raised dots that are felt with the fingertips
[5] with honors: having high academic grades

COMPREHENSION Based on the reading, write T for *true* or F for *false*.

1. _____ Helen Keller became blind and deaf when she was seven years old.

2. _____ Anne Sullivan was Helen's teacher.

3. _____ Helen raised money to build schools for blind people.

THINK ABOUT IT

1. Do you know someone with a disability? Does he or she have any special accommodations?

2. Are there any special laws or rules in your country to help people with disabilities? Explain.

10.1 Adjectives and Adverbs of Manner

EXAMPLES	EXPLANATION
Helen was a **healthy** baby. She became **blind**.	Adjectives describe nouns. We can use adjectives before nouns or after the verbs *be, become, look, seem, sound, taste, feel,* and *smell*.
Anne taught Helen **patiently**. Helen learned **quickly**.	Adverbs of manner tell how we do things. We form most adverbs of manner by putting *-ly* at the end of an adjective.

EXERCISE 1 Listen to the report. Then write T for *true*, F for *false*, or NS for *not stated*. 🎧 10.2

1. _____ Lin was only 21 when she won the contest.

2. _____ There were 15,000 applications in the contest.

3. _____ All veterans liked Lin's design.

EXERCISE 2 Listen again. Fill in the blanks with the words you hear. 🎧 10.2

A ____*popular*____ site in Washington, DC, is the Vietnam Veterans Memorial.
1.

Four million people visit it _____. It is _____ and
2.   3.

_____ with the names of _____ soldiers from the war carved
4.   5.

into _____ stone. Who created this _____ memorial? Was it a
6.   7.

_____ artist? No. It was Maya Lin, a 21-year-old student at Yale University.
8.

In 1980, there was a _____ contest to create a memorial. Lin went to
9.

Washington to study the space _____. She wanted visitors to a war
10.

memorial to look at death _____. A committee looked at almost 1,500
11.

applications and thought Lin's design was _____. She won.
12.

Some war veterans protested _____ against her _____
13.   14.

design. They wanted a more _____ design: statues of soldiers with an
15.

_____ flag. But Lin's design became a reality. In 1982, the memorial was finished.
16.

The Vietnam
Veterans Memorial,
Washington, DC

Adjectives and Adverbs, Noun Modifiers, *Too/Very/Enough* **237**

10.2 Adjectives

EXAMPLES	EXPLANATION
Anne was a **good** friend to Helen. I have many **good** friends.	Adjectives are always singular.
Helen Keller felt **frustrated** when she couldn't communicate. Maya Lin was **excited** to win the contest.	Some -ed words are adjectives: *married, divorced, educated, excited, frustrated, disabled, worried, finished, tired, crowded.*
Helen had an **interesting** life. She was an **amazing** woman.	Some -ing words are adjectives: *interesting, boring, amazing, exciting.*
The Vietnam Veterans Memorial is a **very popular** site.	We can put *very* before an adjective.
Helen was a **normal**, **healthy baby**. The Vietnam Veterans Memorial has a **simple**, **beautiful design**.	We can put two adjectives before a noun. We sometimes separate the two adjectives with a comma.
Some people have an **easy childhood**. Helen had a **hard one**. What about the **other designs**? Were there other **good ones**?	After an adjective, we can substitute a singular noun with *one* or a plural noun with *ones* to avoid repeating the noun.

GRAMMAR IN USE
Don't use the adjectives *asleep, afraid,* or *alone* before a noun. Use these adjectives only after a verb (usually *be*).

> The baby **is asleep**.
>
> NOT: *The asleep baby.*

EXERCISE 3 Fill in the blanks with the adjectives from the box.

blind	excited	frustrated	intelligent	traditional	wild
dead	equal	healthy ✓	patient	unusual	young

1. Helen Keller was a _____ healthy _____ baby.

2. Before Helen learned to communicate, she felt _____.

3. She became _____, sometimes throwing things.

4. Helen's teacher, Anne Sullivan, was a _____ person.

5. When Helen learned to communicate, she became _____.

6. Helen was _____ and did well in school.

7. _____ people can learn to read with braille.

8. Helen wanted _____ treatment for blind people.

9. Maya Lin was very _____ when she won the contest. She was only 21.

10. Her design was _____ because it didn't show soldiers and flags.

11. Some people didn't like her design. They wanted a more _____ design.

12. The Vietnam Veterans Memorial has the names of _____ soldiers.

ABOUT YOU Complete each statement with your opinion. Then find a partner and compare your answers.

1. In my opinion, _____ is a great person.

2. I think _____ is a popular place.

3. I think _____ is a patient person.

4. In my opinion, _____ is a beautiful monument.

5. I think _____ is an unusual woman.

EXERCISE 4 Fill in the blanks with the adjectives from the box. Add *one* or *ones*.

great	long	new	amazing	serious ✓	simple

1. **A:** I prefer funny stories.

   B: I don't. I prefer _____ *serious ones* _____. I especially liked the story of Maya Lin.

2. **A:** I'm reading a book about Helen Keller. It has over 400 pages.

   B: Wow! It's a _____ .

3. **A:** Do you have any good ideas for your next essay?

   B: I have a _____ . I'm going to write about a remarkable woman.

4. **A:** I loved the visitor's stories. Which stories did you like best?

   B: It's hard to decide. She told some _____ .

5. **A:** Many traditional war memorials have soldiers and flags.

   B: I prefer _____ , like the Vietnam Veterans Memorial in Washington, DC.

6. **A:** Maya Lin designed many memorials.

   B: I know. When is she going to design a _____ ?

Lilly LEDBETTER

Read the following article. Pay special attention to the words in bold. 🎧 10.3

Men still earn more money than women in the United States. On average, for every dollar a man makes, a woman makes 79 cents. Even if a woman has the same amount of education, **work experience**, and skills as a man, she will earn 2% less.

Lilly Ledbetter started to work as a manager at a **tire company** in 1979. At that time, her boss told her a **company rule**: Employees must not discuss **salary information** with each other. Nineteen years later, a coworker told her that three men in similar positions made as much as 40 percent more than Ledbetter.

How could this happen? She was a good worker. In fact, one year she won the top **performance award**. She often worked **12-hour shifts**[1] as a **night supervisor** to earn **overtime pay**. She had a lot of expenses: **house** and **car payments** and **college tuition** for her kids. As a result of her lower salary all these years, her **retirement benefits** would be less. Ledbetter was angry.

She decided to fight back. She sued[2] the company. The company moved her to a job lifting **80-pound tires**. (She was 60 years old at the time.) Her case went all the way to the Supreme Court in 2006, but she lost. The Court said it was too late to sue. The limit is 180 days after the first **paycheck**.

Ledbetter didn't give up[3]. She explained to members of Congress how unequal pay affects all women. In 2009, Congress finally passed a law called the "Lilly Ledbetter Fair **Pay Act**." This law says that employees can report discrimination[4] if they discover unfairness not just 180 days after the first **paycheck**, but 180 days after *any* **paycheck**.

Ledbetter didn't benefit from her fight. She received nothing from the company. But she said, "I'm just thrilled that this has finally passed and sends a message to the Supreme Court: You got it wrong."

---

1 shift: a period of paid work time
2 to sue: to go to court to get money from someone who caused you damage or suffering
3 to give up: to stop doing something
4 discrimination: unfair treatment because of race, gender, or religion

Lilly Ledbetter in front of the tire company she worked for

COMPREHENSION Based on the reading, write T for *true* or F for *false*.

1. _____ When Lilly Ledbetter started her job, she had to lift heavy tires.

2. _____ The company didn't let employees discuss their salaries.

3. _____ Ledbetter won her Supreme Court case.

THINK ABOUT IT Discuss the questions with a partner or in a small group.

1. Besides unequal pay, what are some other results of discrimination in the workforce?

2. Do you think it's fair that Lilly Ledbetter didn't benefit from her fight? Why or why not?

10.3 Noun Modifiers

EXAMPLES	EXPLANATION
Workers couldn't discuss **salary information**. Ledbetter had to make **car payments**.	We can use a noun to describe another noun. The first noun acts as an adjective.
The **lawsuit** went to the Supreme Court. How much did she get in each **paycheck**?	Sometimes we write the two nouns as one word. The noun modifier and the noun become a compound noun.
Ledbetter didn't have a **college education**. Some students go to a **city college**.	The first noun makes the second noun more specific. A *college education* is a specific kind of education. A *city college* is a specific kind of college.
She put money in her **checking account**.	Sometimes the first noun ends in *-ing*.
Ellen just got her **driver's license**.	Sometimes the first noun ends in *'s*.
A company that makes tires is a **tire company**. A tire that is 80 pounds is an **80-pound tire**. A woman who is 60 years old is a **60-year-old woman**.	When two nouns come together, the first noun is always singular. When we use a number before the noun, we usually attach it to the noun with a hyphen.

Note:
There are many noun + noun combinations. Here are some common ones:

art museum	*driver's license*	*haircut*	*summer vacation*
bachelor's degree	*drugstore*	*master's degree*	*text message*
baking dish	*earring*	*math course*	*TV show*
cell phone	*eyebrow*	*reading glasses*	*washing machine*
daylight	*fingernail*	*running shoes*	*wedding ring*
dishwasher	*flashlight*	*skiing accident*	*winter coat*
doorknob	*garbage can*	*shopping cart*	

EXERCISE 5 Complete each statement with a noun + noun combination.

1. A memorial about war is a _____ war memorial _____.

2. A student in college is a _____.

3. Language that communicates with signs is _____.

4. Sight with eyes is _____. (*one word*)

continued

5. A wall made from stone is a _____ .

6. A store that sells books is a _____ . (*one word*)

7. A man who is 25 years old is a _____ .

8. A box for mail is a _____ . (*one word*)

9. A shift of 12 hours is a _____ .

10. A trip of 20 miles is a _____ .

EXERCISE 6 Fill in the blanks by putting the words given in the correct order. Make any necessary changes to the nouns. Choose the correct article (*a* or *an*) where you see a choice.

Last night I saw a _____*TV program*_____ about the Paralympic Games. In the Paralympic
           1. program/TV

Games, athletes with physical disabilities compete. One of the athletes in the program was Christina Ripp

Schwab. Christina is in a _____ . But that didn't stop her from becoming a
           2. chair/wheels (*one word*)

_____ . She started playing when she was just a
3. player/basketball

_____ . She played on her _____ at the
4. child/10 years old   **5.** team/college

University of Illinois. In 2005, she got her _____ in
                   6. degree/bachelor's

_____ . In 2008, she won a _____ at the Paralympic
7. community/health   **8.** medal/gold

Games in China.

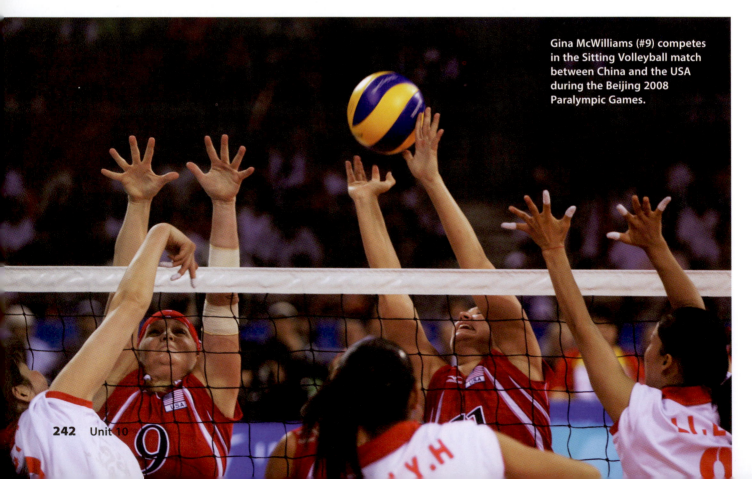

Gina McWilliams (#9) competes in the Sitting Volleyball match between China and the USA during the Beijing 2008 Paralympic Games.

Another great athlete from the Paralympic Games is Gina McWilliams. As a child, she loved sports, but when she was 26 years old, she was in (*a/an*) _____ and lost part of her right leg.

9. accident/car

She tried many sports before deciding on floor volleyball. At the 2008 Paralympic Games, she and her team won the _____ . Now Gina works as (*a/an*) _____

10. silver/medal   **11.** athletic/director

for disabled adults and children.

10.4 Adverbs

EXAMPLES	EXPLANATION
Lilly Ledbetter **acted responsibly**. The company **treated women unfairly**. Helen Keller **learned sign language quickly**.	An adverb of manner tells how we do something. It usually follows the verb or verb phrase. We form most adverbs of manner by putting *-ly* at the end of an adjective.
She was **probably** happy with the new law. The case **eventually** went to the Supreme Court. Her case **finally** went to the Supreme Court.	Other common *–ly* adverbs are *eventually, annually, frequently, certainly, suddenly, recently, directly, completely, generally, repeatedly, naturally, finally, probably, (un)fortunately, extremely, constantly.*
She worked **hard**. (adverb) She had a **hard** job. (adjective) She wakes up **early**. (adverb) She has an **early** shift. (adjective)	Some adverbs and adjectives have the same form: *hard, fast, late, early.*
She did **well** in school. (adverb) She went to a **good** school. (adjective)	The adverb *well* is different in form from the adjective *good*.
The company treated her **very badly**.	We can use *very* before an adverb.

Notes:

1. The adverbs *hard* and *hardly* have different meanings.

   *She works 12 hours a night. She works **hard**.*

   *I **hardly** ever work overtime. (hardly ever = almost never; rarely)*

2. The adverbs *late* and *lately* have different meanings.

   *She came home after midnight. She came home **late**.*

   *She doesn't have much interest in her job **lately**. (lately = recently)*

GRAMMAR IN USE

Really is a synonym for *very*, but it is much less formal. We use *really* frequently in conversation.

  *That cake was **really** good!*

  *You did **really** well on the test.*

EXERCISE 7 Choose the correct words to complete each conversation.

1. **A:** Anne Sullivan was a (great/greatly) teacher.

   B: I agree. She taught Helen Keller (*patient/patiently*).

2. **A:** Did Helen learn (*quick/quickly*)?

   B: Yes, she did. But she never learned to speak (*clear/clearly*).

3. **A:** Did Helen do (*good/well*) in college?

   B: Yes. She was an (*excellent/excellently*) student.

4. **A:** Maya Lin's Vietnam Veterans Memorial is very (*beautiful/beautifully*).

   B: I agree. It deals with death (*honest/honestly*).

5. **A:** Did Lilly Ledbetter benefit (*direct/directly*) from her fight for equality for women?

   B: No, she didn't, because she learned about her pay inequality (*late/lately*). But workers will

   (*definite/definitely*) benefit from the Fair Pay Act in the future.

6. **A:** Lilly Ledbetter worked (*hard/hardly*).

   B: I know. She felt (*happy/happily*) when the Fair Pay Act (*final/finally*) passed in Congress.

   But equal pay for women isn't changing (*fast/fastly*).

7. **A:** I work the night shift and sleep during the day. I (*hard/hardly*) ever have time to see my family.

   B: That's (*certain/certainly*) a difficult way to live.

10.5 Spelling of *-ly* Adverbs

ADJECTIVE	ADVERB	RULE
glad honest	glad**ly** honest**ly**	For most adjectives, add *-ly* to form the adverb.
eas**y** luck**y**	eas**ily** luck**ily**	For adjectives that end in *y*, change *y* to *i* and add *-ly*.
simp**le** comfortab**le**	simp**ly** comfortab**ly**	For adjectives that end in consonant + *le*, drop the *e* and add *-y*.
ful**l**	full**y**	For adjectives that end in *ll*, add *-y*.
nic**e** fre**e**	nic**ely** fre**ely**	For adjectives that end in *e*, add *-ly*.*

Note:

* One common exception is: *true—truly*.

EXERCISE 8 Write the adverb form of each adjective.

1. bad   _badly_   8. polite   _____

2. good   _____   9. fast   _____

3. lazy   _____   10. constant   _____

4. true   _____   11. terrible   _____

5. brave   _____   12. beautiful   _____

6. full   _____   13. responsible _____

7. probable _____   14. early   _____

EXERCISE 9 Fill in the blanks with the adverb form of the adjectives given.

1. Congress _____ _finally_ _____ passed a new law.

            final

2. Companies should treat everyone _____ .

                                equal

3. Lilly Ledbetter works _____ for women's rights.

                       hard

4. At first, Helen Keller talked very _____ .

                             slow

5. She wanted to live life _____ .

                     full

6. Maya Lin studied the space in Washington, DC, _____ .

                                      careful

7. She designed the wall _____ .

                     simple

8. Four million people visit the Vietnam Veterans Memorial _____ .

                                          annual

9. At first, some people protested _____ against Maya Lin's memorial.

                            strong

10. When you visit the wall, you will _____ feel sad.

                                probable

11. The wall is _____ beautiful.

               real

EXERCISE 10 Fill in the blanks with the adjectives given, or change the adjectives to adverbs if necessary.

I know two people who are opposites. One is my coworker Paula. She complains _____ _constantly_ _____

                                                                           1. constant

about everything. She's never _____ . She says that everyone is _____ . When

                                2. happy   3. impolite

she drives, she behaves _____ to other drivers. She says nobody drives _____ .

                            4. rude   5. good

She finds something wrong with everyone. I met her for lunch last week. I arrived about five minutes

_____ , and she was _____ with me.

    6. late   7. angry

continued

My friend Karla is _____ different from Paula. She works _____ but never
8. complete   9. hard

complains. She has a _____ attitude about life. She's an _____ person and
10. positive   11. active

travels _____. She's always learning new things. She's studying French and can speak it
12. frequent

_____ now. She learns _____ and is _____ about everything.
13. fluent   14. quick   15. curious

She goes to museums _____ and knows a lot about art. She is a _____ friend.
16. frequent   17. good

EXERCISE 11 Choose the correct words to complete this report.

When Helen Keller was a (small child/child small), she behaved (wild/wildly) because she couldn't
1.   2.

communicate (good/well) with her family. When she was seven years old, her parents found a (good/well)
3.   4.

teacher, Anne Sullivan, to work with her.

Anne was from a (poorly/poor) immigrant family. She had a (hard/hardly) life. When she was a child,
5.   6.

she had a disease that made her almost blind. When she was an eight-(year/years)-old girl, her mother
7.

died. A few years later, her father left the family.

When she was 14 years old, she could not see (clear/clearly) and she could not read. But
8.

she got the opportunity to go to a school for blind students. At the age of 14, she started

(school elementary/elementary school). She was (intelligent/intelligently) and graduated from
9.   10.

high school as the best student.

After graduation, she heard about a job teaching a blind girl, Helen Keller. Anne went to live with

Helen's family. Anne taught Helen that things had names. Within a month, Helen learned (signs/sign)
11.

language. After that, Helen learned (quick/quickly) and wanted to study in school. Anne attended
12.

(classes college/college classes) with Helen to help her understand lectures and read textbooks. She
13.

continued to help Helen for the rest of her life. Her (sight eyes/eyesight) became worse, and she became
14.

(complete/completely) blind. She died in 1936. Helen lived until 1968.
15.

Michelle OBAMA

Read the following article. Pay special attention to the words in bold. 🎧 10.4

On January 17th, 1964, a baby was born into a middle-class family in Chicago. She had a happy childhood. Her family had **enough money**, but they were definitely not rich. This little girl grew up to be Michelle Obama—one of the most famous women in the world.

Michelle's parents believed in the importance of education. They always encouraged[1] her to study hard and try her best. Michelle's grades were **very good**. They were **good enough** to get into Harvard Law School. When she graduated, she worked to help people and communities.

Michelle met Barack Obama at her law firm. They fell in love, got married, and had two daughters. When Barack became president in 2009, Mrs. Obama became first lady. They were in the White House for eight years. During that time, Mrs. Obama worked hard to improve the lives of young people.

Mrs. Obama was concerned about children's health. Many American children do not get **enough exercise**, and their diets aren't **healthy enough**. They eat **too much fat and sugar**. In 2010, Mrs. Obama started a program[2] called *Let's Move!* It helped schools and parents make healthier choices for kids, and it helped kids get more exercise.

Mrs. Obama was also concerned about children's education. She believed many young people stopped their education **too early**. She felt that a high school degree did not provide **enough education**. In 2014, Mrs. Obama started the Reach Higher program. Because of the program, thousands of young people continued their education in community colleges and four-year colleges. In 2015, Mrs. Obama started Let Girls Learn, a program to help girls around the world go to school and stay in school.

The Obamas are no longer in the White House. However, Mrs. Obama is still busy. She often visits schools and talks to students about the importance of education. Mrs. Obama continues to be a popular role model[3] for young people—not just in America—but around the world.

---

[1] encouraged: made someone hopeful or confident
[2] program: a plan of things done in order to reach a certain goal
[3] role model: someone who other people try to be like

COMPREHENSION Based on the reading, write T for *true* or F for *false*.

1. _____ Michelle Obama was a good student.

2. _____ Michelle Obama encouraged young people to get more exercise.

3. _____ After she left the White House, Michelle Obama stopped being a role model.

THINK ABOUT IT Discuss the questions with a partner or in a small group.

1. What do you know about other First Ladies? Was Michelle Obama different from the others?

2. How much difference do you think that one person can make in the world?

10.6 *Very* and *Too*

EXAMPLES	EXPLANATION
Michelle Obama believes that education is **very important** for girls. She did **very well** in school.	*Very* shows a large degree. We can put *very* before adjectives and adverbs.
Some veterans said Maya Lin's design was **too simple** to honor the soldiers. Lilly Ledbetter brought her case to the Supreme Court, but it was **too late**.	*Too* shows that there is a problem. We can put *too* before adjectives and adverbs. We sometimes use an infinitive phrase after the *too* phrase.

GRAMMAR IN USE

To make a statement stronger, we use *much too* + adj/adv.

> She arrived **much too late**. *Everyone was gone.*

Don't confuse *much too* (+ adj/adv) with *too much* (+ noun).

> *I ate* **much too fast**.
> *I ate* **too much candy**.

EXERCISE 12 Fill in the blanks with *very* or *too*. Both answers may be possible.

1. Helen Keller was _____ *very* _____ intelligent.

2. She became _____ wild, and her parents needed help with her.

3. Anne Sullivan worked _____ patiently with Helen.

4. At first, some people thought Maya Lin's design was _____ unusual. They wanted

    a more traditional design.

5. Most people love her memorial. They think it's _____ beautiful.

6. She was _____ happy when the committee chose her design.

7. Lilly Ledbetter worked _____ hard for her company.

8. Ledbetter learned about pay inequality for women _____ late to do anything about it.

9. Christina Ripp Schwab is _____ talented. She won a gold medal at the Paralympics.

10.7 Enough

EXAMPLES	EXPLANATION
American children's diets aren't **healthy enough**. Michelle Obama was **concerned enough** to start a program called *Let's Move*.	*Enough* means "as much as needed." We use *enough* after adjectives and adverbs.
American children don't get **enough exercise**.	We use *enough* before nouns.

Note:

We often use an infinitive after *too* and *enough*. Remember that an infinitive often expresses a purpose.

> I wake up early **enough to go** for a run before work.

EXERCISE 13 Fill in the blanks with the words given and *enough*.

1. Helen Keller was ____determined enough____ to graduate from college.
                         determined

2. Anne Sullivan was _____ to work with Helen.
                              patient

3. She had _____ to teach Helen many things.
                      time

4. Maya Lin's project was _____ to win the competition.
                                   good

5. Lilly Ledbetter didn't have _____ about
                                        information

   the salaries of other workers.

6. She wasn't _____ to lift heavy tires.
                       strong

7. Did she make _____ to send her children to college?
                          money

8. Michelle Obama's grades were _____ to get into Harvard Law School.
                                           good

FUN WITH GRAMMAR

Write test-taking tips. Work in a small group. Imagine a friend is going to take an important test tomorrow. Write advice for your friend using adjectives, adverbs, *very*, *too*, and *enough*. Then compare your advice as a class. Cross out any advice that another group also has. The group with the most unique sentences wins.

Don't worry too much.

Work quickly but carefully.

Leave enough time to review your answers.

SUMMARY OF UNIT 10

Adjectives and Adverbs

ADJECTIVE	ADVERB
Anne Sullivan was **patient**.	She taught Helen **patiently**.
The Vietnam Veterans Memorial is **beautiful**.	Maya Lin designed it **beautifully**.
Helen Keller was a **good** student.	She did **well** in school.
Lilly Ledbetter had a **late** shift.	She worked **late**.
Pay discrimination is a **frequent** problem.	Pay discrimination occurs **frequently**.

Adjective Modifiers and Noun Modifiers

ADJECTIVE MODIFIER	NOUN MODIFIER
a **hard** job	a **factory** job
a **new** company	a **tire** company
good sight	**eye**sight
expensive tuition	**college** tuition
a **young** child	a **seven-year-old** child

Very, Too, and *Enough*

very + adjective	Lilly Ledbetter was **very brave**.
very + adverb	She worked **very hard**.
too + adjective	You're never **too old** to learn something new.
too + adverb	Some workers work **too slowly**.
adjective + *enough*	Ledbetter was **brave enough** to fight for her rights.
adverb + *enough*	Visitors to the Vietnam Veterans Memorial move **slowly enough** to read all the names.
enough + noun	Ledbetter didn't make **enough money**.

REVIEW

Choose the correct word(s) to complete the essay.

We just read a story about Grandma Moses. We learned that you are never (*too old/too much old*) to
1.

learn something new. Grandma Moses was a 72-(*year/years*)-old grandmother when she started to paint.
2.

She couldn't do many things because of (*health problems/problems health*), but she could hold a
3.

(*brushpaint/paintbrush*). She made many beautiful (*paintings oil/oil paintings*). She continued painting until
4.   5.

she died at the age of 101. I think her story is (*too/very*) interesting.
6.

I always thought I was (*too old/very old*) to learn a (*foreign language/language foreign*), but now that
7.   8.

I'm in the United States, I need to learn it. Most of the students in my (*English class/class English*) are
9.

(*too/very*) young and learn (*quick/quickly*). But I am 59 years old, and I don't learn (*fast/fastly*). However,
10.   11.   12.

most of my (*mates class/classmates*) have a job, so they (*hard/hardly*) ever have time to study. Some of them
13.   14.

have small children, so they are very (*busy/busily*). I'm not working, and my children are
15.

(*enough old/old enough*) to take care of themselves. My kids are (*proud/proudly*) of me for going to college
16.   17.

at my age. My teacher always tells me I'm doing (*too/very*) well in her class.
18.

After learning English, I'm planning to get a (*history degree/degree history*). I am (*too/very*) interested
19.   20.

in history. When I finish my degree, I'll be in my sixties. It will (*probable/probably*) be too (*late/lately*) for
21.   22.

me to find a job, but I don't care. I know I'll have to study (*hard/hardly*) because history books are
23.

(*hard/hardly*) to read. But I am (*too/very*) interested, so I know I can do it. Besides, if Grandma Moses
24.   25.

could learn to paint in her seventies and write a book when she was 92, I can (*certain/certainly*) study
26.

history at my age. Grandma Moses is a very (*well/good*) example for me.
27.

FROM GRAMMAR TO WRITING

PART 1 Editing Advice

1. Don't make adjectives plural.

   Helen Keller and Michelle Obama were ~~excellents~~ excellent students.

2. Put the specific noun before the general noun.

   The Vietnam Veterans Memorial is a ~~memorial war~~ war memorial.

3. Some adjectives end in *-d* or *-ed*. Don't omit the *-d* or *-ed*.

   She was tire_d_ after the long game.

4. If the adjective ends in *-ed*, don't forget to include the verb *be*.

   Helen _was_ excited to learn to communicate.

5. A noun modifier is always singular.

   Lilly worked for a ~~tires~~ tire company.

6. Put the adjective before the noun.

   Anne Sullivan had a _hard_ childhood ~~hard~~.

7. Don't confuse *too* and *very*. *Too* indicates a problem.

   Helen was ~~too~~ very intelligent.

8. Don't confuse *too much* and *too*. A noun follows *too much*. An adjective or adverb follows *too*.

   You're never too ~~much~~ old to learn.

9. Put *enough* after the adjective.

   Maya was ~~enough~~ talented _enough_ to win the contest.

10. Put *late, early, fast,* or *hard* at the end of the verb phrase.

    She ~~late~~ came home _late_ from work last night.

11. Don't separate the verb phrase with an adverb of manner.

    Anne taught ~~patiently~~ Helen _patiently_.

12. Use an adverb, not an adjective, to describe a verb.

    Companies should treat men and women equal_ly_.

    Christina plays basketball very ~~good~~ well.

PART 2 Editing Practice

Some of the shaded words and phrases have mistakes. Find the mistakes and correct them. If the shaded words are correct, write C.

     really   *C*

I ~~real~~ admire my aunt Rosa. She's very intelligent. She is marry and has three adults children. When
  1.   **2.**   **3.**   **4.**

her children became enough old to take care of themselves, she decided to go back to college. She wants
                                        5.

to study programming computer. Some people say she's too much old to start a new career, but she doesn't
               6.   **7.**   **8.**

care. She loves computers. She also works part-time at a flowers shop. She thinks it's a job very interesting.
                                         9.   **10.**

She's very nicely to everyone, and everyone loves her. Whenever I need advice, I can go to her. She listens
          11.

patiently and treats everyone kind.
 12.   **13.**

    Rosa came to the United States from Guatemala when she was 18. She had five younger sisters and

brothers. Her mother died when she was young, and she had to take care of her brothers and sisters. She
                                 14.

took care of them wonderfully. She didn't speak one word of English when she left Guatemala. She learned
                    15.

quickly English, and now she speaks English very good.
    16.   **17.**

    Rosa is not only my aunt—she's a good friend.
                             18.

WRITING TIP

To find more information about a topic, you should do some research on the Internet. Include a list of the sources you used at the end of your paragraph. Ask your teacher what type of information you should include in this list besides the web address.

PART 3 Write

Read the prompts. Choose one and write one paragraph about it.

1. Write about a person you know who accomplished something at an older age or with a disability. Do some research to find information.
2. Write about a woman whom you admire very much. You may write about a famous woman or any woman you know. If you write about a famous woman, do some research to find information about her.

PART 4 Edit

Reread the Summary of Unit 10 and the editing advice. Edit your writing from Part 3.

UNIT

11

Comparatives and Superlatives

A mirror illusion makes an entertainer at the State Fair of Texas look like half a man.

AMERICAN
EXPERIENCES

STATE FAIR OF TEXAS

America is not a country, it is a world.
OSCAR WILDE

Climbing DENALI

Read the following article. Pay special attention to the words in bold. 🎧 11.1

We often hear about people climbing Mount Everest, **the highest** mountain in the world. What about **the tallest** mountain in the United States?

The highest peak[1] in the United States is Denali in Denali National Park in Alaska. If you measure it from the base to the peak, it's actually **much higher than** Mount Everest. The base of Mount Everest is at 17,000 feet above sea level. It is 12,000 feet from the base to the top of Mount Everest. The base of Denali is at 2,000 feet above sea level. It is 18,000 feet from the base to the top of Denali.

Denali is one of **the most difficult** challenges in the Western Hemisphere for mountain climbers. Denali is

closer to the North Pole **than** other tall mountains. This means that the air is **thinner**, so it's **harder** for climbers to breathe. June is **the busiest** month for climbers. **The deadliest** season was May 1992, when 11 climbers died.

The first group of climbers reached the top of Denali in 1909. Two other groups were successful after that. The next group reached the top in 1947. This group included a husband and wife team, Bradford and Barbara Washburn. Barbara was the first woman to successfully climb the mountain.

The Washburns were not climbing for sport; they were explorers. In the field of mountain mapping, Bradford Washburn was one of **the best**. The Washburns mapped many mountains and the Grand Canyon. Bradford dreamed of mapping Mount Everest. Finally, in 1981, the Washburns worked on the Mount Everest project. They produced **the most detailed**[2] and **most accurate**[3] map ever made of Mount Everest.

---

[1] peak: the top of a mountain
[2] detailed: full of small bits of information
[3] accurate: exact

EVEREST
29,029 ft

DENALI
20,320 ft

Base to peak
12,000 ft

Elevation (ft)

30,000
25,000
20,000
15,000
10,000
5,000
Sea level

Base to peak
18,000 ft

A mountain ranger climbs on Denali. Every year, mountain rangers of the Denali National Park Service help climbers in need.

COMPREHENSION Based on the reading, write T for *true* or F for *false*.

1. _____ Denali is the tallest mountain in the world.

2. _____ The first person to reach the top of Denali was a woman.

3. _____ Between 1909 and 1947, many climbers reached the top of Denali.

THINK ABOUT IT Discuss the questions with a partner or in a small group.

1. Why do you think people like to climb tall mountains?

2. Would you like to try mountain climbing? Why or why not?

11.1 Comparatives and Superlatives—An Overview

EXAMPLES	EXPLANATION
Denali is **closer** to the North Pole than Mount Everest. Most climbers think Mount Everest is **more difficult** to climb than Denali.	We use comparatives to compare two items.
Mount Everest is **the highest** mountain in the world. This is **the most accurate** map of Mount Everest.	We use superlatives for the number one item in a group of three or more.

EXERCISE 1 Listen to the report. Then write T for *true*, F for *false*, or NS for *not stated*. 🎧 11.2

1. _____ The United States is the largest country in the world.

2. _____ California is the flattest state in the country.

3. _____ It is very expensive to live in San Jose, California.

EXERCISE 2 Listen again. Fill in the blanks with the words you hear. 🎧 11.2

1. The _____ city in the United States is New York. It has about 8.5 million people.

   It is _____ than Los Angeles.

2. In population, the United States is the third _____ country in the world.

   Only China and India are _____ .

3. In area, the United States is also the third _____ country in the world. Only Russia

   and Canada are _____ .

4. San Jose, California, has the _____ cost of living in the United States. But the cost

   of living in Singapore is much _____ .

5. The _____ waterfall in the United States is Yosemite Falls in California.

   But Niagara Falls is _____ .

continued

6. California is the _____ state. It has about 40 million people. There are

   _____ people in California than in New York State.

7. Alaska is the _____ state in area. Alaska is even _____ than Texas.

8. Phoenix, Arizona, gets the _____ sunshine. Bellingham, Washington,

   gets the _____ sunshine.

9. The _____ state is Delaware. The _____ state is Hawaii.

11.2 Some Common Comparatives and Superlatives

	SIMPLE	COMPARATIVE	SUPERLATIVE
One-syllable adjectives and adverbs	tall fast	taller faster	the tallest the fastest
Two-syllable adjectives that end in -y	easy deadly	easier deadlier	the easiest the deadliest
Other two-syllable adjectives	famous active	more famous more active	the most famous the most active
Some two-syllable adjectives that have two forms	simple quiet	simpler more simple quieter more quiet	the simplest the most simple the quietest the most quiet
Adjectives with three or more syllables	important difficult	more important more difficult	the most important the most difficult
Adjectives that end in -ed	tired worried	more tired more worried	the most tired the most worried
Adverbs that end in -ly	quickly brightly	more quickly more brightly	the most quickly the most brightly
Irregular comparatives and superlatives	good/well bad/badly far	better worse farther	the best the worst the farthest
Quantity words	little few	less fewer	the least the fewest
	a lot much many	more	the most

GRAMMAR IN USE

Generally for two-syllable adjectives that have two forms, the -er forms are much more common than the *more* forms.

angry → angrier/more angry	narrow → narrower/more narrow
friendly → friendlier/more friendly	polite → politer/more polite
gentle → gentler/more gentle	pretty → prettier/more pretty
handsome → handsomer/more handsome	stupid → stupider/more stupid

EXERCISE 3 Write C for *comparative statements* and S for *superlative statements*.

1. Los Angeles is smaller than New York City. _____C_____

2. Alaska has more snow than Wyoming. _____

3. In the United States, Denali is the most challenging mountain for climbers. _____

4. Mount Everest is farther from the North Pole than Denali. _____

5. The United States is smaller than Russia. _____

6. Canada is bigger than the United States in area. _____

7. Wyoming is the least populated state in the United States. _____

8. May 1992 was the deadliest season on Denali. _____

11.3 Short Adjectives and Adverbs—Spelling of Comparatives and Superlatives

RULE	SIMPLE	COMPARATIVE	SUPERLATIVE
For short adjectives and adverbs, add -er or -est.	tall fast	tall**er** fast**er**	tall**est** fast**est**
For adjectives that end in -e, add -r or -st.	nice late	nice**r** late**r**	nice**st** late**st**
For adjectives that end in -y, change y to i and add -er or -est.	easy happy	eas**ier** happ**ier**	eas**iest** happ**iest**
For one-syllable words that end in consonant-vowel-consonant, double the final consonant and add -er or -est.	big sad	big**ger** sad**der**	big**gest** sad**dest**

EXERCISE 4 Write the comparative and superlative forms of these words. There may be more than one correct answer.

	Comparative	Superlative
1. interesting	more interesting	the most interesting
2. young		
3. beautiful		
4. good		

continued

	Comparative	Superlative
5. quiet	_____	_____
6. thin	_____	_____
7. carefully	_____	_____
8. pretty	_____	_____
9. bad	_____	_____
10. famous	_____	_____
11. lucky	_____	_____
12. simple	_____	_____
13. high	_____	_____
14. important	_____	_____
15. far	_____	_____
16. foolishly	_____	_____

11.4 Using Superlatives

EXAMPLES	EXPLANATION
New York is **the biggest** city in the U.S. California is **the most populated** state in the U.S. China has **the largest** population in the world.	We use *the* before superlatives. We often put a prepositional phrase at the end of a superlative. *in the world* *in my family* *in my class* *in the U.S.*
Niagara Falls is **one of the most popular attractions** in the U.S. One World Trade Center is **one of the tallest buildings** in the world.	We often put *one of the* before the superlative. Then we use a plural noun.

Note:

We can substitute a possessive adjective for *the* before a superlative.

*What was **your** most exciting vacation?*

GRAMMAR IN USE

You can use the superlative without a noun if the meaning is clear.

*I have three brothers. Enrique is **the tallest**.*

*I have three tests this week. My history test will be **the hardest**.*

EXERCISE 5 Fill in the blanks with the superlative form of the words given. Include *the* before the superlative.

1. Alaska is _____<u>the largest</u>_____ state in area.
   <small>large</small>

2. _____ lake in the United States is Lake Superior.
   <small>big</small>

3. _____ river in the United States is the Missouri River.
   <small>long</small>

4. _____ mountain in the United States is Denali.
   <small>high</small>

5. The Vietnam Veterans Memorial is one of _____ tourist
   <small>popular</small>

   attractions in Washington, DC.

6. New York City is one of _____ cities in the United States.
   <small>expensive</small>

7. San Francisco is one of _____ American cities.
   <small>beautiful</small>

8. Harvard is one of _____ universities in the United States.
   <small>good</small>

9. Crime is one of _____ problems in big cities.
   <small>bad</small>

10. Boston is one of _____ cities in the United States.
    <small>old</small>

11. _____ state to join the United States is Hawaii.
    <small>recent</small>

12. The state that is _____ north is Alaska.
    <small>far</small>

EXERCISE 6 Write a true superlative sentence using the words given. You may use *one of the +* superlative *+ a plural noun.* Then find a partner and compare your sentences.

1. long street in this city

   <u>Western Avenue is the longest street in this city.</u>

2. interesting place in this city

   _____

3. good restaurant in this city

   _____

4. beautiful city in the United States

   _____

5. big problem in the United States

   _____

continued

6. important invention of the last 100 years

_____

7. popular movie star in the United States

_____

8. pretty neighborhood in this city

_____

11.5 Word Order with Superlatives

EXAMPLES	EXPLANATION
Denali is **the highest mountain** in the United States. In Boston, 2015 was one of **the worst winters**.	We put a superlative adjective before a noun.
The population of Seattle, Washington, **is increasing the most rapidly**.	We can put a superlative adverb after the verb.
It **rains the least** in Las Vegas. It **snows the most** in Alaska.	We can put _the most, the least, the best,_ and _the worst_ by themselves after the verb.

EXERCISE 7 Fill in the blanks by putting the words given in the correct order. Use _the_ and the superlative form of the adjectives and adverbs given.

1. Rhode Island is _____the smallest state_____ in the United States.

small/state

2. _____ in the United States is Lake Superior.

big/lake

3. _____ of Latinos is in New Mexico.

large/population

4. California has _____ in the United States.

diverse/population

5. The Asian American population in the United States _____.

fast/is increasing

6. Latinos are _____ in the United States.

young/minority group

7. Alaska has _____ in the United States.

cold/weather

8. School children in Lakewood, Ohio, _____ because they

a lot/walk
   have no school buses.

9. _____ in the world are in California.

old/trees

10. The population of Seattle, Washington, _____.

rapidly/is growing

Doing Things DIFFERENTLY

Read the following article. Pay special attention to the words in bold. 🎧 11.3

Travel to any country in the world, and you will discover something. The country is similar to your own in some ways, and different in others. Each country has its own unique[1] ways of doing things. That is certainly true for the United States. Some of these things may surprise you.

For example, Americans use ounces, feet, and Fahrenheit to measure. But most other countries of the world use the metric system of grams, meters, and Celsius.

Food portions in the United States are usually **much larger than** in other parts of the world. Researchers found that the average size of a meal in a restaurant in Paris is 25 percent **smaller than** the size of a meal in a restaurant in Philadelphia. The serving sizes in stores are **larger** in Philadelphia, too. Sodas are 52 percent **bigger**, and yogurt servings are 82 percent **bigger!**

American money looks different from money in most other countries. The green, white, and black design of American bills is **plainer** and **less interesting than** the colorful bills of other countries.

In most countries, sales tax is included in the price of items. In the U.S., the price tag doesn't include the tax. Visitors to the U.S. often don't know this. They are surprised that items are **more expensive than** the price on the tag.

But it's not just food, measurements, and money that are different in the United States. Americans may act differently, too. For example, Americans often make small talk[2] with strangers. Because of this, some people think Americans are **friendlier than** people in other countries. However, many people say that Americans talk **louder** and laugh **more frequently**. This makes them think that Americans are **ruder than** people from other countries!

Do these differences make the United States **better** or **worse than** other countries? No, they don't. They just give the United States its own unique personality[3].

---

[1] unique: very unusual; the only one of its kind
[2] small talk: friendly conversation about unimportant subjects
[3] personality: the set of qualities that makes a person or place different from other people or places

The Grand Canyon is a popular tourist destination. It is 277 miles (446 km) long, up to 18 miles (29 km) wide, and a mile (1.6 km) deep.

COMPREHENSION Based on the reading, write T for *true* or F for *false*.

1. _____ Restaurants in the United States serve a lot of food to their customers.

2. _____ Americans often seem friendly because they make a lot of small talk.

3. _____ The United States uses Celsius to measure temperature.

THINK ABOUT IT Discuss the questions with a partner or in a small group.

1. Why do you think the United States does not use the metric system?

2. Why do you think serving sizes of food are so much bigger in the U.S. than in other places?

11.6 Using Comparatives

EXAMPLES	EXPLANATION
U.S. money is **plainer than** European money. Is Celsius **more common than** Fahrenheit? It's **better** to use the metric system **than** other forms of measurement.	When making a comparison between two items, we use *than* before the second item.
People from other countries don't make a lot of small talk. Americans seem **friendlier**.	We don't use *than* when the second item of comparison is understood.
In other countries, there is **less laughter** in the streets. In other countries, you may see **fewer smiles**.	The opposite of *more* is *less* or *fewer*. (Remember: we use *less* with noncount nouns and *fewer* with count nouns.)
Denali is **much taller** than Mount Everest. In the U.S., prices are **a little more expensive** than the amount on the tag.	We can use *much* or *a little* before a comparative form.

GRAMMAR IN USE

In speaking, when we compare two people, we usually use object pronouns after *than*.

> *You walk faster than **me**.*
> *He is friendlier than **her**.*

In formal situations, we use the subject pronoun followed by an auxiliary verb after *than*.

> *You walk faster than **I do**.*
> *He is friendlier than **she is**.*

EXERCISE 8 Fill in the blanks with the comparative form of the words given. Add *than*.

1. The top of Mount Everest is _____*higher*_____ above sea level _____*than*_____ Denali.

high

2. Climbing Mount Everest is _____ climbing Denali.

difficult

3. Bradford Washburn was four years _____ his wife, Barbara.

old

4. The air in the mountains is _____ the air at sea level.

thin

5. European money is _____ U.S. money.

colorful

6. Many people are surprised when items are _____ the amount on the price tag.
   expensive

7. The American way of doing things is not _____ the ways other countries do things.
   bad

8. Boots dry _____ shoes.
   slow

9. Mount Everest is _____ from the North Pole _____ Denali.
   far

EXERCISE 9 Look at the information in the chart. Then fill in the blanks to make comparisons between Chicago, Illinois, and San Francisco, California. Use the words in the box and *than*.

	CHICAGO, ILLINOIS	SAN FRANCISCO, CALIFORNIA
Population	2,705,994	883,305
Average household income	$68,403	$101,714
Area	227.34 square miles	46.87 square miles
Average home cost	$226,400	$1,362,200
Average rent for a 2-bedroom apartment	$2,310	$4,690
Average snowfall	37.1 inches per year	0 inches per year
Average high temperature in July	82°F	67°F
Average low temperature in January	17°F	46°F
People over 65	11.7 percent	15.7 percent

bad	big	cheap	cool	expensive	large ✓	high	pleasant	wealthy

1. The population of Chicago is _____ *larger than* _____ the population of San Francisco.

2. San Franciscans are _____ Chicagoans. The average income is higher in San Francisco.

3. In area, Chicago is _____ San Francisco.

4. Homes in San Francisco are _____ homes in Chicago.

5. A two-bedroom apartment in Chicago is _____ a two-bedroom apartment in San Francisco.

continued

Chicago

San Francisco

6. For people who don't like snow, winters in Chicago are _____

   winters in San Francisco.

7. San Francisco is _____ Chicago in the summer.

8. For people who don't like cold weather, winters in San Francisco are

   _____ winters in Chicago.

9. There is a _____ percentage of older people in San Francisco than in Chicago.

ABOUT YOU Write sentences comparing your city to San Francisco or Chicago. Use the comparative form of the words given. Share your answers with a partner.

1. small _____

2. crowded _____

3. cold _____

4. interesting _____

5. noisy _____

6. modern _____

7. sunny _____

8. beautiful _____

9. pleasant _____

10. old _____

11. amazing _____

12. confusing _____

13. expensive _____

11.7 Word Order with Comparatives

EXAMPLES	EXPLANATION
Houses in San Francisco **are more expensive** than houses in Chicago.	We put comparative adjectives after the verb *be*.
San Francisco has **more sunshine** than Chicago. San Francisco has **less rain** than Chicago.	We put *more, less, fewer, better, worse,* and other comparative adjectives before the noun.
The Asian population **is growing more quickly** than the Latino population.	We put comparative adverbs after the verb.
It **rains less** in San Francisco than in Chicago.	We put *more, less, better,* and *worse* by themselves after the verb.

EXERCISE 10 Look at the information in the chart. Then fill in the blanks to make comparisons between Miami, Florida, and Los Angeles, California. Use the words given and the comparative form.

	MIAMI, FLORIDA	LOS ANGELES, CALIFORNIA
Population	463,347	3,999,759
Percentage change in population 2010–2017	16.0	5.5
Median household income	$33,999	$54,501
Average household size	2.63	2.83
Average rent for a 2-bedroom apartment	$2,437	$3,256
Average rainfall	51.73 inches	14.93 inches
Average high temperature in January	73.8°F	68.2°F
Average high temperature in July	88.1°F	83.1°F
Average travel time to work	28.1 minutes	30.9 minutes

1. The trip to work takes _____ for people in Los Angeles than for people in Miami.
   long

2. In January and July, the weather in Miami is _____
   hot

   than the weather in Los Angeles.

3. It is much _____ in Miami than in Los Angeles.
   rainy

4. It is _____ to rent a two-bedroom apartment in Miami than in Los Angeles.
   expensive

5. In Miami the average household is _____ than in Los Angeles.
   small

6. People in Los Angeles have a _____ median income than people in Miami.
   high

7. There are _____ in Los Angeles than in Miami.
   people

8. The population is _____ in Miami than in Los Angeles.
   growing/fast

ABOUT YOU Compare the city you live in now to another city you know. Use comparative adjectives and the words given. Share your answers with a partner.

1. public transportation _____

2. factories _____

3. crowded _____

4. clean _____

5. tall buildings _____

6. snow _____

7. sunny _____

continued

8. traffic _____

9. beautiful _____

10. job opportunities _____

EXERCISE 11 Fill in the blanks with the comparative form of the words given. Put the words in the correct order. Add *than* where necessary.

I'm from Genoa, a small town in Illinois. Now I live in Chicago. Chicago is ___*much bigger than*___
                                                                      1. much/big

Genoa, but there are many other differences. In Genoa, it's _____ to go from place to
                                                   2. easy

place because there is _____. So I spend _____ in my car.
                         3. traffic/little   **4.** little/time

Parking is _____ in Chicago. I also have to walk _____ in
                   5. expensive   **6.** much/far

Chicago to get to my destination, so I get _____. Of course, Chicago has
                                          7. exercise

_____ Genoa.
    8. good/public transportation

People in Genoa are _____ people in Chicago. Neighbors talk to each other,
                            9. friendly

help each other, and watch out for each other. As a result, Genoa is _____
                                                 10. safe

Chicago.

In Chicago, there are _____ such as movies, concerts, plays, and sporting
                          11. activities

events. I like these activities, but I spend _____ I do in Genoa.
                                  12. money

The climate is the same in both places. But in winter, when there's a lot of snow, Chicago usually

clears the snow _____. Genoa has _____ and
                       13. quickly   **14.** little/equipment

_____ for snow removal.
    15. few/workers

For me, life in Genoa is _____ it is in Chicago. Genoa is
                          16. much/comfortable

_____, and the town is _____ Chicago.
    17. much/relaxed   **18.** quiet

EXERCISE 12 Fill in the blanks with the comparative or superlative form of the word given. Add *than* or *the* where necessary.

1. August is usually ___*hotter than*___ May in Miami.
                         hot

2. January is usually ___*the coldest*___ month of the year in Minneapolis.
                            cold

3. Los Angeles is _____ San Francisco.
                          warm

4. Los Angeles is _____ city in California.
   big

5. The state of Hawaii is _____ south in the United States.
   far

6. New York City is _____ Los Angeles.
   crowded

7. Niagara Falls is one of _____ U.S. tourist attractions.
   popular

8. San Francisco is one of _____ U.S. cities.
   beautiful

9. _____ mountain in the United States is in Alaska.
   tall

10. _____ city in the United States is San Jose, California.
    expensive

ABOUT YOU Discuss the questions with a partner.

1. What is the best thing about living in the United States? What is the worst thing?

2. In choosing where to live, what is the most important thing to consider?

3. In your opinion, which is better: life in a small town or life in a big city?

4. What is the most beautiful part of this city?

5. Do you think that it's better to own a house or rent an apartment in this city?

6. In your opinion, what is the most pleasant month in this city?

7. In your opinion, what is the worst month in this city?

8. In this city, is it easier to drive or use public transportation?

FUN WITH GRAMMAR

Race to write. Work in small groups. Write as many sentences as you can comparing the people in your group. Use comparatives and superlatives. The team with the most comparisons after three minutes wins.

Sara is taller than Steve.

Janet is the tallest.

Steve speaks more languages than Sara or Janet.

SUMMARY OF UNIT 11

Comparatives and Superlatives with Adjectives

ADJECTIVES WITH ONE SYLLABLE OR WITH TWO SYLLABLES THAT END IN -Y	
Chicago is a **big** city.	Madison, Wisconsin, is a **happy** U.S. city.
Chicago is **bigger than** Houston.	Irvine, California, is **happier** than Madison.
New York is **the biggest** U.S. city.	Plano, Texas, is **the happiest** U.S. city.

ADJECTIVES WITH TWO OR MORE SYLLABLES
Houston is a **populated** city.
Chicago is **more populated than** Houston.
New York is **the most populated** U.S. city.

Comparatives and Superlatives with Adverbs

ADVERBS WITH ONE SYLLABLE
He walks **fast**.
He walks **faster than** you do.
I walk **the fastest**.

-LY ADVERBS
The population of Phoenix is increasing **rapidly**.
The population of Austin is increasing **more rapidly**.
The population of Seattle is increasing **the most rapidly**.

Comparisons with *Less* and *Fewer*

COUNT NOUNS
Seattle has **fewer people** than Los Angeles.

NONCOUNT NOUNS
Los Angeles has **less rain** than Seattle.

Word Order in Comparison

BE + COMPARATIVE/SUPERLATIVE ADJECTIVE	
Comparative	Bradford Washburn **was older** than his wife.
	Mount Everest **is more challenging** than Denali.
Superlative	Mount Everest **is the tallest mountain** in the world.
	The tallest mountain in the world **is** Mount Everest.

COMPARATIVE/SUPERLATIVE ADJECTIVE + NOUN	
Comparative	Bradford Washburn had **more experience** than his wife.
Superlative	New York City is **the most populated state** in the U.S.

VERB + COMPARATIVE/SUPERLATIVE ADVERB	
Comparative	Some people say Americans **laugh more frequently** than people from other countries.
Superlative	We **eat** at this restaurant **the most frequently**.

REVIEW

Fill in the blanks using the comparative or superlative form of the word(s) given. Put the words in the correct order. Add *than* or *the* where necessary.

A: I'm planning to visit Chicago.

B: You're going to love it. It's one of _____ *the most beautiful cities* _____ in the U.S.

1. beautiful city

A: It's the second largest city, isn't it?

B: No. It's the third. Los Angeles and New York are _____ Chicago.

2. big

When you're there, you can visit the Willis Tower. It's one of _____

3. tall/building

in the U.S. It has 110 stories. Go on a sunny day. You can see _____ . When

4. far/much

I was there, it was cloudy. I hope you have _____ I had. When

5. good/weather

are you going?

A: In August.

B: Ugh! August is _____ of the summer. It's often 90 degrees or more. If

6. month/bad

it's too hot, you can always go to the beach and cool off. Chicago is near Lake Michigan.

A: Is it big like Lake Washington?

B: It's _____ Lake Washington. In fact, it's one of

7. big/much

_____ in the U.S.

8. lake/large

A: Is Chicago very rainy?

B: Not in the summer. It's sunny. In fact, it's _____ Seattle.

9. sunny/much

A: What do you like about Chicago?

B: The architecture downtown is amazing. The _____ in the

10. architects/good

U.S. designed the buildings.

A: Do I need to take taxis everywhere?

B: Taxis are so expensive! They're _____ the

11. much/expensive

buses and trains. Use public transportation. But be careful at night. It's _____ to travel in

12. safe

the daytime.

A: Does Chicago have _____ Seattle?

13. crime/more

B: Yes. But if you're careful, you'll be OK. I'm sure you'll enjoy it. It's an interesting place. I think it's one of

_____ in the United States.

14. interesting/city

FROM GRAMMAR TO WRITING

PART 1 Editing Advice

1. Don't use *more* and *-er* together.

    The weather in May is ~~more~~ better than the weather in January.

2. Use *than* before the second item in a comparison.

    Mount Everest is higher ~~that~~ **than** Denali.

3. Use *the* before a superlative form.

    China has **the** biggest population in the world.

4. Use a plural noun after the phrase *one of the*.

    Willis Tower is one of the tallest building**s** in the United States.

5. Use the correct word order.

    People in big cities farther ~~travel~~ **travel** to get to work.

    There is traffic ~~less~~ **less** in a small town.

    Denali is the ~~mountain~~ most challenging **mountain** in the United States.

6. Don't use *the* with a possessive form.

    My ~~the~~ most interesting vacation was in Alaska.

7. Use correct spelling.

    Miami is ~~sunnyer~~ **sunnier** than Seattle.

PART 2 Editing Practice

Some of the shaded words and phrases have mistakes. Find the mistakes and correct them. If the shaded words are correct, write C.

    I used to live in Mexico City. Now I live in St. Louis. These cities are very ~~different~~. Mexico City is

                                                                                  C
                                                                                 1.

bigger

~~more biger~~ than St. Louis. In fact, it's one of the biggest city in the world. It's certainly the most large
  2.   3.   4.

city in Mexico. St. Louis has no mountains. Mexico City is surrounded by tall mountains. I think Mexico
                                                                  5.

City is prettyer that St. Louis. It has beautiful parks. Mexico City is more interesting St. Louis. It has
       6.   7.   8.

great museums.

    But Mexico City has a few serious problems: it has pollution more than St. Louis. My the oldest brother
                                               9.   10.

still lives there, and he always complains about the air quality. I think it has the worst air quality in the
                                                             11.

Americas. And I hate the subway. I think it's the subway most crowded in the world.
                                                      12.

    No city is perfect. Each one has advantages and disadvantages. But my heart is in Mexico City because

my family and best friends live there.
            13.

WRITING TIP

When you compare two places, it's a good idea to choose three factors (e.g., size, weather, cost of living). Write one or two sentences about each factor, comparing the two places. For each factor, write one sentence using a comparative and a second sentence that gives more detail.

    Miami is smaller than Los Angeles. Miami has a population of 463,347 people, and Los Angeles has a population of 3,999,759.

PART 3 Write

Read the prompts. Choose one and write one paragraph about it.

1. Write a paragraph comparing two cities you know well.
2. In choosing where to live, what are the most important things to consider?

PART 4 Edit

Reread the Summary of Unit 11 and the editing advice. Edit your writing from Part 3.

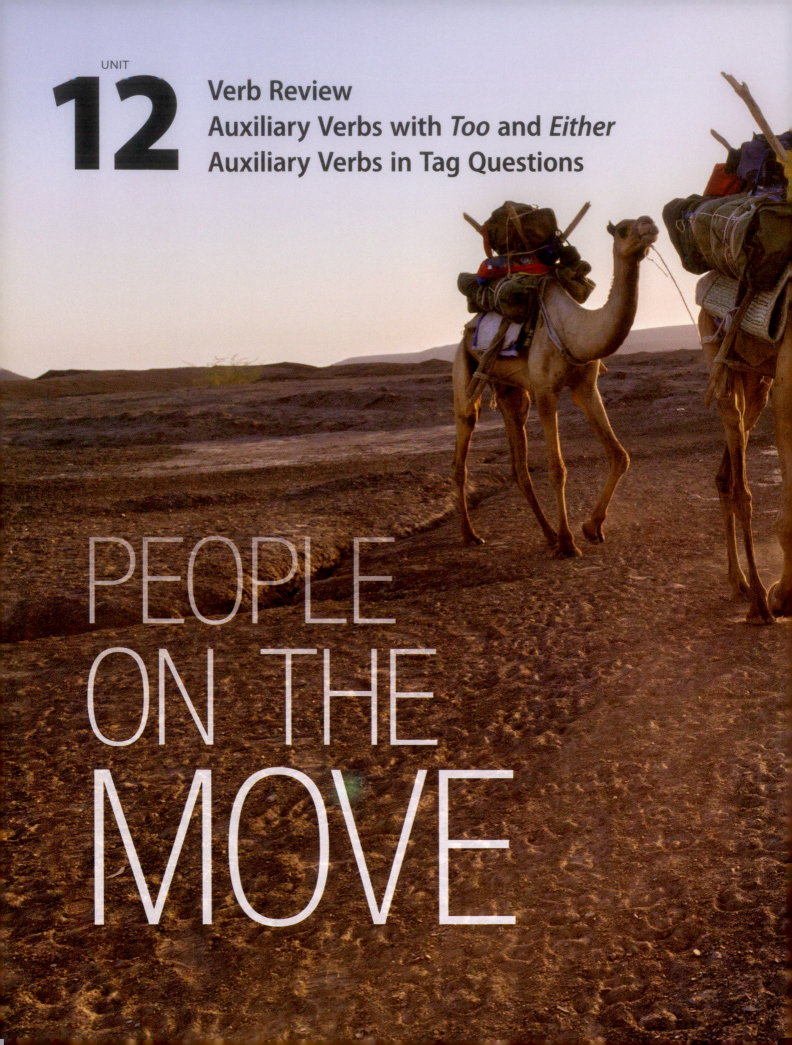

UNIT

12

Verb Review
Auxiliary Verbs with _Too_ and _Either_
Auxiliary Verbs in Tag Questions

PEOPLE ON THE MOVE

National Geographic Explorer
Paul Salopek traveling across
Ethiopia's Afar desert in East Africa

We keep moving forward, opening new doors,
and doing new things, because we're curious
and curiosity keeps leading us down new paths.

WALT DISNEY

Barrington Irving:
FLYING TO INSPIRE[1]

Read the following article. Pay special attention to the words in bold. 🎧 12.1

Barrington Irving **was born** in Jamaica and **moved** to Miami when he **was** six years old. When he **was** 15, he **had** a job in his parents' bookstore. A man **came** in one day in an unfamiliar uniform and **told** Irving that he **was** a professional pilot. Irving **said**, "I **don't think** I'**m** smart enough **to become** a pilot." The next day, the man **invited** Irving **to sit** in his plane. Irving **knew** immediately: he **wanted to become** a pilot. He **washed** airplanes **to earn** money for flight school.

In college, Irving **studied** aeronautical science[2] and **graduated** with honors. In 2007, at the age of 23, he **became** the youngest person **to fly** alone around the world. After 97 days and 26 stops, he **returned** to the United States.

After that experience, Irving **wanted to inspire** kids **to follow** their dreams. If you **have** a dream, he **says**, you **can do** great things. But there **is** another important thing kids **need**: powerful learning experiences. If they **have** meaningful, real-world experiences, they'**ll want to continue** their education and **start** a career.

In 2005, Irving **started** an organization called Experience Aviation. He **wanted to develop** programs **to inspire** students **to learn** about science, technology, engineering, and math. Irving **says**, "I **want to use** aviation **to excite** and **empower**[3] a new generation **to become** scientists, engineers, and explorers."

Irving's students **are working** on different projects. Some **are building** cars; some **are building** airplanes. All of them **are gaining** confidence. He **told** a group of kids in his program, "I not only **believe** you **can build** an airplane, but I'**ll fly** it if you **do**." In just 10 weeks, 60 students **built** an airplane and then **watched** Irving fly it away.

Irving **continues to fly** to locations around the world with his Flying Classroom project and **to share** information with his students on the ground.

---

[1] to inspire: to cause to work hard or be creative
[2] aeronautical science: the science of flight
[3] to empower: to give someone confidence to do something

Based on the reading, write T for *true* or F for *false*.

1. _____ Barrington Irving decided to become a pilot after meeting one as a teenager.

2. _____ Irving built a plane for his students to fly.

3. _____ Irving says that children need real-life learning experiences.

THINK ABOUT IT Discuss the questions with a partner or in a small group.

1. Irving says students need real-life learning experiences. What does he mean by that?

2. What do you think the Flying Classroom is?

12.1 Verb Review—Uses

THE SIMPLE PRESENT

EXAMPLES	EXPLANATION
Children **learn** from powerful experiences. Irving always **tries** to help students. Irving **comes** from Jamaica.	We use the simple present with facts, general truths, habits, customs, regular activities, repeated actions, and a place of origin.
He **has** a lot of experience as a pilot. He **loves** to help students.	We use the simple present with nonaction verbs.
If you give kids fun activities, they'll want to learn. **When you finish college,** you will find a good job.	We use the simple present in future *if* clauses and time clauses.

THE PRESENT CONTINUOUS

EXAMPLES	EXPLANATION
Look at those kids. They**'re building** a car.	We use the present continuous with actions that are happening now.
The kids **are gaining** confidence. Irving **is trying** to inspire kids.	We use the present continuous with longer actions that are in progress but may not be happening at this exact moment.

THE FUTURE

EXAMPLES	EXPLANATION
Careers in technology **will grow.** Careers in math **are going to grow,** too.	We use *will* or *be going to* with simple facts or predictions about the future.
I**'ll help** you with your airplane project.	We use *will* with offers.
My friend **is going to study** aeronautical science.	We use *be going to* when there is a previous plan to do something.

THE SIMPLE PAST

EXAMPLES	EXPLANATION
A pilot **invited** Irving to see his airplane. Irving **flew** around the world in 2007.	We use the simple past with short or long actions that began and ended in the past.
He **made** 26 stops on his flight around the world.	We use the simple past with repeated past actions.

continued

THE VERB *BE*

EXAMPLES	EXPLANATION
Barrington Irving **is a pilot**. He'**s interested** in helping students. His parents' store **was in Miami**.	We use *be* with descriptions and the location of the subject.
Irving **was 15** when he decided to become a pilot.	We use *be* with the age of the subject.
There are many ways to teach children.	We use *be* with *there* to say that something exists.
It is warm in Miami. When **it's 6:00** in Miami, **it's 3:00** in Los Angeles.	We use *be* to talk about weather and time. The subject is *it*.
Irving **was born** in Jamaica.	We use *be* with *born*.

MODALS

EXAMPLES	EXPLANATION
Children **can do** great things. **Could** you **teach** me to fly? People **should follow** their dreams. I **may major** in math. She **might study** engineering. A pilot **must have** a license.	We use modals to add more meaning to the main verb. The modals are *can* (ability, possibility, request, permission), *could* (request, permission), *should* (advice), *may* (possibility, permission), *might* (possibility), *would* (request), and *must* (necessity). After a modal, we use the base form.
Children **have to gain** confidence. They **are able to build** an airplane. They **are not allowed to fly** it.	Phrasal modals are *have to* (necessity), *be able to* (ability), and *be allowed to* (permission). After a phrasal modal, we use the base form.

INFINITIVES

EXAMPLES	EXPLANATION
Irving **wants to help** young people. **It's important to empower** children. Irving was **lucky to meet** a pilot.	We use infinitives after certain verbs, certain expressions beginning with *it*, and certain adjectives.
Irving uses aviation **to excite** students.	We can use infinitives to show purpose.

EXERCISE 1 Listen to each sentence and fill in the blanks with the words you hear. Then write whether you heard the simple present, present continuous, future, simple past, a modal, or an infinitive. 🎧 12.2

1. Irving _____*wanted*_____ to become a pilot. _____*simple past*_____

2. Someone _____ in him. _____

3. He _____ to help young people. _____

4. He wants _____ young people. _____

5. Jobs in science and engineering _____. _____

6. Young people _____ from Irving. _____

7. Irving _____ to fly. _____

8. Teachers _____ empower students. _____

9. It's interesting _____ about Irving's life. _____

EXERCISE 2 Choose the correct word(s) to complete this essay by a college student. If both answers are correct, circle both choices.

I'm a pre-law student at Michigan State University. I'm going (*graduate/to graduate*) next year and
                                                                                                    1.
then (*go/going*) to law school. Last year, my counselor (*told/tell*) me about internship programs in
      2.   **3.**
Washington, DC. She said I (*might/should*) apply. I (*must/had to*) get recommendations from three
                           4.   **5.**
professors. I was so excited when I (*received/receive*) my letter of acceptance. Now my life is (*move/moving*)
                                    6.   **7.**
in a new direction.

I'm an intern this semester. Besides my work, I (*take/am taking*) classes at Georgetown University.
                                                 8.
(*I'm gaining/I gain*) so much experience here. I (*know/am knowing*) much more now about the law. When I
 9.   **10.**
(*go/will go*) to law school next year, (*I have/I'll have*) a greater understanding of U.S. law.
 11.   **12.**
(*I have/I'm having*) a roommate now. Her name is Nicole. She (*graduate/graduated*) from the
 13.   **14.**
University of California last year. (*She's planning/She planned*) to (*becoming/become*) a biology teacher
                                    15.   **16.**
when (*she'll finish/she finishes*) her internship. (*It'll be/It's going to be*) easy for her (*find/to find*) a job
      17.   **18.**   **19.**
because (*there/they*) aren't enough science teachers now.
        20.
Nicole and I are serious about our jobs and classes, but we (*like/are liking*) to (*having/have*) fun, too.
                                                             21.   **22.**
Last weekend, we (*did go/went*) to the Air and Space Museum. Next weekend, we might (*to go/go*) to the art
                  23.   **24.**
museum if we (*have/will have*) enough time. (*There's/It's*) one thing Nicole and I don't like: we can't
             25.   **26.**
(*wear/to wear*) jeans to work. It's important (*look/to look*) very professional at our jobs.
 27.   **28.**
An internship is a wonderful experience. I (*think/am thinking*) all college students should (*do/to do*) an
                                             29.   **30.**
internship in preparation for their future professions.

FUN WITH GRAMMAR

Play a game of chance. With your classmates, write the names of each of these forms on slips of paper: simple present, present continuous, simple past, future (*will* and *be going to*), modals, and infinitives. Write one slip for affirmative and one for negative. There should be 14 slips of paper total. Put them in a bag. Then write each of the following topics on a separate slip of paper: *you, a classmate, a friend, a family member, a famous person*. Put these in a separate bag.

Now form two teams. Your teacher will take a slip of paper from each bag. One member of each team writes a sentence on the board using that grammar and topic. Repeat with two new slips. When the game is over, the team with the most correct sentences wins.

1 Man, 7 Years, 21,000 Miles

Read the following article. Pay special attention to the words in bold. 🎧 12.3

Can you **imagine** walking across the world? That's what journalist Paul Salopek **is doing** right now. He **started** his journey[1] in Ethiopia in 2013. By the end of his trek[2], he**'ll be** in Tierra del Fuego, South America. **Why is** he **doing** this? **How long will** it **take** him? **What is** he **going to learn** from this experience?

Salopek's project is called the Out of Eden Walk. He **is following** the path of our distant ancestors. He **wants** to understand the story of human migration[3]. Humans **started** this movement across the planet 60,000 years ago. He **estimates**[4] that he **will take** 30 million footsteps to reach his destination. He **will walk** 21,000 miles.

According to Salopek, we **are** now **living** through the greatest migrations of humans. Nearly a billion people **are moving** across the planet.

People often **ask** Salopek, "Are you crazy?" But Salopek **is learning** so much along the way. For example, he **learned** that water is like gold in the desert of Ethiopia.

About every 100 miles, Salopek **records** his journey in photographs and sounds. He **interviews** local people. He **is sharing** his journey in real time[5] with people around the world.

Salopek is a journalist and National Geographic Explorer. He often **does** unusual things. Once he **rode** a mule for a year across the mountains of Mexico to write a story. Another time, he **worked** in a gas station in Chicago to write about oil. He often **puts** himself in dangerous situations. He **traveled** by canoe for several weeks down the Congo River to report on the Congo civil war. Salopek **won** the Pulitzer Prize for his Congo report—the highest award for a journalist.

---

[1] journey: a long trip
[2] trek: a long, difficult journey
[3] human migration: a movement of people from one place to another
[4] to estimate: to guess a number using your knowledge
[5] in real time: as it happens

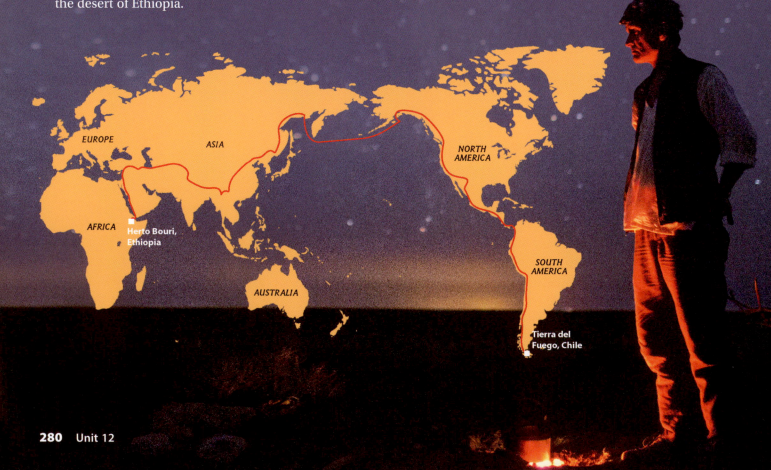

EUROPE

ASIA

NORTH AMERICA

AFRICA

Herto Bouri, Ethiopia

AUSTRALIA

SOUTH AMERICA

Tierra del Fuego, Chile

COMPREHENSION Based on the reading, write T for *true* or F for *false*.

1. _____ Salopek expects to finish his journey in Tierra del Fuego.

2. _____ Salopek's canoe trip down the Congo River put him in danger.

3. _____ Salopek will walk 60,000 miles.

THINK ABOUT IT Discuss the questions with a partner or in a small group.

1. If Salopek travels through your country, what will he learn?

2. Would you like to go on a journey like this? Why or why not?

12.2 Verb Review—Forms

THE SIMPLE PRESENT

AFFIRMATIVE STATEMENT	Barrington Irving **teaches** kids.
NEGATIVE STATEMENT	He **doesn't teach** in a school.
YES/NO QUESTION	**Does** he **teach** science?
SHORT ANSWER	Yes, he **does**.
WH- QUESTION	**Where does** he **teach**?
NEGATIVE WH- QUESTION	**Why doesn't** he **teach** in a school?
SUBJECT WH- QUESTION	**Who teaches** in a school?

THE PRESENT CONTINUOUS

AFFIRMATIVE STATEMENT	Paul Salopek **is walking** a long distance.
NEGATIVE STATEMENT	He **isn't walking** for sport.
YES/NO QUESTION	**Is** he **walking** across the United States?
SHORT ANSWER	No, he **isn't**.
WH- QUESTION	**Where is** he **walking**?
NEGATIVE WH- QUESTION	**Why isn't** he **walking** across the United States?
SUBJECT WH- QUESTION	**Who is walking** across the United States?

THE FUTURE WITH *WILL*

AFFIRMATIVE STATEMENT	The students **will learn** about science.
NEGATIVE STATEMENT	They **won't learn** about sports.
YES/NO QUESTION	**Will** they **learn** about math?
SHORT ANSWER	Yes, they **will**.
WH- QUESTION	**What** else **will** they **learn**?
NEGATIVE WH- QUESTION	**Why won't** they **learn** about sports?
SUBJECT WH- QUESTION	**Who will learn** about sports?

continued

THE FUTURE WITH *BE GOING TO*

AFFIRMATIVE STATEMENT	They **are going to study** science.
NEGATIVE STATEMENT	They **aren't going to study** math.
YES/NO QUESTION	**Are** they **going to study** biology?
SHORT ANSWER	No, they **aren't**.
WH- QUESTION	When **are** they **going to study** science?
NEGATIVE WH- QUESTION	Why **aren't** they **going to study** math?
SUBJECT WH- QUESTION	**How many** students **are going to study** math?

THE SIMPLE PAST

AFFIRMATIVE STATEMENT	Paul Salopek **started** his walk in Ethiopia.
NEGATIVE STATEMENT	He **didn't start** his walk in the United States.
YES/NO QUESTION	**Did** he **start** his walk this year?
SHORT ANSWER	No, he **didn't**.
WH- QUESTION	**When did** he **start** his walk?
NEGATIVE WH- QUESTION	**Why didn't** he **start** in South Africa?
SUBJECT WH- QUESTION	**Who** else **started** a walk?

MODALS

AFFIRMATIVE STATEMENT	I **can imagine** walking for 50 miles.
NEGATIVE STATEMENT	I **can't imagine** walking across the world.
YES/NO QUESTION	**Can** you **imagine** walking across the United States?
SHORT ANSWER	No, I **can't**.
WH- QUESTION	**How far can** you **imagine** walking?
NEGATIVE WH- QUESTION	**Why can't** you **imagine** walking across the United States?
SUBJECT WH- QUESTION	**Who can imagine** walking across the world?

EXERCISE 3 Fill in the blanks with the negative form of the underlined verb.

1. Paul Salopek <u>is</u> a journalist. He _____*isn't*_____ a pilot.

2. Salopek <u>started</u> his walk in Africa. He _____ his walk in Asia.

3. He<u>'ll finish</u> his walk in South America. He _____ his walk in Africa.

4. He<u>'s walking</u> to learn about human migration. He _____ for sport.

5. He<u>'s going to walk</u> across many countries. He _____ across Poland.

6. He <u>rode</u> across Mexico on a mule. He _____ on a horse.

7. He <u>sends</u> his stories to people around the world. He _____ stories every day.

8. He'<u>s</u> brave. He _____ afraid.

9. He <u>should be</u> careful. He _____ foolish.

EXERCISE 4 Read each statement. If the statement is about Paul Salopek, write a question about Barrington Irving. If the statement is about Barrington Irving, write a question about Paul Salopek. Write short answers.

1. Salopek is brave.

   Is Irving brave? Yes, he is. _____

2. Salopek likes to teach children.

   Does Irving like to teach children? Yes, he does. _____

3. Salopek is walking around the world.

   _____

4. Salopek named his project the Out of Eden Walk.

   _____

5. Irving flew solo around the world.

   _____

6. Salopek is sharing his knowledge with schoolchildren.

   _____

7. Irving knows a lot about the world.

   _____

8. Irving can teach children about the world.

   _____

9. Irving will meet many people around the world through his project.

   _____

10. Salopek will finish his project after seven years.

   _____

EXERCISE 5 Write *wh-* questions using the words given. Then discuss your answers to the questions with a partner. Answers may vary.

1. Kids need learning experiences.

   (what kind of) _What kind of learning experiences do kids need?_

2. Irving's students are working on a project.

   (what kind of) _____

3. Irving washed airplanes when he was young.

   (why) _____

4. Someone created the organization Experience Aviation.

   (who) _____

5. Teachers can inspire students.

   (how) _____

6. Irving didn't believe in himself at first.

   (why) _____

7. Salopek is going to walk to Tierra del Fuego.

   (why) _____

8. Salopek's journey is going to take many years.

   (how many years) _____

9. Salopek will finish his walk in a few years.

   (when) _____

EXERCISE 6 Listen to the conversation between a mother and daugher. Then write T for *true*, F for *false*, or NS for *not stated*. 🎧 12.4

1. _____ Lena doesn't call her mother very often.

2. _____ Nicole is Lena's boss.

3. _____ Lena is going home for the weekend.

EXERCISE 7 Listen again. Fill in the blanks with the words you hear. 🎧 12.4

A: Hi, Mom. This is Lena.

B: Hi, Lena. I 'm _____ happy to _____ your voice. You
                    1.   2.

_____ . You just send short text messages.
           3.

A: I'm sorry, Mom. I _____ much time.
                      4.

B: Why _____ time?
                  5.

A: I have to work, go to classes, and participate in activities all day. Last weekend, we _____
                                                6.

to Virginia.

B: Who _____ ?
            7.

A: No one. We _____ the subway. Public transportation is really good here.
                  8.

B: _____ enough to eat this summer? Who _____ for you?
            9.   10.

A: I _____ to cook this summer. _____ surprised?
           11.   12.

B: Yes, I am. When you were home, you never _____ .
                                  13.

A: Nicole and I often _____ and _____ our friends for dinner
                      14.   15.

on the weekends.

B: Who _____ Nicole?
            16.

A: I _____ you about Nicole in my text yesterday. She's my roommate. She
           17.

_____ from California.
           18.

B: Oh, yes. Now I _____ . How _____ ? _____ it?
            19.   20.   21.

A: It's great! I _____ so much this summer.
           22.

B: _____ enough money?
           23.

A: No, I don't. I _____ most of my money. I _____
           24.   25.

professional clothes when I arrived.

B: _____ home for a weekend? We _____ for your ticket.
           26.   27.

A: I can't, Mom. We sometimes _____ activities on weekends, too.
                              28.

B: _____ again next week?
           29.

A: If I _____ time, I _____ you.
           30.   31.

ABOUT YOU Write sentences about each of the topics in the chart. Use the simple present, the present continuous, the future, and the simple past. Then find a partner and compare your answers.

	SCHOOL	JOB	FAMILY
Simple present	I have class every day from 9:00 a.m. until 1:00 p.m.	I work in a store in the afternoon after class.	I have two brothers and one sister.
Present continuous			
Future			
Simple past			

EXERCISE 8 Find a partner. Write questions to ask Barrington Irving and Paul Salopek. Use the simple present, the present continuous, the simple past, the future, modals, and infinitives.

Barrington Irving

1. _Why do you like your job?_

2. _____

3. _____

4. _____

Paul Salopek

5. _____

6. _____

7. _____

8. _____

Chimene Ntakarutimana: FROM Africa TO America

Read the following essay. Pay special attention to the words in bold. 🎧 12.5

I'm the second of four children. Our names are Gentille, Chimene (that's me), Joseph, and Joy. When we lived in Africa, our family was in great danger. We moved from country to country. I was born in Burundi, but my siblings[1] **weren't**. We were each born in a different country. Gentille was born in the Congo. Joseph was born in Zambia. And Joy was born after we left Africa. It's hard to believe, **isn't it?** My parents dreamed of a better future, and we kids **did, too.** You can't imagine what it's like to live in fear all the time, **can you?** But that was our life in Africa.

I was six when we came to the United States. My youngest sister, Joy, was born in the United States. She was an American citizen from birth, but the rest of us **weren't**.

At first, we lived in a small apartment in Chicago. Life was hard. We didn't speak English. My parents didn't have jobs. But a refugee[2] agency[3] helped us, and an American woman **did, too**. We started to call her "Grandma Sandy."

After three years in Chicago, my family moved to Kentucky. Grandma Sandy was sad when we left, and we **were, too**. But she visits us often, and we always spend part of our summer vacations in Chicago. I love Chicago, and my sisters and brother **do, too**.

I now speak English fluently. I don't speak my native language, Kirundi, anymore. Joseph and Joy **don't, either**, but my oldest sister, Gentille, **does**. I understand it, but Joseph and Joy **don't**.

I'm now a senior in college. My major is psychology. I hope we can learn from history and that the future will be better. I'm an optimist[4], **aren't I?**

After college, I plan to go to law school. I want to be an immigration lawyer. I want to help other people and make a difference in the lives of others.

---

1 sibling: a person's brother or sister
2 refugee: a person who leaves his or her country to escape war, natural disaster, or other dangerous situations
3 agency: an organization
4 optimist: someone who thinks good things will happen

COMPREHENSION Based on the reading, write T for *true* or F for *false*.

1. _____ Chimene lives in Chicago.

2. _____ All four children were born in Africa.

3. _____ Only Chimene's oldest sister still speaks the family's native language.

THINK ABOUT IT Discuss the questions with a partner or in a small group.

1. Do you think it is possible to keep your language when you move to another country? If not, why not? If yes, how?

2. How do you think Chimene's experiences will help her later in life?

12.3 Auxiliary Verbs with *Too* and *Either*

We use auxiliary verbs (*be, have,* or *do*) with *too* and *either* to show similarity and to avoid repetition.

EXAMPLES	EXPLANATION
Chimene was born in Africa. Joseph **was, too.** Chimene speaks English fluently, and Joseph **does, too.**	For affirmative statements, we use an auxiliary verb + *too* to avoid repetition.
Joy doesn't understand Kirundi, and Joseph **doesn't, either.** Chimene wasn't born in the United States, and Joseph **wasn't, either.**	For negative statements, we use an auxiliary verb + *not* + *either*. We usually use a contraction before *either*.
I was born in Africa. Joy **wasn't.** I can't speak Kirundi, but Gentille **can.** I **am** in high school. Joseph **isn't.**	We can use an auxiliary verb to avoid repetition in opposite statements. We sometimes connect opposite statements with *but*.

GRAMMAR IN USE

In informal speech, we often say *me, too* and *me, neither* in short answers about ourselves.

> A: *I'm interested in Chimene's story.*
> B: ***Me, too.***
> A: *I don't know much about Burundi.*
> B: ***Me, neither.***

EXERCISE 9 Complete the statements about the things Chimene and her family have in common. Use an auxiliary verb + *too*.

1. Chimene was born in Africa, and Joseph _____ *was, too* _____ .

2. She speaks English now, and her sisters _____ .

3. She dreamed of a better future, and her parents _____ .

4. She can understand Kirundi, and Gentille _____ .

5. She is getting a good education, and her brother and sisters _____ .

6. She was sad to leave Chicago. Her brother and sisters _____ .

EXERCISE 10 Complete the statements about the things Chimene, her family, her friends, and her teachers have in common. Use an auxiliary verb + *either*.

1. Chimene can't speak Kirundi, and Joseph _____ can't, either _____.

2. Chimene isn't in high school. Joseph _____.

3. Chimene wasn't born in the United States, and Joseph and Gentille _____.

4. Chimene's father didn't speak English when they arrived. Her mother _____.

5. Chimene doesn't remember much about Africa, and Joseph _____.

6. Chimene's friends don't know much about Burundi. Some of her teachers _____.

EXERCISE 11 Fill in the blanks to complete the opposite statements.

1. Burundians speak Kirundi, but Zambians _____ don't _____.

2. Chimene doesn't speak Kirundi, but Gentille _____.

3. Chimene is in college now, but Joy _____.

4. Chimene speaks English. Her grandmother _____.

5. The name *Gentille* is sometimes hard for Americans to say. The name *Joy* _____.

6. Joy was born in the United States, but her brother and sisters _____.

EXERCISE 12 Complete the conversation between two friends. Use an auxiliary verb and *too* or *either* when necessary.

A: I'm moving on Saturday. Maybe you and your brother can help me. Are you working on Saturday?

B: My brother is working on Saturday, but I 'm not _____. I can help you.

1.

A: I need a van. Do you have one?

B: I don't have one, but my brother _____. I'll ask him if we can use it. By the way, why are

2.

you moving?

A: There are a couple of reasons. I like my apartment, but my wife _____. She says it's too small

3.

for two people.

B: How many rooms does your new apartment have?

A: The old apartment has two bedrooms, and the new one _____. But the rooms are much

4.

bigger in the new one. Also, we'd like to live downtown. We spend too much time traveling to work.

B: I _____, but apartments downtown are so expensive.

5.

continued

A: We found a nice apartment that isn't expensive. Also, I'd like to own a dog, but my present landlord

doesn't permit pets.

B: Mine doesn't, _____ . What kind of dog do you plan to get?
6.

A: I like small dogs, but my wife _____ .
7.

B: Me, _____ . They just make a lot of noise.
8.

A: Now you know my reasons for moving. Will you help me on Saturday?

B: Of course I will.

12.4 Auxiliary Verbs in Tag Questions

We use a tag question to ask if the statement is correct or if the listener agrees.

EXAMPLES	EXPLANATION
Chimene is from Africa, **isn't she?** You lived in Zambia, **didn't you?** You speak English fluently now, **don't you?**	An affirmative statement has a negative tag question. For a negative tag question, we contract the auxiliary verb with *not* and follow with a subject pronoun.
I'm an optimist, **aren't I?**	For *I*, use *are* in the tag question (not *am*).
You don't speak Kirundi, **do you?** You weren't born in the United States, **were you?** Sandy didn't move to Kentucky, **did she?**	A negative statement has an affirmative tag question. For an affirmative tag question, we use an auxiliary verb + a subject pronoun.
There are many languages in Africa, **aren't there?**	If the sentence begins with *there*, we use *there* in the tag question.
This is a long name, **isn't it?** That was an interesting story, **wasn't it?**	If the sentence begins with *this* or *that*, we use *it* in the tag question.
These aren't long questions, **are they?** Those were hard times, **weren't they?**	If the sentence begins with *these* or *those*, we use *they* in the tag question.

GRAMMAR IN USE

When we use tag questions, we expect people to agree with the main statement, not the the tag.

> *She speaks English,* **doesn't she?** (We expect the answer to be *yes*.)

> *She doesn't speak Russian,* **does she?** (We expect the answer to be *no*.)

To agree with a negative question (for example, *She doesn't speak Russian, does she?*), answer like this:

> **No,** *(she doesn't)*. (You may omit the short answer.)

To disagree, answer like this:

> **Yes, she does**. (You must include the short answer.)

EXERCISE 13 Complete the conversation between two people at a party. Use tag questions.

A: Hi, Sam.

B: Uh, hi . . .

A: You don't remember me, _____*do you*_____ ?
1.

B: You look familiar, but I can't remember your name. We were in the same chemistry class last semester,

_____ ?
2.

A: No.

B: Then we probably met in math class, _____ ?
3.

A: Wrong again. I'm Nicole's brother.

B: Now I remember you. Nicole introduced us at a party last summer, _____ ? Your name
4.

is Max, _____ ?
5.

A: That's right.

B: How are you, Max? You did an internship in Washington last year, _____ ?
6.

A: No. Nicole did the internship.

B: So how's Nicole doing? She isn't in Washington anymore, _____ ?
7.

A: No. She finished her internship and started teaching.

B: I never see her anymore. She moved back to California, _____ ?
8.

A: No, she's still here. But she's married now.

B: Who did she marry?

A: Dan Tripton. You met him, _____ ?
9.

B: Yes, I think so. This is a great party, _____ ? There are a lot of interesting people here,
10.

_____ ?
11.

A: Yes, there are. But I have to leave early.

B: It was great seeing you again, Max. Say hello to Nicole when you see her.

FUN WITH GRAMMAR

Find things in common with a classmate. Work with a partner. You have five minutes to find out what you have in common. Share information about your families, work, studies, likes, dislikes, etc. After you finish, share with the class what you have in common with your classmate using auxiliary verbs with *too* and *either*. For example: *I have three siblings, and Julia does, too. Julia doesn't eat meat, and I don't, either.* The pair with the most things in common wins.

SUMMARY OF UNIT 12

Verb Review

	EXAMPLES	EXPLANATION
Simple Present	Irving **loves** to fly. He often **helps** kids. Irving **comes** from Jamaica.	We use the simple present with facts, general truths, habits, customs, regular activities, repeated actions, and a place of origin.
Present Continuous	Salopek **is walking** around the world. We **are reviewing** verbs.	We use the present continuous with actions that are happening right now, or with longer actions that are in progress but may not be happening at this exact moment.
Future	Salopek **is going to end** his journey in South America. He **will arrive** in Tierra del Fuego.	We use the future with simple facts or predictions about the future.
Simple Past	Chimene's family **left** Africa in 2004. She **learned** English quickly.	We use the simple past with actions that began and ended in the past.
Be	Salopek and Irving **are adventurous**. **There are** many ways to teach kids about science. Chimene **was born** in Africa.	We use *be* with descriptions, location, age, weather, time, *there*, and *born*.
Modals	Chimene **can speak** English fluently. She **might be** a lawyer in a few years.	We use modals to add meaning to the main verb.
Infinitives	She **wants to become** a lawyer. **It's necessary to choose** a major. She's **pleased to be** in the U.S. She's studying **hard to get** into a good law school.	We use infinitives after certain verbs, certain expressions beginning with *it*, and certain adjectives. We use infinitives to show purpose.

Auxiliary Verbs

EXAMPLES	EXPLANATION
Irving likes adventure. Salopek **does, too.** I wasn't born here. You **weren't, either.**	We use auxiliary verbs with *too* and *either* to avoid repetition of the same verb phrase.
Chimene can't remember her native language, but her older sister **can.** Chimene is in college, but Joseph **isn't.**	We use auxiliary verbs to avoid repetition in opposite statements.
Irving helps kids, **doesn't he?** Salopek won't stop in France, **will he?**	We use auxiliary verbs to make tag questions.

REVIEW

PART 1 Choose the correct word(s) to complete the statements.

1. Barrington Irving (*borned*/*was born*) in Jamaica.

2. When he (*was*/*were*) 15, he (*meet*/*met*) a pilot.

3. He (*become*/*became*) interested in aviation.

4. He (*is loving*/*loves*) to fly.

5. He (*flied*/*flew*) around the world when he was 23.

6. He (*wants*/*want*) (*inspire*/*to inspire*) kids.

7. Irving's students (*working*/*are working*) on different projects.

8. The kids in this program (*gain*/*are gaining*) confidence.

9. He's going (*to fly*/*fly*) around the world again.

10. When (*he'll fly*/*he flies*) around the world again, (*he'll share*/*he shares*) information with schoolchildren.

PART 2 Write the negative form of the underlined word(s).

1. Chimene <u>was</u> born in Africa. She _____ wasn't _____ born in the United States.

2. Her last name <u>is</u> hard for Americans to say. It _____ easy to pronounce.

3. She <u>spoke</u> Kirundi when she arrived in the United States. She _____ English.

4. Her family <u>had</u> a hard time in Africa. They _____ an easy life.

5. Her family <u>lives</u> in Kentucky. Her family _____ in Chicago.

6. I <u>can imagine</u> life in another city in my country. I _____ life in another country.

7. Joy <u>is preparing</u> for college. She _____ for a career yet.

8. Chimene <u>knows</u> that she wants to go to law school. She _____ which law school she will attend.

9. She <u>has to complete</u> her applications in the spring. She _____ the applications in the fall.

10. She<u>'ll start</u> law school next year. She _____ law school in the summer.

PART 3 Complete the sentences with the question form of the underlined word(s). Fill in the correct form for short answers.

1. **A:** <u>Paul Salopek isn't</u> in the United States now.

   B: Where _____ is he _____ now?

2. **A:** <u>Salopek will travel</u> around the world.

   B: _____ to South Africa?

   A: No, he _____.

3. **A:** <u>He worked</u> in a gas station in Chicago.

   B: Why _____ in a gas station?

4. **A:** <u>He's writing</u> about his experiences.

   B: Why _____ about his experiences?

5. **A:** <u>He's going to walk</u> through North America.

   B: _____ through New York?

   A: No, he _____.

6. **A:** <u>He won't walk</u> through Brazil.

   B: Why _____ through Brazil?

7. **A:** <u>He will be</u> in Tierra del Fuego, South America.

   B: When _____ in Tierra del Fuego?

8. **A:** <u>Human migration started</u> many years ago.

   B: When _____ ?

9. **A:** <u>He is sharing</u> his information on his website.

   B: _____ his information with schoolchildren?

   A: Yes, he _____.

10. **A:** <u>He can learn</u> about the world.

    B: What _____ about the world?

PART 4 Complete the statements with the correct auxiliary verb. Add *too* or *either* when necessary.

1. Barrington Irving likes adventure. Paul Salopek _____ *does, too* _____.

2. Irving is interested in teaching children, and Salopek _____.

3. Irving will share his knowledge with young people. Salopek _____.

4. Irving is a pilot, but Salopek _____.

5. Chimene was born in Burundi, but her sisters and brother _____.

6. Chimene didn't speak English when she arrived in the United States, and her parents

   _____.

7. She doesn't need ESL classes anymore, and her brother _____.

8. She doesn't live in Chicago, but Grandma Sandy _____.

9. She wants to go to the University of Chicago, but her sister _____.

10. She should study hard. Her brother _____.

PART 5 Complete the sentences with a tag question.

1. Salopek is brave, _____ *isn't he?* _____

2. He started his journey in 2013, _____

3. Salopek isn't finished with his journey, _____

4. He won't go to Brazil, _____

5. There's a lot to learn about the world, _____

6. Irving comes from Miami, _____

7. Irving's students built an airplane, _____

8. They didn't believe it was possible, _____

9. This was an interesting unit, _____

10. We should always practice in English, _____

FROM GRAMMAR TO WRITING

PART 1 Editing Advice

1. Use the correct question formation.

   does Chimene go   _did her family come_
   Where ~~Chimene goes~~ to school? When ~~her family came~~ to the United States?

   Barrington
   Where was born ~~Barrington~~?

2. Don't use *be* with a simple present or past verb.

   Children ~~are~~ need confidence.

   Sixty kids ~~were~~ built an airplane.

3. Use the base form after *do*, *does*, and *did*.

   speak
   She didn't ~~spoke~~ English when she arrived in the United States.

   _go_
   Where does she ~~goes~~ to school?

4. For the simple present, use the *-s* form when the subject is *he*, *she*, *it*, *family*, or a singular noun.

   _s_
   Lena love Washington, DC.

5. Use the correct past form for irregular verbs.

   left
   Salopek ~~leaved~~ Ethiopia in 2013.

6. Use the base form after *to*.

   study
   He wants to ~~studies~~ human migration.

7. Use the base form after a modal.

   study
   Lena should ~~studies~~ hard.

   She must ~~to~~ wear professional clothes to work.

8. Use an infinitive after some verbs (but not after a modal), adjectives, and certain expressions with *it*.

   _to_   _to_
   She needs choose a major. She's not ready make a decision.

   _to_
   It's important inspire kids.

9. Don't use the present continuous with nonaction verbs.

   wants
   Irving ~~is wanting~~ to inspire kids now.

10. Don't forget to include a form of *be* in a present continuous sentence.

    are
    We learning about people on the move.

11. Don't use the future in a time clause or an *if* clause. Use the simple present.

    _s_
    When she ~~will~~ graduate from college, she'll go to law school.

PART 2 Editing Practice

Some of the shaded words and phrases have mistakes. Find the mistakes and correct them. If the shaded words are correct, write C.

             C   live

A: Does your family ~~lives~~ in the United States?
     1.   2.

B: Yes, but I doesn't live with them.
               3.

A: Why you don't live with them?
           4.

B: They live in Miami. I finded a job here, so I was moved.
       5.   6.   7.

A: When you moved here?
          8.

B: Three years ago. I don't like to be this far from my parents, but I have no choice. I didn't realized how
                 9.   10.   11.

   much I would miss them. I lonely at times, but my mom call me almost every day, so that helps.
                           12.   13.   14.

A: I'm know how you feel. When I left home, it was very hard for me be away from my family.
      15.   16.   17.   18.

B: Where your family lives?
           19.

A: They live in Vietnam. They want visit me very much. When I will save enough money, I'm going to send
      20.   21.   22.   23.

   them plane tickets. I'm having two jobs now, so soon I'll be have enough money for their trip.
                    24.   25.

B: How long they'll stay here?
           26.

A: My mom will to stay for six months. But my dad can stay for only two weeks.
         27.   28.

B: How often do you talk to your parents?
              29.

A: It's expensive talk by phone, so we usually send email. Sometimes I use a phone card.
              30.   31.

WRITING TIP

After you finish a piece of writing, it's a good idea to have a classmate or friend read it for mistakes. This is called peer editing. Someone else will often notice grammar, punctuation, spelling, and content errors in your writing that you don't because you're too close to it.

PART 3 Write

Read the prompts. Choose one and write one paragraph about it.

1. Write about a time you or someone you know moved. How was your life before the move? How was your life after?
2. Write about an unusual person you know or read about. Tell what that person did or is doing.

PART 4 Edit

Reread the Summary of Unit 12 and the editing advice. Edit your writing from Part 3.

SUMMARY OF VERB TENSES

VERB TENSE	FORM	MEANING AND USE
SIMPLE PRESENT	I **have** class Mondays. He **doesn't have** class today. **Do** you **have** class today? **What do** you **do** every day?	• facts, general truths, habits, and customs • used with frequency adverbs, e.g., *always, usually, sometimes, never* • regular activities and repeated actions
PRESENT CONTINUOUS	I **am studying** biology this semester. He **isn't studying** now. **Are** you **studying** this weekend? **What** is she **studying** at college?	• actions that are currently in progress • future actions if a future time expression is used or understood
FUTURE WITH *WILL*	I **will go** to the store. He **won't go** to the store. **Will** you **go** to the store? **When will** you **go** to the store?	• future plans/decisions made in the moment • strong predictions • promises and offers to help
FUTURE WITH *BE GOING TO*	He**'s going to study** all weekend. He **isn't going to study** Saturday. **Are** you **going to study** Saturday? **What are** you **going to study** Saturday?	• future plans that are already made • predictions
SIMPLE PAST	They **liked** the story. I **didn't like** the story. **Did** you **like** the story? **What did** you **like** about the story?	• recent or historical events • a narrative, or story, that is real or imagined • events in a person's life • the result of an experiment
PAST CONTINUOUS	She **was watching** TV when I called. I **wasn't watching** TV when you called. **Were** you **watching** TV around 10? **What were** you **watching**?	• an action in progress at a specific past time • often with the simple past in another clause to show the relationship of a longer past action to a shorter past action
PRESENT PERFECT	I **have seen** the movie *Black Panther*. He **has seen** *Black Panther* five times. **Have** you **seen** *Black Panther*? **Why have** you never **seen** *Black Panther*?	• actions that started in the past and continue to the present • actions that repeat during a period of time from the past to the present • repeated actions at indefinite times in the past
PRESENT PERFECT CONTINUOUS	She **has been working** there for years. I **haven't been working** regularly in awhile. **Have** you **been working** here long? **Where have** you **been working** lately?	• actions that started in the past and continue to the present

APPENDIX B

NONACTION VERBS

DESCRIPTION	FEELINGS	DESIRES	MEASUREMENTS	MENTAL STATES	SENSES
appear*	appreciate	hope	cost	agree	belong
be*	care	need	measure*	believe	contain
consist of	dislike	prefer	weigh*	concern	feel*
look*	forgive	want		disagree	have*
look like	hate	wish		doubt	hear*
resemble	like			forget	hurt
seem	love			guess	notice
	mind			know	own
	miss			imagine	possess
				mean	see*
				recognize	smell*
				remember*	sound*
				suppose	
				surprise	
				think*	
				understand	

*Words that also have an active meaning

APPENDIX C

IRREGULAR VERB FORMS

BASE FORM	PAST FORM	PAST PARTICIPLE	BASE FORM	PAST FORM	PAST PARTICIPLE
be	was/were	been	fight	fought	fought
bear	bore	born/borne	find	found	found
beat	beat	beaten	fit	fit	fit
become	became	become	flee	fled	fled
begin	began	begun	fly	flew	flown
bend	bent	bent	forbid	forbade	forbidden
bet	bet	bet	forget	forgot	forgotten
bid	bid	bid	forgive	forgave	forgiven
bind	bound	bound	freeze	froze	frozen
bite	bit	bitten	get	got	gotten
bleed	bled	bled	give	gave	given
blow	blew	blown	go	went	gone
break	broke	broken	grind	ground	ground
breed	bred	bred	grow	grew	grown
bring	brought	brought	hang	hung	hung
broadcast	broadcast	broadcast	have	had	had
build	built	built	hear	heard	heard
burst	burst	burst	hide	hid	hidden
buy	bought	bought	hit	hit	hit
cast	cast	cast	hold	held	held
catch	caught	caught	hurt	hurt	hurt
choose	chose	chosen	keep	kept	kept
cling	clung	clung	know	knew	known
come	came	come	lay	laid	laid
cost	cost	cost	lead	led	led
creep	crept	crept	leave	left	left
cut	cut	cut	lend	lent	lent
deal	dealt	dealt	let	let	let
dig	dug	dug	lie	lay	lain
dive	dove/dived	dove/dived	light	lit/lighted	lit/lighted
do	did	done	lose	lost	lost
draw	drew	drawn	make	made	made
drink	drank	drunk	mean	meant	meant
drive	drove	driven	meet	met	met
eat	ate	eaten	mistake	mistook	mistaken
fall	fell	fallen	overcome	overcame	overcome
feed	fed	fed	overdo	overdid	overdone
feel	felt	felt	overtake	overtook	overtaken

BASE FORM	PAST FORM	PAST PARTICIPLE	BASE FORM	PAST FORM	PAST PARTICIPLE
overthrow	overthrew	overthrown	stick	stuck	stuck
pay	paid	paid	sting	stung	stung
plead	pled/pleaded	pled/pleaded	stink	stank	stunk
prove	proved	proven/proved	strike	struck	struck/stricken
put	put	put	strive	strove	striven
quit	quit	quit	swear	swore	sworn
read	read	read	sweep	swept	swept
ride	rode	ridden	swell	swelled	swelled/swollen
ring	rang	rung	swim	swam	swum
rise	rose	risen	swing	swung	swung
run	ran	run	take	took	taken
say	said	said	teach	taught	taught
see	saw	seen	tear	tore	torn
seek	sought	sought	tell	told	told
sell	sold	sold	think	thought	thought
send	sent	sent	throw	threw	thrown
set	set	set	understand	understood	understood
sew	sewed	sewn/sewed	uphold	upheld	upheld
shake	shook	shaken	upset	upset	upset
shed	shed	shed	wake	woke	woken
shine	shone/shined	shone/shined	wear	wore	worn
shoot	shot	shot	weave	wove	woven
show	showed	shown/showed	wed	wedded/wed	wedded/wed
shrink	shrank/shrunk	shrunk/shrunken	weep	wept	wept
shut	shut	shut	win	won	won
sing	sang	sung	wind	wound	wound
sink	sank	sunk	withdraw	withdrew	withdrawn
sit	sat	sat	withhold	withheld	withheld
sleep	slept	slept	withstand	withstood	withstood
slide	slid	slid	wring	wrung	wrung
slit	slit	slit	write	wrote	written
speak	spoke	spoken			
speed	sped	sped			
spend	spent	spent			
spin	spun	spun			
spit	spit/spat	spit/spat			
split	split	split			
spread	spread	spread			
spring	sprang	sprung			
stand	stood	stood			
steal	stole	stolen			

Note:

The past and past participle of some verbs can end in *-ed* or *-t*.

burn	burned or burnt
dream	dreamed or dreamt
kneel	kneeled or knelt
learn	learned or learnt
leap	leaped or leapt
spill	spilled or spilt
spoil	spoiled or spoilt

APPENDIX D

CAPITALIZATION AND PUNCTUATION

Capitalization Rules

RULE	EXAMPLES
The first word in a sentence	**M**y friends are helpful.
The word *I*	My sister and **I** took a trip together.
Names of people	**A**braham **L**incoln; **G**eorge **W**ashington
Titles preceding names of people	**D**octor (**D**r.) **S**mith; **P**resident **L**incoln; **Q**ueen **E**lizabeth; **M**r. **R**ogers; **M**rs. **C**arter
Geographic names	the **U**nited **S**tates; **L**ake **S**uperior; **C**alifornia; the **R**ocky **M**ountains; the **M**ississippi **R**iver **Note:** The word *the* in a geographic name is not capitalized.
Street names	**P**ennsylvania **A**venue (**A**ve.); **W**all **S**treet (**S**t.); **A**bbey **R**oad (**R**d.)
Names of organizations, companies, colleges, buildings, stores, hotels	the **R**epublican **P**arty; **C**engage **L**earning; **D**artmouth **C**ollege; the **U**niversity of **W**isconsin; the **W**hite **H**ouse; **B**loomingdale's; the **H**ilton **H**otel
Nationalities and ethnic groups	**M**exicans; **C**anadians; **S**paniards; **A**mericans; **J**ews; **K**urds; **I**nuit
Languages	**E**nglish; **S**panish; **P**olish; **V**ietnamese; **R**ussian
Months	**J**anuary; **F**ebruary
Days	**S**unday; **M**onday
Holidays	**I**ndependence **D**ay; **T**hanksgiving
Important words in a title	*Grammar in Context; The Old Man and the Sea; Romeo and Juliet; The Sound of Music* **Note:** Capitalize *the* as the first word of a title.

Punctuation Rules

PUNCTUATION	EXAMPLES
A period (.) is used at the end of a declarative sentence.	This is a complete sentence**.**
A question mark (?) is used at the end of a question.	When does the movie start**?**
An exclamation mark (!) is used at the end of an exclamation. It expresses a strong emotion.	This book is so interesting**!**
A comma (,) is used: • before the connectors *and*, *but*, *so*, and *or* in a compound sentence. • between three or more items in a list. • after a dependent clause at the beginning of a complex sentence. Dependent clauses include time clauses, *if* clauses, and reason clauses. • between the day and the date, and between the date and the year. • between and after (if in the middle of a sentence) city, state, and country names that appear together. • after time words and phrases, prepositional phrases of time, and sequence words (except *then*) at the start of a sentence.	 • She gave Tomas a pen**, but** he wanted a pencil. • He needs **a notebook, a pen, and a calculator.** • **If it's cold outside,** you should wear a coat. • The test will be on **Friday, May 20.** The school opened on **September 3, 2010.** • She lived and taught in **Shanghai, China,** for five years. • **Finally,** the test was over, and the student could leave. **After the movie,** they decided to go out for coffee.
An apostrophe (') is used to indicate either a contraction or a possession: • Use an apostrophe in a contraction in place of the letter or letters that have been deleted. • Add an apostrophe and the letter *-s* after a word to show possession. If a plural word already ends in *-s*, just add an apostrophe.	 • **I'm** happy to see you. **You've** read a lot of books this year. • That is **Yusef's** book. The **teachers'** books include the answers.
Quotation marks (") are used to indicate: • the exact words that were spoken by someone. Notice that the punctuation at the end of a quote is inside the quotation marks. • language that a writer has borrowed from another source. • when a word or phrase is being used in a special way.	 • Albert Einstein said, **"I have no special talent. I am only passionately curious."** • The dictionary defines *punctuation* as **"the use of specific marks to make ideas within writing clear."** • The paper was written by a **"professional"** writer.

APPENDIX E

VOWEL AND CONSONANT SOUNDS

Vowels

SYMBOL	EXAMPLES
ʌ	love, cup
a	father, box
æ	class, black
ə	alone, atom
ɜ	ever, well
i	eat, feet
ɪ	miss, bit
ɔ	talk, corn
ʊ	would, book
oʊ	cone, boat
u	tooth, school
eɪ	able, day
aɪ	mine, try
aʊ	about, cow
ɔɪ	join, boy

Consonants

SYMBOL	EXAMPLES
b	bread, cab
d	door, dude
f	form, if
g	go, flag
h	hello, behind
j	use, yellow
k	cook, hike
l	leg, meal
m	month, sum
n	never, win
ŋ	singer, walking
p	put, map
r	river, try
s	saw, parks
ʃ	show, action
ɾ	atom, lady
t	take, tent
tʃ	check, church
θ	thing, both
ð	the, either
v	voice, of
w	would, reward
z	zoo, mazes
ʒ	usual, vision
dʒ	just, edge

APPENDIX F

USES OF ARTICLES

The Indefinite Article

A. To define or classify a subject

EXAMPLES	EXPLANATION
Chicago is **a** city. Illinois is **a** state. Abraham Lincoln was **an** American president.	• We use *a* before a consonant sound. • We use *an* before a vowel sound. • We can put an adjective before the noun.
Chicago and Los Angeles are cities. Lincoln and Washington were American presidents.	We do not use an article before a plural noun.

B. To make a generalization about a noun

EXAMPLES	EXPLANATION
A dog has sharp teeth. **Dogs** have sharp teeth.	We use an indefinite article (*a/an*) + a singular count noun or no article with a plural noun.
An elephant has big ears. **Elephants** have big ears.	Both the singular and plural forms have the same meaning.
Coffee contains caffeine. **Love** makes people happy.	We do not use an article to make a generalization about a noncount noun.

C. To introduce a new noun into the conversation

EXAMPLES	EXPLANATION
I have **a cell phone**. I have **an umbrella**.	We use the indefinite article *a/an* with singular count nouns.
I have **(some) dishes**. Do you have **(any) cups**? I don't have **(any) forks**. I have **(some) money** with me. Do you have **(any) cash** with you? I don't have **(any) time**.	We use *some* or *any* with plural nouns and noncount nouns. We use *any* in questions and negatives. *Some* and *any* can be omitted.
There's **an elevator** in the building. There isn't **any money** in my wallet.	*There* + a form of *be* can introduce an indefinite noun into a conversation.

continued

The Definite Article

A. To refer to a previously mentioned noun

EXAMPLES	EXPLANATION
There's **a dog** in the next apartment. **The dog** barks all the time.	We start by saying *a dog*. We continue by saying *the dog*.
We bought **some grapes**. We ate **the grapes** this morning.	We start by saying *some grapes*. We continue by saying *the grapes*.
I need **some sugar**. I'm going to use **the sugar** to bake a cake.	We start by saying *some sugar*. We continue by saying *the sugar*.
Did you buy **any coffee**? Yes. **The coffee** is in the cabinet.	We start by saying *any coffee*. We continue by saying *the coffee*.

B. When the speaker and the listener have the same reference

EXAMPLES	EXPLANATION
The number on this page is 306.	The object is present, so the speaker and listener have the same object in mind.
The president is talking about **the economy**.	People who live in the same country have things in common.
Please turn off **the lights** and shut **the door** before you leave **the house**.	People who live in the same house have things in common.
The house on the corner is beautiful. I spent **the money you gave me**.	The listener knows exactly which one because the speaker defines or specifies which one.

C. When there is only one in our experience

EXAMPLES	EXPLANATION
The sun is bigger than **the moon**. There are many problems in **the world**.	The *sun*, the *moon*, and the *world* are unique objects.
Write your name on **the top** of the page.	The page has only one top.
Alaska is **the biggest** state in the U.S.	A superlative indicates that there is only one.

D. With familiar places

EXAMPLES	EXPLANATION
I'm going to **the store** after work. Do you need anything? **The bank** is closed now. I'll go tomorrow.	We use *the* with certain familiar places and people—*the bank, the zoo, the park, the store, the movies, the beach, the post office, the bus, the train, the doctor, the dentist*—when we refer to the one that we habitually visit or use.

Notes:

1. Omit *the* after a preposition with the words *church, school, work,* and *bed.*
   He's **in church**.   They're **at work**.
   I'm going **to school**.   I'm going **to bed**.

2. Omit *to* and *the* with *home* and *downtown.*
   I'm going **home**.   Are you going **downtown** after class?

Special Uses of Articles

NO ARTICLE	ARTICLE

Personal names:
    John Kennedy
	The whole family:
	    the Kennedys

Title and name:
    Queen Elizabeth
	Title without name:
	    the Queen

Cities, states, countries, continents:
    Cleveland
    Ohio
    Mexico
    South America
	Places that are considered a union:
	    the United States
	Place names: *the* _____ *of* _____
	    the District of Columbia

Mountains:
    Mount Everest
	Mountain ranges:
	    the Rocky Mountains

Beaches:
    Palm Beach
    Pebble Beach
	Rivers, oceans, seas:
	    the Mississippi River
	    the Atlantic Ocean
	    the Dead Sea

Streets and avenues:
    Madison Avenue
    Wall Street
	Well-known buildings:
	    the Willis Tower
	    the Empire State Building

Parks:
    Central Park
	Zoos:
	    the San Diego Zoo

Name + *College* or *University*:
    Northwestern University
	The University/College of _____:
	    the University of Michigan

Holidays and dates:
    Mother's Day
    July 4 (month + day)
	The day of month:
	    the fifth of May
	    the Fourth of July

Diseases:
    cancer   AIDS
    polio   malaria
	Ailments:
	    a cold a toothache
	    a headache the flu

Languages:
    English
	The _____ *language*:
	    the English language

APPENDIX G

PREPOSITIONS OF TIME

	TIME EXPRESSION	EXAMPLES
in	in the morning in the afternoon in the evening	He eats breakfast **in** the morning. He eats lunch **in** the afternoon. He eats dinner **in** the evening.
	in the [season]	We have vacation **in** the summer. There are many flowers **in** the spring.
	in [month]	Her birthday is **in** March.
	in the ___ century	People didn't use cars **in** the 19th century.
	in [number] minutes, hours, days, weeks, months, years	We'll leave on vacation **in** three days. I will graduate **in** two weeks.
	in the past in the future	**In** the past, people didn't use computers. **In** the future, we will need more health care workers.
	in the beginning	**In** the beginning, I didn't understand the teacher at all.
at	at night	He likes to watch TV **at** night.
	at [time]	My class begins **at** 12:30.
	at present	**At** present, I'm learning French.
	at the beginning of [something] at the end of [something]	The semester starts **at** the beginning of September. The semester ends **at** the end of May.
on	on [date]	His birthday is **on** March 5.
	on [day]	I have to work **on** Saturday.
	on the weekend	I'm going to a party **on** the weekend.
from	from [time] to [time]	My class is **from** 12:30 **to** 3:30.
	from [time] until/till [time]	My class is **from** 12:30 **until** (or **till**) 3:30.
for	for [number] minutes, hours, days, weeks, months, years	She was in Mexico **for** three weeks. We lived in Paris **for** two years.
by	by [time]	Please finish your test **by** six o'clock.
until/till	until/till [time]	I slept **until** (or **till**) 9 a.m. this morning.
	until /till [event]	I lived with my parents **until** (**till**) I got married.
during	during [event]	He fell asleep **during** the meeting.
about	about [time]	The plane will arrive **about** 6 p.m.
around	around [time]	The plane will arrive **around** 6 p.m.
before	before [time, day, date]	You should finish the test **before** 9:30. You should finish the job **before** Friday.
	before [event]	Turn off the lights **before** you leave.
after	after [time, day, date]	Please don't call me **after** 10 p.m. I'll have more free time **after** next Monday.
	after [event]	Wash the dishes **after** you finish dinner.

APPENDIX H

VERBS AND ADJECTIVES FOLLOWED BY A PREPOSITION

MANY VERBS AND ADJECTIVES ARE FOLLOWED BY A PREPOSITION.

accuse (someone) of	(be) familiar with	(be) prepared for/to
(be) accustomed to	(be) famous for	prevent (someone/something) from
adjust to	(be) fond of	prohibit (someone/something) from
(be) afraid of	forget about	protect (someone/something) from
agree with	forgive (someone) for	(be) proud of
(be) amazed at/by	(be) glad about	recover from
(be) angry about	(be) good at	(be) related to
(be) angry at/with	(be) grateful (to someone) for	rely on/upon
apologize for	(be) guilty of	(be) responsible for
approve of	(be) happy about	(be) sad about
argue about	hear about	(be) satisfied with
argue with	hear of	(be) scared of
(be) ashamed of	hope for	(be) sick of
(be) aware of	(be) incapable of	(be) sorry about
believe in	insist on/upon	(be) sorry for
blame (someone) for	(be) interested in	speak about
(be) bored with/by	(be) involved in	speak to/with
(be) capable of	(be) jealous of	succeed in
care about	(be) known for	(be) sure of/about
care for	(be) lazy about	(be) surprised at
compare to/with	listen to	take care of
complain about	look at	talk about
concentrate on	look for	talk to/with
(be) concerned about	look forward to	thank (someone) for
consist of	(be) mad about	(be) thankful (to someone) for
count on	(be) mad at	think about
deal with	(be) made from/of	think of
decide on	(be) married to	(be) tired of
depend on/upon	object to	(be) upset about
(be) different from	(be) opposed to	(be) upset with
disapprove of	participate in	(be) used to
(be) divorced from	plan on	wait for
dream about/of	pray for	warn (someone) about
(be) engaged to	pray to	(be) worried about
(be) excited about		worry about

INFINITIVES

Verbs Followed by Infinitives

agree	claim	know how	seem
appear	consent	learn	swear
ask	decide	manage	tend
attempt	demand	need	threaten
arrange	deserve	offer	try
be able	expect	plan	volunteer
beg	fail	prepare	want
can afford	forget	pretend	wish
care	hope	promise	would like
choose	intend	refuse	

Adjectives Followed by Infinitives

afraid	easy	lucky	sad
ashamed	embarrassed	necessary	shocked
careful	excited	pleased	sorry
certain	glad	prepared	stupid
challenging	good	proud	surprised
delighted	happy	ready	upset
determined	hard	relieved	useful
difficult	important	reluctant	willing
disappointed	impossible	rewarding	wrong
eager	likely	right	

SENTENCE TYPES

There are three basic sentences types: simple, compound, and complex.

Simple Sentences

Simple sentences usually have one subject and one verb.

Simple sentences can have more than one subject and/or verb.

Children and adults like pizza.

Compound Sentences

Compound sentences are usually made up of two simple sentences (independent clauses) with a **connector** (a coordinating conjunction such as *and*, *but*, *or*, *yet*, *so*, and *for*). Use a comma before the connector in a compound sentence.

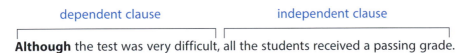

The test was very difficult, **but** all the students received a passing grade.

Complex Sentences

Complex sentences have one independent clause and at least one dependent clause. The dependent clause is often an adverb clause, which begins with a **connector** (a subordinating conjunction such as *while*, *although*, *because*, and *if*). When a dependent clause begins a sentence, use a comma to separate it from the independent clause.

Although the test was very difficult, all the students received a passing grade.

When a dependent clause comes after an independent clause, no comma is used.

All the students received a passing grade **although** the test was very difficult.

GLOSSARY

- **Adjective** An adjective gives a description of a noun.

    It's a *tall* tree.   He's an *old* man.   My neighbors are *nice*.

- **Adverb** An adverb describes the action of a sentence or an adjective or another adverb.

    She speaks English *fluently*.   I drive *carefully*.

    She speaks English *extremely* well.   She is *very* intelligent.

- **Adverb of Frequency** An adverb of frequency tells how often an action happens.

    I *never* drink coffee.   They *usually* take the bus.

- **Affirmative** *Affirmative* means "yes."

    They *live* in Miami.

- **Apostrophe** ʼ We use the apostrophe for possession and contractions.

    My *sister's* friend is beautiful. (possession)

    Today *isn't* Sunday. (contraction)

- **Article** An article comes before a noun. It tells if the noun is definite or indefinite. The indefinite articles are *a* and *an*. The definite article is *the*.

    I have *a* cat.   I ate *an* apple.   *The* teacher came late.

- **Auxiliary Verb** An auxiliary verb is used in forming tense, mood, or aspect of the verb that follows it. Some verbs have two parts: an auxiliary verb and a main verb.

    You *didn't* eat lunch.   He *can't* study.   We *will* return.

- **Base Form** The base form of the verb has no tense. It has no ending (*-s, -ed, or -ing*): *be, go, eat, take, write*.

    I didn't *go*.   We don't *know* you.   He can't *drive*.

- **Capital Letter** A B C D E F G . . .

- **Clause** A clause is a group of words that has a subject and a verb. Some sentences have only one clause.

    She speaks Spanish.

    Some sentences have a **main clause** and a **dependent clause**.

MAIN CLAUSE	DEPENDENT CLAUSE (reason clause)
She found a good job	*because she has computer skills.*
MAIN CLAUSE	DEPENDENT CLAUSE (time clause)
She'll turn off the light	*before she goes to bed.*
MAIN CLAUSE	DEPENDENT CLAUSE (if clause)
I'll take you to the doctor	*if you don't have your car on Saturday.*

- **Colon** :

- **Comma** ,

- **Comparative** The comparative form of an adjective or adverb is used to compare two things.

    My house is *bigger* than your house.

    Her husband drives *faster* than she does.

    My children speak English *more fluently* than I do.

- **Consonant** The following letters are consonants: *b, c, d, f, g, h, j, k, l, m, n, p, q, r, s, t, v, w, x, y, z.*

  NOTE: *Y* is sometimes considered a vowel, as in the world *syllable.*

- **Contraction** A contraction is two words joined with an apostrophe.

  He's my brother.   *You're* late.   They *won't* talk to me.

  (*He's = He is*)   (*You're = You are*)   (*won't = will not*)

- **Count Noun** Count nouns are nouns that we can count. They have a singular and a plural form.

  1 *pen*–3 *pens*   1 *table*–4 *tables*

- **Dependent Clause** See **Clause**.

- **Exclamation Mark** !

- **Frequency Word** Frequency words (*always, usually, generally, often, sometimes, rarely, seldom, hardly ever, never*) tell how often an action happens.

  I *never* drink coffee.   We *always* do our homework.

- **Hyphen** -

- **Imperative** An imperative sentence gives a command or instruction. An imperative sentence omits the subject pronoun *you.*

  Come here.   *Don't be* late.   Please *help* me.

- **Infinitive** An infinitive is *to* + the base form.

  I want *to leave.*   You need *to be* here on time.

- **Linking Verb** A linking verb is a verb that links the subject to the noun, adjective, or adverb after it. Linking verbs include *be, seem, feel, smell, sound, look, appear,* and *taste.*

  She *is* a doctor.   She *looks* tired.   You *are* late.

- **Main Clause** See **Clause**.

- **Modal** The modal verbs are *can, could, shall, should, will, would, may, might,* and *must.*

  They *should* leave.   I *must* go.

- **Negative** *Negative* means "no."

  She *doesn't speak* Spanish.

- **Nonaction Verb** A nonaction verb has no action. We do not use a continuous tense (*be* + verb *-ing*) with a nonaction verb. Nonaction verbs include: *believe, cost, care, have, hear, know, like, love, matter, mean, need, own, prefer, remember, see, seem, think, understand, want,* and sense-perception verbs.

  She *has* a laptop.   We *love* our mother.   You *look* great.

- **Noncount Noun** A noncount noun is a noun that we don't count. It has no plural form.

  She drank some *water.*   He prepared some *rice.*

  Do you need any *money*?   We had a lot of *homework.*

- **Noun** A noun is a person, a place, or a thing. Nouns can be either count or noncount.

  My *brother* lives in California.   My *sisters* live in New York.

  I get *advice* from them.   I drink *coffee* every day.

- **Noun Modifier** A noun modifier makes a noun more specific.

  fire department   *Independence* Day   *can* opener

- **Noun Phrase** A noun phrase is a group of words that form the subject or object of a sentence.

    A very nice woman helped me.   I bought *a big box of cereal*.

- **Object** The object of a sentence follows the verb. It receives the action of the verb.

    He bought *a car*.   I saw *a movie*.   I met *your brother*.

- **Object Pronoun** We use object pronouns (*me, you, him, her, it, us, them*) after a verb or preposition.

    He likes *her*.   I saw the movie. Let's talk about *it*.

- **Paragraph** A paragraph is a group of sentences about one topic.

- **Parentheses ( )**

- **Period .**

- **Phrasal Modal** Phrasal modals, such as *have to* and *be able to,* are made up of two or more words.

    You *have got to* see the movie.   We *have to* take a test.

- **Phrase** A group of words that go together.

    Last month my sister came to visit.   There is a strange car *in front of my house*.

- **Plural** *Plural* means "more than one." A plural noun usually ends with *-s*.

    She has beautiful *eyes*.   My *feet* are big.

- **Possessive Form** Possessive forms show ownership or relationship.

    Mary's coat is in the closet.   *My* brother lives in Miami.

- **Preposition** A preposition is a short connecting word. Some common prepositions are: *about, above, across, after, around, as, at, away, back, before, behind, below, by, down, for, from, in, into, like, of, off, on, out, over, to, under, up,* and *with*.

    The book is *on* the table.   She studies *with* her friends.

- **Present Participle** The present participle of a verb is the base form + *-ing*.

    She is *sleeping*.   They were *laughing*.

- **Pronoun** A pronoun takes the place of a noun.

    John likes Mary, but *she* doesn't like *him*.

- **Punctuation** The use of specific marks, such as commas and periods, to make ideas within writing clear.

- **Question Mark ?**

- **Quotation Marks " "**

- **Regular Verb** A regular verb forms the simple past with *-ed*.

    He *worked* yesterday.   I *laughed* at the joke.

- **-s Form** A simple present verb that ends in -s or -es.

  He *lives* in New York.   She *watches* TV a lot.

- **Sense-Perception Verb** A sense-perception verb has no action. It describes a sense. Some common sense-perception verbs are: *look, feel, taste, sound,* and *smell.*

  She *feels* fine.   The coffee *smells* fresh.   The milk *tastes* sour.

- **Sentence** A sentence is a group of words that contains a subject and a verb and gives a complete thought.

  SENTENCE: She came home.

  NOT A SENTENCE: When she came home

- **Singular** *Singular* means "one."

  She ate a *sandwich.*   I have one *television.*

- **Subject** The subject of the sentence tells who or what the sentence is about.

  My sister got married last April.   *The wedding* was beautiful.

- **Subject Pronoun** We use a subject pronoun (*I, you, he, she, it, we, you, they*) before a verb.

  They speak Japanese.   *We* speak Spanish.

- **Superlative** The superlative form of an adjective or adverb shows the number one item in a group of three or more.

  January is the *coldest* month of the year.

  My brother speaks English the *best* in my family.

- **Syllable** A syllable is a part of a word. Each syllable has only one vowel sound. (Some words have only one syllable.)

  change (one syllable)   after (af·ter = two syllables)

  look (one syllable)   responsible (re·spon·si·ble = four syllables)

- **Tag Question** A tag question is a short question at the end of a sentence. It is used in conversation.

  You speak Spanish, *don't you?*   He's not happy, *is he?*

- **Tense** Tense shows when the action of the sentence happened. Verbs have different tenses.

  SIMPLE PRESENT: She usually *works* hard.

  PRESENT CONTINUOUS: She *is working* now.

  SIMPLE PAST: She *worked* yesterday.

  FUTURE: She *will work* tomorrow.

- **Verb** A verb is the action of the sentence.

  He *runs* fast.   I *speak* English.

  Some verbs have no action. They are linking verbs. They connect the subject to the rest of the sentence.

  He *is* tall.   She *looks* beautiful.   You *seem* tired.

- **Vowel** The following letters are vowels: *a, e, i, o, u.*

  NOTE: *Y* is sometimes considered a vowel, as in the world *syllable.*

INDEX

CREDITS

ILLUSTRATIONS

© Cengage Learning

PHOTOS